A ▣ CORNISH CHILDHOOD

A CORNISH CHILDHOOD
A. L. Rowse

AUTOBIOGRAPHY
OF A CORNISHMAN

Clarkson N. Potter, Inc./Publishers
DISTRIBUTED BY CROWN PUBLISHERS, INC., NEW YORK

FIRST PUBLISHED 1942
REPRINTED 1942, 1943, 1945, 1946, 1956, 1965
REISSUED IN THIS FORMAT 1974
BY
JONATHAN CAPE LTD, 30 BEDFORD SQUARE, LONDON WCI

Printed in the United States of America

Published simultaneously in Canada by
General Publishing Company Limited

Library of Congress Cataloging in Publication Data

Rowse, Alfred Leslie, 1903-
    A Cornish childhood.

    Includes index.
    1. Rowse, Alfred Leslie, 1903-   —Biography—Youth.   2. Au-
thors, English—20th century—Biography.   3. Cornwall, Eng.—Social life
and customs.   I. Title.
PR6035.084Z5 1979   828'.9'1209 [B]   79-14610
ISBN: 0-517-538458
10 9 8 7 6 5 4 3 2

CONTENTS

PREFACE

I DO not know that an autobiography requires an apology. Autobiographies to my mind make interesting reading; among them I reckon some of my favourite books — books which have a meaning and an appeal for me beyond any other. Newman's *Apologia pro Vita Sua* and Renan's *Souvenirs d'Enfance et de Jeunesse* have a place apart in the life of my mind: something more than books to me, they have entered into and become part of my experience.

But if not an apology, perhaps I may offer an explanation. This Autobiography has its origin in a very far-going and severe illness a few years ago which I was afraid I might not survive. As I lay in hospital in London, it was some consolation to turn back in my mind to the surroundings of my childhood in Cornwall, along with its memories to evoke its very atmosphere, to enter once more into its feeling. I recalled Renan's saying: *On ne doit pas écrire que de ce qu'on aime.* Remembering gave me so much pleasure, when I was helpless and could do nothing else, that I resolved then that I would write this book.

The book has been written now, not without thought of the uncertainty of the time, of dangers from another side, beyond one's control; there is the natural desire to leave some memorial of oneself, whatever may come to us.

With previous books, on history and politics, I have had occasion to complain of the difficulties I had in writing them. Not so with this: it seemed, after those months of illness and day-dreaming, that the book was there waiting to write itself.

As it formed in my mind, it struck me that such a book might have a distinctive contribution of its own to make to our literature. For, numerous as have been the autobiographies of the past, almost all have come from the upper or middle class, and most recent ones of distinction (Connolly's *Enemies of Promise*, Isherwood's *Lions and Shadows*, Henry Green's *Pack my Bag*, for example) have a public-school background. There are very few autobiographies that come out of the working class and reveal its ways of behaviour and feeling from within, its standards and reflections upon itself. And it is curious, considering that since the war of 1914-1918 a whole generation has come up in the normal course from elementary and secondary school to the university, forming almost a new educated class, that not a single autobiography has yet appeared, so far as I know, which gives any account of that process of education and emergence, though it has become the more usual one for the nation at large. I cannot claim that the story told in this book is necessarily typical, yet I have some hope that, when complete, it may be regarded as representative of its generation.

The account has the advantage of being to some extent a documented one. The book begins with a portrait of my native Cornish village, as it remained virtually unchanged from Victorian days, with its old customs, characters and stories, up to the war of 1914-1918. For this part I have relied upon a note-book which I kept while my father was alive, in which I jotted down stories and memories of his that take us back to the village as it was in the 1860s. While for the later chapters I had my own schoolboy diaries, which I kept during my last years at school, to go upon and keep me straight. A historian would feel lost without some at least of his material being in documentary form; in writing this I could feel at times that I was engaged upon a work of research!

With these aids I hope that the book may reveal something of the inner process of a working-class child's education, and may have some value for the discussions as to the future shaping of our educational system. I am sure from my own experience that day-school education has, to place against certain advantages that the public schools have, some qualities, and still greater potentialities, of its own: for example, independent-mindedness and intellectual self-reliance as against too great an emphasis upon character. It may well be that in the dangers and insecurity of the contemporary world we need to put more emphasis on the former qualities than we have been accustomed to in the last half-century.

I am indebted to Lord Berners and Lord David Cecil for their kindness in reading parts of my typescript for me. To the usual good offices of a publisher, Mr. Jonathan Cape has added the accomplishments of a literary critic. I am deeply indebted to Mr. Jack Simmons of Christ Church, as with previous books, for his invaluable literary counsel, his sternness and discretion. For all faults of taste and obstinate prejudices, nevertheless, I am wholly and solely responsible.

My deepest debt is to my mother, whose wonderful memory has helped me time and again. Some small part of what I owe to her and to my father in writing this book is indicated in the dedication.

A. L. ROWSE

Oxford
March 1942

To
my mother
and the memory of
my father

CHAPTER I

THE VILLAGE

THERE is the village in my mind's eye, as it was in those years before
the last war, the age-long routine of Cornish life still unbroken, though
perhaps like an old grandfather clock it was winding down slowly,
imperceptibly, to a stop. The War — till lately 'the War' still meant
in these parts the Great War of 1914 to 1918: evidence perhaps of the
slowness of adaptation, the tenacity, of our minds — the War brought
all that life of habit to a sudden full stop, held it suspended, breathless
for a full four years in the shadow of its wing, and meanwhile set in
being motions and tendencies which came to full flood the moment
the War was over and swept away the old landmarks in a tide of
change. I remember the momentary return to the old ways, for we
celebrated the Armistice with a Flora Dance through the town. There
was something instinctive, pathetic about it, like a gesture remembered
from some former existence, which had no meaning any more.
Hardly anybody knew how to dance it by now: we just crowded the
narrow, tortuous Fore Street of St. Austell town, treading on each
other's heels in a snake-walk, for the most part walking for we had
forgotten the steps, though all of us knew the tune. Never was there
such a crush as in our town on the night of November 11th, 1918; the
old instinctive impulse brought in hundreds, thousands from all the
villages round, from the populous china-clay district, and as the night
wore on the little twisting street was impassable, jammed with happy,
released humanity. But not all the good will in the world could reconstruct the fabric of the old ways; in the years immediately
after the War, they vanished like snows touched by the sun, like a
dream 'remembered on waking'.

In the pre-war years of which I am writing, the continuity of custom
was still unbroken. One thing of interest to the social historian, for
example: the families, the family names which for generations and even
for centuries had belonged to some particular spot had not as yet been
disturbed, uprooted by the revolution in transport. Though many

Cornish families sent a large quota of their sons abroad, to the United States and South Africa especially, the parent stock remained at home in the old place. So there were always Jenkinses at Phernyssick, Pascoes at Holmbush, Tretheweys at Roche; Kellows, Blameys, Rowses at Tregonissey. Now as I write, there is neither a Kellow nor a Blamey nor a Rowse at Tregonissey any more. The old social structure has at length been broken, like a pitcher at the well, the pieces dispersed. And the same with many of the old customs and ways.

By the time of my childhood years, some of them had irretrievably gone from the village. For example, the interesting custom of crying the neck at the end of the harvest. The last sheaf, rigged up in the form of a figure and dressed with flowers, was brought into the house ceremonially, the harvesters crying 'A-neck, A-neck' and some other words which my father couldn't remember: some rigmarole perhaps which went back to the Celtic past. This last sheaf brought into the house presided over the harvest-supper and was left in possession till the next harvest. Sir James George Frazer tells us that it was the corn-spirit which was being thus invoked: I dare say he was right. My father as a lad was present at crying the neck on Kellow's farm, at the end of the village; but by my time it had quite died out. Then, too, there was the Christmas mumming of St. George and the Dragon which used to be given in his boyhood in the courtyard of the Seven Stars inn in the town. He could never give me a coherent account of the proceedings, only a few scraps of phrases and gestures of the actors; but the mumming has been studied and its form is quite well known to scholars. [1]

Whether the 'shivaree' was a really old custom, or of recent intro-duction by returned miners from America, I do not know; some reader may inform me. But this was in full swing when my father and mother were married and set up house in the village. It was a way of keeping up a wedding, and apt to be an awkward one for the couple that did not take the proceedings in the right spirit, though productive of merriment for the others. All the village turned out to parade the road on the night of the wedding; there was a procession headed by the bride and bridegroom, impersonated by two of the villagers

[1] cf. R. J. E. Tiddy, *The Mummer's Play*; and E. K. Chamber's *The English Folk Play* for an account of the Mylov Play.

dressed for the part. There was music — concertina, flautina, trombone, mouth-organ — and dancing. 'Everybody danced up and down' — says my mother. The married pair were supposed to provide a barrel of beer, and at the end of all there was a bonfire. My father, who was a steady, sober-sided fellow, did not approve of such goings-on and refused to provide the beer at his 'shivaree'. He was thought mean; and indeed he was not 'givish', as we say, by nature. There were other, more primitively suggestive, accompaniments to these festivities. It was customary, while the bridal couple were away for the day, to perform some mischief of a broad sort: stuff up the chimney so that the fire would not light next morning, nail up the door, or *faute de mieux* hang a chamber-pot on the door to greet the returning wedded. The most splendid of 'shivarees' given at Tregonissey was for the wedding of Eliza Dyer to Eneas (pronounced Enas) Kellow. The bride was fifty, the groom twenty: surely an occasion for special celebration and merry-making. A farm-wagon was hired to do honour to it; the wedding garments were of a realist extravagance (Jim Blamey the groom, my father's youngest brother Edwin, merry and impish, the bride); the bonfire of the most resplendent. But Eliza and Eneas did not respond; they were annoyed by the special point lent to the celebrations and remained indoors all the evening while all the village danced up and down outside their house. That 'shivaree', as it was the most splendid, was also the last. I never remember even hearing about them in my childhood: they were too recent to be matter of history.

I can throw no light upon this curious custom; I do not even know that it was general in Cornwall; it may have been peculiar to Tregonissey. But it is certainly reminiscent of the junketings that attended a wedding in Elizabethan days, such as are described by Carew, as when William Carnsew could attend a wedding at St. Germans, ride into Devonshire to see the bishop, and back by way of Plymouth, and so return to the wedding, for the celebrations lasted a week.

Though these amenities had gone, feast-week and fairs still held their ancient reign. For our parish of St. Austell the high point was the week following Trinity Sunday, for that was the dedication feast of our Church, or rather of its re-dedication, since the time in the dim middle ages when the reforming, energetic bishop, Walter Bronescombe, had swept down upon the county, consecrating fifteen churches and chapelries, in one fell swoop of a fortnight's tour of the county, often as in our case extruding the old Celtic saint unknown to the Roman Calendar and making everything conform to the magnificent, the immutable order of Rome.

How well one remembers the sacred routine of St. Austell Feast-week, as it still obtained in undiminished splendour in my youth! The Feast lasted, with us, four days, from Monday to Thursday. Monday was Charlestown Regatta. Tuesday was Mount Charles Feast, when the children from all four Sunday schools, Bridge United Methodist, the Wesleyans from Victoria Road and from Charlestown, with the Primitives, met together in procession, who were so divided all the rest of the year, and enjoyed a common bun-fight, or 'tay-drink', as it is called with us. Wednesday was perhaps the high spot: it was the Town Feast, with sports held in the Rocky Park, donkey-races, jumping, competitions, stalls, fights, what not. Again all the different Sunday schools had their tea-drinks, I think in different fields: Wesleyans, Baptists, Primitives, Bible Christians, Reform — though what the last was a Reform of, or from, I do not now remember, if I ever knew. So many schools, so many parades, so many separate bands. It must have been not unlike the church-ales of Elizabethan times which Carew describes in his *Survey*. We church-people held rather aloof from such popularity, and in my day at church Sunday-school we moved away from the mêlée to the sobriety of a tea-drink on our own on the Winnick at Pentewan. On Thursday the Feast came to an end with Trethurgy Feast, a remote little granite village at the bounds of the parish, high up in its moorland fastness, defended by the prodigious ascent of Trethurgy Hill, that straight, white road beyond which I had never been, which dominated the northward view from the village. The townspeople hired wagonettes for the ascent; they all went up and, according to my mother, 'had fine fun'. It always rained for Trethurgy Feast — also according to my mother. So Feast-week came to an end. Friday was market-day at St. Austell; so to-morrow, after the fun and frolics of the week, back to the serious business of life.

The week after, St. Peter's-tide, was Mevagissey Feast, which went on, very suitably for a fishing village, for the whole week, Monday to

Saturday. Of this I knew nothing; six miles was quite beyond my radius as a child; my father went once or twice, but he wouldn't have thought of taking us. But I remember Bernard Walke telling me how, there, processions from the chapels came down to the waterside, hung about singing hymns not knowing what to do and then trooped back again; that in fact it was a dim memory of the days when they would bring the image of St. Peter down from the church to bless the waters and their increase. I have no doubt that he was right; it was just like his intuition of our old Catholic past to have seen that. But of course it was a hopeless dream to try and re-live all that in our day; as he must have come to realize at the end of his life — though no man ever came nearer to causing a dream of the beauty of the past to live again than he did at St. Hilary. All honour to him for that brave attempt, hopeless in its very nature; for it is such failures that redeem the drabness and commonness of everyday life. He was an artist and a saint; his name will for ever be associated with a rare and lovely experience in Cornish life.

Then there were the fairs. Summercourt Fair, held in September, was the chief one in our neighbourhood. The men from the china-clay works — 'claywork men' in our vernacular — would go off with a couple of horses and a big clay wagon, the horses decorated with coloured ribbons, the men singing:

> 'Ere we'm off to Summercourt Fair:
> Me mother said 'Ess',
> Me faather said 'No';
> An' dash me buttons if I dunt go.

My father usually went to Summercourt Fair, though I don't remember his bringing home any fairings for us, at least not in my time; he may have done in earlier years. The view was that we had the shop and were better off than other people by that fact already. We were — and he was a careful man. In October was St. Lawrence's Fair at Bodmin — 'St. Larrence' it was always called; but that was mainly a horse fair and he didn't often go. Only gaddabouts, 'gaddivantin' about the plaace fur want ov somethin' better to do', went as far afield as Liskeard Honey Fair; nobody we knew ever did. Money wouldn't run to that.

It is extraordinary to look back upon how circumscribed were our lives, in what a confined space, within what narrow grooves they were lived. What else could be expected when a clayworker's wage was something less than £1 a week? We never had any pocket-money. There was no money for anybody of the working class to travel, except very occasionally for a day's outing to relations within the county, or once in a lifetime to London — unless it were abroad to America, from which it was expected that you came home 'made'. Life proceeded therefore along very well-worn ruts, as deep as the tracks the heavily-laden clay-wagons wore in our road on the way to the station, or down Slades to the little port of Charlestown. So that market night (Friday) and Saturday night were the regular occasions for jollity — along with feasts and fairs, the ordained safety-valves of a hard-working, high-spirited community.

My father religiously went to market every Friday night, arrayed in his favourite attire, pepper-and-salt jacket and waistcoat, dark grey breeches and shining black leggings. (He liked to look like a farmer.) I think it was matter of some disappointment to him that he hadn't a gold watch, or at least chain, to wear in his waistcoat, as some others had: the farmers (it was his dearest ambition to farm a small-holding of his own: he never attained it) or the men who had returned from America or South Africa. What he did at market was a sacred mystery, at any rate to me, for I was never taken. I had to stay at home on Friday nights, as indeed on most nights, to help 'mind the shop'. But later on, my profane elder brother discovered from a friend of his working in a pub that my father's regular order on Friday night was 'a pint of bitter and two-pennorth of rum'. That was the limit of his weekly indulgence. No liquor was allowed inside our home by my mother: it was in practice, without any nonsensical theory attached to it, a teetotal household. That was more than made up for by the oceans of strong tea consumed in it.

Sometimes a little later, on my way home from choir-practice or from an errand in the town, I would venture up those busy steps into the buzz and bustle of the crowded market-house. Avoiding the butchers' standings down below, with the fearsome carcasses hanging in subterranean gloom, I went up the steps to the dazzling brilliance, the hissing gas-lamps, the flaring jets of upstairs. This was my palace of

Haroun-al-Raschid. I remember the sensation to the eyes of so much dazzle after the semi-darkness of the vaulted crypt below. Here were the standings that interested me: Emmie Cundy's (she lively-eyed and bustling about, talking all the time) with jars of sweets in rows, golden and ruby and brown, slabs of toffee and long pink sticks of peppermint rock. Then there were all the pretty things that hung inside – glistening stockings, the crackers and paper-hats and coloured decorations of Christmas-time. (Father invariably brought home a sprig of mistletoe from Christmas market.) Upon a long trestle-table spread with a clean white cloth were tiny plates of limpets in vinegar, mussels, winkles, shrimps and other tasty delicacies, I think a penny a time. But, alas, it was so very rarely that I had a penny to dispose of in those years. 'Market' was for me almost entirely a feast of the eyes and ears, for the whole of the vast space (there was no vaster known to my experience) buzzed with the excitement of a high-spirited Cornish crowd out to enjoy itself after the week's work, the sibilant murmur of a hundred conversations, the shrill cries of stall-holders, the higgling and haggling of customers. Unsatisfied, alone, expecting something, which never came, from all that excitement, I made my way out by the Market Hill entrance, my head dizzy and confused with the intoxicating clamour, and so up Tregonissey Hill homewards.

I call to mind now as I write the comfortable sound which was the regular accompaniment of my going to sleep on Friday nights as a child, of the chaps of the 'higher quarter' coming home in droves, after a less frugal visit to market than father's, singing hymns and sacred songs, usually Moody and Sankey, as they went, some singing steadily and keeping together in part, others tipsy and breaking the melody. Their voices sounded sweet in the road outside, approaching, then receding uphill from the house, fading away in the distance. Even then they held an incurable nostalgia for the small boy who heard them mingled with sleep and drowsy warmth, the security of the walls of home. I recognize it well, that nostalgia which has underlain all my experience of life, in one form or another, like the not always explicit burden of a song.

But where are the voices of those young men that sang? Some of them extinguished for ever in the Great War, at the bottom of the North Sea, in France, in Flanders, in Palestine, for these Cornish lads were in all those theatres of the War. Some of them who died were at school with me: I recognized their names on a tablet outside the little chapel at Bethel the other day when walking that way. Most of them grown up, become fathers of families, grown old, worn and marked in the way they do with their toil, toothless or grizzled or bald: no longer recognizable for the lithe youths of my childhood's dream who sang coming home from market. Others of them, perhaps the greater part, dispersed, gone away, flown from the nest that gave them birth — where I, by a curious conjunction of circumstances, have remained.

Those were the years in which when 'clay was goin' away' the great wagons drawn by two or three or four horses rumbled through the village all day, the horses straining and sweating; wagons rattling and bumping along merrily, chains clanking on the way back. Then there were the voices of the men, soft-toned though loud, urging their teams. 'Taager! Gee up, Lion', I can hear one of them saying now; or it was 'Gee up, Triumph! Gee up, Victor!' Years later when I have been working at my Elizabethan researches in the Public Record Office, coming upon a list of ships among the State Papers perhaps, the names *Tiger, Lion, Triumph* have sent a shiver down my spine and in that dusty place brought tears to my eyes. It seemed that I heard again the golden voice, saw the fresh red complexion of George Oxenham driving his team through the village: 'Lion! Gee up, Taager! Triumph!' For he came back to the village no more, when he went away to the War. He went down, I think, at Jutland.

Those were the years when, at night, you looked out at the bay, you would often see a hive of little golden lights, moving like glow-worms upon the water: the Mevagissey fishing fleet out. One never sees them now.

There was the village of Tregonissey, then, half-way up the hillside to the north-east from the town of St. Austell to the china-clay uplands — the 'Higher Quarter' we called them. The words 'Higher Quarter' conveyed to our minds the sense of a civilization altogether rough and raw and rude compared with ourselves — or rather of an absence of civilization as we understood it, living next to the town, three-quarters of a mile away. The men of the Higher Quarter, the china-clay villages that clustered in the high bleak uplands, were known to be fierce, fearsome creatures; there was no taking liberties with them: they were much more likely to take liberties with you. The best policy was to give them no cause of offence, avoid their company, give them a wide berth, especially if, as was usually the case, they were travelling the roads in groups. And indeed, when my father was a lad, a very primitive state of hostility subsisted between one village and another. The Tregonissey lads wouldn't allow the village to be invaded by Mount Charles men; Mount Charles men couldn't endure the townsmen. The cry 'Hands off Mount Charles' held up a very desirable extension of urban boundaries at St. Austell for years — until in fact the War put an end to that sort of local separatism along with much else.

The principle of hating most your next-door neighbour held good all over Cornwall. (There never was a greater joke that 'One and All' as the Cornish motto, for Cornish people, like all Celts, are notoriously individualist and incapable of co-operating.) Roche and Bugle never agreed; Penryn and Falmouth were at daggers drawn: they held the lowest opinion of each other; a centuries-long feud sundered Lostwithiel from Fowey. But the most notorious dislike of all was that which Redruth and Camborne mutually entertained, since of all Cornish towns they were nearest together. A friend of mine when a young man was talking one day with old Cap'n Thomas, a well-known Redruth man, and happened to mention that some celebrated person was coming to speak at Camborne: would the Cap'n like to go in and hear him? The old man replied politely, in a melancholy tone: 'Aw, noa, thank'ee my lad all the saame: I dunt go into Camborne fur nothin'.' But the War and post-war legislation brought these two mutually incompatibles into one town council — though I must say the new urban area of 'Camborne-Redruth' is a horrid monstrosity to any right-minded Cornishman. I rather fancy that they had to begin with a chairman from Illogan to hold the balance. The latest news is that they are getting to tolerate each other quite well.[1]

Nor is this at all surprising. The same principle of hating most your

---

[1] I am sorry to have to record that since writing the above there has been a back-sliding, further dissension and exchange of compliments between the two groups on the town council.

next-door neighbour, generalized over Europe, gives you, according to Sorel's *L'Europe et la Révolution Française*, the classical principle of eighteenth-century diplomacy: friends with your next-door neighbour but one: France — Poland, Prussia — Russia. Nor is the contemporary world any better. The independent existence of Poland brought Germany and Russia together before this war; the mutual antagonism of Poland and Russia enabled Nazi Germany to undermine the stability of Eastern Europe and make the war. It is very disheartening how human affairs always follow the same patterns — as against Herbert Fisher's view that he could detect no pattern in history; nobody ever learns anything, nobody ever profits by the mistakes that have been made before, but lets himself (and others, more intelligent, who would emancipate themselves if they could) in for the same mess of blood and misery as before.

Back to the village! There we find that fifty years ago, or even thirty, in the 'Higher Quarter', it was quite possible for a stranger coming into a village to be stoned by the children of the place — as in the villages up in the hills in Southern Italy.

The village was a straggle of houses along one side of the road, where for a bit it was level before mounting the hill to Lane End, then to Carclaze, then Penwithick, with which you were in the Higher Quarter proper. The other side of the road — it was no more than a ribbon of a lane, with high hedges on either side and many twists and bends, very convenient for the game of frightening people, which was much to the fore as an amusement in that simple society — was bordered by elms; so that the village had a not unattractive appearance in my early years, with its cob-walled cottages washed yellow and cream, the colour of the clotted cream on top of the pans in the dairy at the farm. A few were a deeper shade, saffron. A little group of thatched cottages in the middle of the village had a small orchard attached; and I remember well the peculiar purity of the blue sky seen through the white clusters of apple-blossom in spring. I remember being moon-struck looking at it one morning early on my way to school. It meant something for me; what, I couldn't say. It gave me an unease at heart, some reaching out towards perfection such as impels men into religion, some sense of the transcendence of things, of the fragility of our hold upon life, mixed up with a schoolboy's dream of an earlier world (I was then reading Q.'s *The Splendid Spur*), of England in the time of the Civil War, the gallant bands of young horsemen careering out in the morning, Spring, the pure sunlight falling over the hills in waves under that cloudless blue. It was always morning, early morning, in that day-dream — and here was I, a schoolboy loitering a little, hugging that experience, incapable then of describing it to anyone, even myself, on my way to school.

I could not know then that it was an early taste of aesthetic sensation, a kind of revelation which has since become a secret touchstone of experience for me, an inner resource and consolation. Later on, though still a schooboy — now removed downhill to the secondary school — when I read Wordsworth's *Tintern Abbey* and *Intimations of Immortality*, I realized that that was the experience he was writing about. In time it became my creed — if that word can be used of a religion which has no dogma, no need of dogma; for with this ultimate aesthetic experience, this apprehension of the world and life as having value essentially in the moment of being apprehended *qua* beauty, I had no need of religion. That I never understood in my childhood, and in my adolescence sometimes wondered why, with the best will in the world and my own dedication of myself from my earliest years to the Church, I could not believe — or rather that the things they said, 'God is Love' and such-like conundrums, never conveyed anything to my intelligence. I will not say that in truth they had nothing to convey, but here simply that my intelligence was pre-empted, in the literal sense, pre-occupied. There was really no room for doctrine, not much room for ethical precepts. Nothing of all that corresponded with my inner experience.

Years later at Oxford, when I had just ceased to be an undergraduate and had some time as a young Fellow of All Souls to look round and reflect in, I tried to think it out for myself. I was trying to determine what gave value to an experience and in what the value of this consisted, since to me it represented the ultimate secretion of value in my universe. It seemed to me, after no very long but most intense reflection — I remembered no more intense effort of thought — that what was characteristic of the experience was that in the moment of undergoing it, in contemplating the light come and go upon the façade of a building, the moon setting behind St. Mary's spire outside my window — Newman's St. Mary's — in listening to Beethoven or Byrd, or seeing the blue sky through the apple-blossom of my childhood, in that very moment it seemed that time stood still, that for a moment time was held up and one saw experience as through a rift across the flow of it, a shaft into the universe. But what gave such poignancy to the experience was that, in the very same moment as one felt time standing still, one knew at the back of the mind, or with another part of it, that it was moving inexorably on, carrying oneself and life with it. So that the acuity of the experience, the reason why it moved one so profoundly, was that at bottom it was a protest of the personality against the realization of its final extinction. Perhaps, therefore, it was bound up with, a reflex action from, the struggle for survival. I could get no further than that; and in fact have remained content with that.

With the elms to give us shade in the hot summer days, the leaves making bright and glittering patterns with the light, the yellow-washed cottages in the sun, the village in my early years was not unattractive, though nobody could call it beautiful. In fact a very ordinary little old Cornish hamlet. It was in a healthy situation on the slope of the hill looking south, with a good view of the bay enclosed within the two headlands, the Gribbin and the Black Head at Trenarren. On the left we could see the high hilly country that marked the further bank of the River Fowey; on the right we looked across to the dark woods of Penrice, constant in the landscape, the mysterious-looking opening in the woods where the house was; from the bedroom windows we could see as far as Goran church-tower erect upon the skyline. There was, of course, no view at the back: sheer hillside up which the cottage gardens climbed and down which poured torrents of mud when it rained.

It was a good thing the village was in a healthy situation for man had done nothing to make it hygienic. I doubt if there was a single water-closet in the whole place. Most houses shared earth-closets, one to two or three houses; you can imagine to what quarrels that led with regard to respective rights and duties. However, the lives of the simple must be filled with something, and their innumerable quarrels and incessant bickerings helped to fill the gap. Some houses had no closets at all. Ours was situated at the very top of the gardens at the back of the house, half-way up the hillside: hardly conducive to that good regulation of the bowels upon which the French are so candidly, and so volubly, insistent. Nobody, I think, had water inside the house: the villagers fetched all their water from the two public taps, which were, along with our shop, the chief news-centres and meeting-places the village afforded. We were the nearest to the unwonted luxury of having water within the house, for we had a tap of our own at the door — and a very capricious and skittish instrument it was to those who did not know its ways: it sent up a ferocious squirt of water in the face of the inexpert. Small children who could not resist its appeal were always getting into trouble with it, drenching themselves and their elders. For years I was afraid of it.

Sometimes water failed altogether and we took our pitchers to the clear-running stream which came out of the springs in the hillside and ran along in front of the houses at the other end of the village. That stream was a constant resource to us children: walking in the water was a fearful pleasure, all the more exquisite because we knew the penalties it would entail on arriving home; then there was damming it up with mud and floating sticks down its course, once even trying to track its lower reaches down through the fields below the village as far as Donkey Lane — that adventure gave me at least the sensation of an earlier discoverer of America. Very rarely even this stream gave out and we were forced, with carts and barrels and buckets and pails, to go all the way to Phernyssick, half a mile uphill for water. It was almost worth the journey; for in that deep cranny in the earth, a little dell overshadowed by elder-trees, there was the most delicious, the purest and coldest water you ever drank. Perhaps because, too, of the effort of getting there, we sat down and drank cup after cup of icy water as if it were pure nectar. Years later, when an undergraduate undergoing an operation in hospital, hot with fever and thirst, I remember asking my father to bring me a bottle of water from Phernyssick as the thing above all I wanted. He brought me a bottle from the deepest depths of the clay pit where he was working, a pure cold stream: it did not disappoint. When we sang the psalm in church, 'By the waters of Babylon we sat down and wept', it was always the waters of Phernyssick that I saw myself sitting by, and upon the elder-trees there that I hangèd up my harp.

Such drains as Tregonissey possessed were open drains: I am not sure that even the plural here is not a mistake. All your slops and dish-water you had to take across the road and empty into the open drain which ran along in front of our house, if on the opposite side of the road—a distinction which made little difference in hot, smelly summer weather. My bedroom window, which was downstairs, was directly opposite the grating of the drain. I did not much notice the smell, for I was much too possessed by night-terrors ever to sleep with my window open. I was often terrified as it was, with the window shut and the catch fast. In such circumstances, it was a wonder, perhaps, that the health of the village was good; but it was — attributable, no doubt, to our living so much in the open air. Sometimes in summer there would be thunder and a tremendous downpour: the drains would be quickly blocked and the road become a swimming lake, into which pattered the myriad silver pennies of the raindrops. I watched fascinated from inside, nose pressed against window, my mind cherishing the thought that, if only those were real pennies dropping down, how lovely it would be to go out and shovel them up in barrowsful. But more enduring than this conceit was the extraordinary sense of comfort and well-being which it always gave me to be inside the window and watching the rain pelt down outside. It made me hug myself with glee and *wohlgemut*. Nor did it detract from the pleasure to see other people caught out in it hurrying and skurrying for shelter. I still get something of that curious thrill with a really heavy downpour to-day — I remember something of the same sort at the beginning of a story of Nathaniel Hawthorne's; and I have a corresponding, and quite inexplicably savage, dislike of being rained upon. It even makes me slightly crazy — I have never understood why.

The shop was not quite midway on in the village, coming from the town. At that end, the first thing you came to was the farm. In my childhood the farm played no very active part in our lives; there was a shadow upon it: all those years the farmer was away at the Lunatic Asylum at Bodmin, and the place was managed by his wife, a brave-hearted woman who brought up her children alone and ran the farm with the help of a hind and the children. But in my father's boyhood the farm had been a great place in the life of the villagers. It was held by old Mr. and Mrs. Kellow, who were still spoken of with great respect. They had owned the large posting establishment which supplied relays for the coaches travelling the south road through the county. In those days fifty horses would be stabled at Tregonissey. The farm gave employment to half the village in one capacity or another — hinds, labourers, stable-boys, maidservants. Something of the air of decayed prosperity hung about the place still, in spite of large empty stables, overgrown gardens. The garden in front of the house went uncultivated, but all along the southward wall there were the plum trees of former days, unpruned, no longer bearing. In the little side garden there were two splendid camelias which regularly bore their crop of rose-like flowers, red and white.

Next the farm was the cottage in which lived my Uncle Harry, my father's brother, and his wife. We were not on speaking terms with them in my childhood, and it was not until I grew up and went to Oxford that I effected a reconciliation, at any rate for myself, and saw the interior of that odd *ménage*. Before them the house had been Grandfather Rowe's, my father's grandfather on his mother's side, and father of my great-uncle George Rowe, who played a very important part in the life of the village, and still more so in ours. Great-grandfather Rowe had been a hind of the Kellows and came, I believe, from St. Stephen's parish. I have forgotten what little I once elicited from my father of his ways, except that he was a sweet, gentle-natured old man. Of his family, three of the children had been born before wedlock and three after: very Cornish, after an older mode. My father's mother was one of those born before, Uncle George after. My father was very sensitive on this point and never mentioned it — as if it mattered. The important point, as we can appreciate in these days of declining population, is that they did get born. My father as a boy lived there with the old people, and used to play the pranks on them which were *de rigueur* in village life. He would steal from his bed when they were asleep, insert himself under their bed, which in those days was hung upon sacking, and lift it up on his back by way of giving the old people a fright, or a treat. It was always very patiently received, and I am sure that he was fond of them — he hadn't much reason, poor dear, to be very fond of his own home.

At the back of this little house was my Uncle Rowe's stable. Next

came two cottages·with green porches and laurel bushes; the second
of these was my father's home. His father, who combined tin-mining
with a little smallholding of fields at the other end of the village, had
died of miner's phthisis in the forties or early fifties, leaving his widow
with a family of nine sons and one daughter to bring up. It must have
been a great struggle, for they were a hungry, rough, spirited, fighting,
musical lot; the little woman fought her way on bravely, uncomplain-
ingly, but when death came to her in her early sixties she was glad to
lay down her burden. I never knew her. My father was rather late in
marrying, and I was the youngest child; all these things happened years
before I was born. That was the home of the Rowses at Tregonissey,
and to that house my father took my mother when they were married.
It had two rooms up and two down, the back-kitchen having, as was
usual in the village, an earthen floor. Here my sister and brother were
born.

Next along came Uncle Rowe's china-shop, then the shop itself,
where he and Aunt Rowe had lived in good fellowship, much gaiety
and merriment, and to considerable profit, though without children,
until within a year or two of my birth. Then they made way for
my mother and father, who succeeded, but not to the same position
that Uncle and Auntie had occupied: they were regarded with good
humour as lord and lady of the village. They behaved accordingly,
made money, were beholden to no one, and did what they liked.
'Shop' was a peculiar composite house, made out of two former
cottages, and my Uncle and Aunt with their servant occupied even a
third. Though they had no children, and we were three, we gave up
that—an indication of the difference in our respective positions. In front
the house had a little high-up porch, and a fine cotoneaster with its red
berries in autumn; one day a brewery-wagon halted outside and the
great dray-horses pulled it up by the roots and ate it. At the side my
father had a 'rockery' with fine ferns, Solomon's seal, and a bay-tree
growing at the door.

Outside and up was the 'court', partly cobbled, the scene of most of
our public appearances: it played the part of the back-alley in East End
life, if not of the piazzetta in a little Italian town. Three or four houses
ran up from it. In the next lived old Mrs. Cornelius, who had had a
tragedy in her life: she had been deserted years before by her husband,

who left her with a family of children to rear, which she did, honourably and honestly, by dint of incessant charring and hard work. She was a hard, bitter old woman, who looked like a witch; but very faithful and loyal to us, and with a core of sweetness for me. In the top house lived Mrs. Vague, who had an even more tragic story. In the middle house there was a young married couple whose life together was a growing tragedy, which became irremediable and impinged on us in time—matter for a novel. Later the top house was taken by a cousin of my mother's, Annie Courtenay, whose husband lived all his life as a miner in South Africa. Then one of her daughters followed him, the other two married and went to America; her only boy followed in the bad years of unemployment after the War. She lived on there alone, fat, dark as a Zulu, proud-spirited, a small property-owner, too — pathetic in the end. At last her children in America sent for her; she went out, and died shortly after. In its way an epitome of a Cornish family's history, very many of them. Not one is left in this country: all of them gone abroad, not to return, the home broken up.

Their Courtenay name is interesting, too. There is no doubt that they would go back to the original stock of the Courtenays, Earls of Devon, who threw out several offshoots in this part of the county, and in course of time had come down to the level of working people. The Courtenays knew in a vague way from whom they had descended, though it meant little to them. I remember my cousin and schoolmate, Sidney Courtenay, one day telling me at school that his ancestors had been Earls of Devon or some such thing. Neither he nor I knew, at the age of ten or eleven, that he was probably quite right. One recalls Gibbon's chapter and their remoter ancestry, from Louis VI and the Paleologus Emperor at Constantinople: curious to think of them after all those descents, all those generations, side by side with the villagers. Charlie Courtenay, so far as I remember seeing him, was a fine-looking man: fair, with noble features, clear, pale, rather transparent skin, who held himself well and had rather a way with him. Is it mere fancy on my part to suppose that he had rather a Norman cast of face and feature?

Under Annie's garden were the foundations of a little old chapel, long since vanished, which my father attended as a boy. He once told me that it had a mud floor and benches without any backs and was lit by candles. During the service, an old woman used to go round and snuff the candles. Mr. Tredinnick, the town missionary, used to come there and preach. And 'pitch the tune'. Pitching the tune was a very important performance and a highly thought-of ability. It demanded not only voice but confidence, not merely confidence but judgment: in short, a head. Granny Vanson, my mother's mother, could pitch the tune, and sometimes used to pitch it at prayer meetings at chapel. The old people used to set great store upon not giving out the same tune twice in the course of the day. No hymn books: only the preacher had a hymn book and gave out each verse, told them the tune and they would sing after.

The houses at the other end of the village, for the most part grey granite as against our yellow cob-walls, do not count in my story. Except perhaps Pearce's, the little dairy-farm, where I went every day of my life for years to fetch the milk, sometimes accompanied as far by my cat. And except, too, for the houses opposite which had been built by my Uncle William, and in one of which lived our chief friends, with whom we were linked by ties not merely, I presume, of friendship. These houses were built on a plot of the holding of several fields hereabouts which belonged to my grandfather, and before him to the Rowses time out of mind, beyond which there is no memory to the contrary — according to the old formula of the twelve men of the homage.

The tenure that chiefly prevailed in the village was still, I fancy, the old Cornish three-lives system. Household property was broken up among a number of small sub-holders, chief among whom was my Uncle Rowe and his brother's widow and her daughter, Annie Courtenay. The farm belonged to the Duchy, as did the land on our side of the road; some land below the village belonged to 'Sir Charles' — that distant, rumoured figure whom we never saw, who lived at Penrice and was the chief landowner of St. Austell. So that Tregonissey, like all the china-clay villages of the 'Higher Quarter', escaped the stifling embrace of the squirearchy. And that fact, I realize now, though it was never thought of then, had a profound effect on our upbringing and social outlook. We were an independent folk; we never saw anybody in the village better than ourselves. I never remember seeing any sign of servility among any of its inhabitants. We were not in the habit of saying 'sir' to anybody. I cannot recall my father saying 'sir' to anyone; nor did the china-clay workers as a whole, any more than, I suppose, the free and independent tinners from whom they sprang had done in their day. The result was that I never said 'sir' to anybody except at school, and then as little as possible, and have since never been able to contract the habit, let alone say 'my lord' to anyone enjoying that rank.

My friend Charles Henderson, most remarkable of Cornish scholars, once observed to me that it was the exceptional position held by the Duchy, with all its manors and lands in the county, which rather prevented the growth of an aristocracy of large landowners in Cornwall. Carew remarks on the fact that there were no Cornish families which had attained to the peerage. On the whole, historically, Cornish landholdings were on a small scale, except for the Duchy, the Courtenays and Arundells. I see now that there is, and always has been, a marked difference in social structure and outlook between the people of the rough moorlands of the Cornish interior, themselves rough, independent, free, and the people of the coastal plains and arable lands, brought up under the eye of their local gentry, their tenants or employees, more polite, submissive, apt to be yes-men. The former were Radical in politics, the latter Conservative, or, more precisely, conformist. Geographically we were on the border-line; but socially, though one would never have believed it then, we belonged to the 'Higher Quarter'.

In later years, when at Oxford, I always regretted that I knew nothing about the history of our village; it was too unimportant, it seemed, ever to have been mentioned anywhere, by anyone. It had never produced anybody known to history, or with an approach to a name. Tregrehan Mills even had produced a Samuel Drew; Trevellas an Opie; Tregurry a medieval Archbishop. Tregonissey was too obscure. In all my researches into Cornish history at the Public Record Office and British Museum I had never come across a mention of it. I asked Charles Henderson what was the meaning of the name, supposing myself that it bore some reference to the saint whose name occurs in Mevagissey and St. Issey. Charles thought not: he had seen earlier references to the name as Tregonedwed, and was of the opinion that it incorporated a personal name, something like Cunedwed, or

Cunedwith. I daresay he was right: nobody was likely to know more about such a matter than he. Curious to think back to this unknown man who must have been a personage of a sort and gave his name to our village!

Then one day in the Public Record Office I came upon a Tudor survey of the manor of Treverbyn Courtenay which gave me a picture of the village as it had been in the days of Queen Elizabeth. Imagine my excitement and the pleasure, after having given up hope of ever finding anything about it. I felt that curious thrill, the authentic sensation of the researcher, which is so well described by the present Regius Professor of History at Oxford: 'It is as if you were to sit down and find you have sat on the cat.' The thing comes alive in your hand. So Tregonissey was part of the great holdings of the Courtenays, Earls of Devon, in Cornwall. One saw the payments, hard-wrested from the soil, going up to help maintain those splendid, extravagant personages living their precarious lives, so close to the Royal blood, in London. There were two references, the first to Tregonhesewith, the second to Tregonhise — practically the modern form of the name.

The second came from a survey made in the last year of Elizabeth's reign, 1602, when the hamlet consisted of two main holdings. There was John Treleaven's with various closes and 'parks' — which meant patches of open downs, furze and heath — including 'Down Park', which still goes by that name. The second holding was that of Gregory Rowse: 'a messuage and tenement containing a fair hall, a buttery, a kitchen, a milk house, a sheep house, a linhay house and other small houses, a back side and a town place' [i.e. farmyard]. There was a garden before the house, an orchard, a little meadow, a close called Cavorres, closes above the house and under the church-way, Polkear, Cross park (where there must have been a Cornish cross, since vanished), pasture on Gwallon downs. The total value was £17 1s. 10d. per annum; the fine on renewal — it was copyhold tenure — £90. For an idea of contemporary value, you have to multiply Tudor figures by twenty or twenty-five. It was evidently an important holding, slightly larger than John Treleaven's. Together they must have occupied most of the village and the fields about.

It is pretty clear that Treleaven's holding is the present Duchy farm. But Gregory Rowse's holding has vanished as a unit. It would seem that my grandfather's two or three fields at the other end of the village were all that remained by the last century. What happened to the family to lose hold over the centuries? They belonged to the class of copyhold tenants squeezed out by time and the tightening up of the property system. They took to tin-mining, a harder and more speculative mode of living. Perhaps, after all, more remarkable than that they should have lost most of their holding in the course of three centuries is the tenacity with which they held on in the village at all. There is no evidence of any other family which did. The Treleavens have long since gone. And though there are no Rowses in Tregonissey now, the house to which I have moved, on the site of old Polmear Mine, with its view of the bay and the lovely Gribbin in the background, its memories of the miners (for the drive is the old mine-road), looks out across the cornfields and the woods of Charlestown to Appletree Mine where my grandfather worked, the shell of a ruined engine-house upon the cliffs.

CHAPTER II

VILLAGE LIFE

NOTHING gave me greater pleasure as a small child than to get my father, when he was in a good humour, to tell me about the 'old days' in the village. It would be hard to analyse the peculiar, nostalgic pleasure it was — though I recognize now that nostalgia in some form or other has been the underlying emotion, the undertone, of my whole life. (The religious-minded would have their explanation: they might not be far wrong.) To hear about the old days and the old people, sitting by my father, putting him questions, encouraging him to go on, drawing him out, gave me an exquisite sense of comfort. It opened a window into a realm of the mind away from the present, which I never liked much — it needed to become the past before it had much savour for me — a region in which my imagination, still more my curiosity, could wander free and content. I suppose it was the first beginnings of the historical sense in me: that peculiar, razor-edge sensation, at once a joy and a grief, for life that was gone and was so valued because irrevocable.

I was an exceedingly curious child, always wanting to know and always being snubbed for 'inquisitiveness'. Therein lay the dissatisfaction lurking round the corner of that charmed experience of hearing about the old days. For my father wasn't often in such a good humour as that. I drew him out for a bit, out of his impenetrable shell of reserve; for a brief time he forgot his inhibitions in reminiscence, and then some harmless question would put him on his guard. The momentary pleasure was over; it was no use plaguing him any more; nothing would induce him to go on. The small boy might fret or sulk or wheedle; but all to no purpose. My father just shut up like an oyster. Even many years later, when he was getting on for seventy and I a man in my early thirties, his willingness to talk about the past was very limited. The curious thing was that there was pleasure for him, too, in recalling the old days: he quite liked talking about them at moments.

Something in my father had been deeply hurt by the circumstances of his early family life; recollections of the past, though they began well, brought up associations which gave him acute pain. He was a man of simple texture, upright, hard-working, honourable, of a distinctly Puritan cast of character; but he was uneducated, unintrospective, unsubtle and naturally incapable, as all such men are, of seeing himself and his environment objectively, of locating the pain, diagnosing it and gaining relief from it by self-expression. Like all such men he had no means of self-expression, apart from work and sex; and so resentment at his early life was bottled up in him. It made him silent, reserved, discontented, a less satisfactory man, and less successful than he might have been; some obscure feeling of that only added to the resentment. And, of course, the reserve was so great, intensified by his deafness, that no one could do anything for him. It never occurred to me, for instance — I had always been so halted short along a certain line of approach that my own reaction to the situation had become fixed and automatic — it did not occur to me to consider him as a person in the light of his environment. I give credit to my brother, himself a working man, for understanding something of my father's difficult personality along these lines, long before I did — though he got on with him even less well than I.

My father, Richard Rowse, born January 31st, 1864, was the seventh of a family of nine sons and one daughter born to William and Fanny Rowse in that house in the village. His father, in addition to his holding, was a tin-miner who worked independently 'on contract' and had to provide his own ventilation in the workings — so my father told me: 'No laws to see to it in they days.' There would be a boy eighty or one hundred feet down blowing with a handle, pumping air up through a pipe to where a man was working. The mines were flourishing around St. Austell in the middle years of the nineteenth century and brought in great wealth to the Carlyons who received the dues from many of them — and spent it freely, living in opulent state in their fine house at Tregrehan. But my grandfather died of miner's phthisis, brought on by the poor air in the workings at Appletree Mine. He was about fifty. That was in the year 1881. And he was one of the first to be buried in the new cemetery at St. Austell.

I know hardly anything about him, except that he was gay and good-tempered, a regular miner in his ways, for he had a tin-whistle on which he could play any tune and would dance to it. He used to take it to work with him and at crib-time (i.e. lunch-time) would entertain his fellows with it. Once, in his last years, my father played him a trick — the kind of turn which it was everybody's ambition to play everybody else in the village, one of their chief forms of amusement in a civilization without cinemas, wireless, or motor-transport. Father brought home from market a pair of spectacles for him and asked how he could see with them; grandfather replied gravely, 'Aw! Iss, my son, I can see lovely with they.' They were, of course, only frames with no glasses in them. The joke was all the more appreciated because the victim was so vexed by it — an essential part of the game.

That family of sons, all of them miners, were a rough crowd, a hard-drinking, hard-fighting, swearing, dancing, singing lot, up to every kind of mischief, fun and pranks — not at all respectable. It seems that the struggle for survival inside such a family was a hard one. Not that they were exactly poor or went hungry. They had the little holding with four or five cows and pigs, and there were the older boys working in the mines. As my mother says: 'A great eatin' an' drinkin' party, the Rowses was.' But when the hand of the father was removed from a family of such high-spirited, turbulent miners — well, life must have been rough for the younger boys, who got more kicks and cuffs than ha'pence. My father's younger brother, Harry, became a complete neurasthenic, who could hardly bear to be seen outside of his house from the time of middle-age. It has only now occurred to me what must have been the explanation. My father, who was made of tougher stuff, though not so tough as those bullies his elder brothers, shut himself up in reserve and silence, said nothing because he was afraid of them, became a slave and a drudge for them about the house, did all the outdoor work about the cows and pigs and poultry, brought all his wages home as soon as he started to work while his brothers spent a good deal of theirs on drink — all which he resented and stored up till the day when he married and succeeded to his mother's house, when he refused to have any of them in what was now his home. They were all 'no good', he said, and he maintained that attitude pretty much through life. After various unfortunate experiences, he ceased to be on speaking terms with some of them. I had to persuade him, when I was an undergraduate at Oxford, to go to his brother Harry's funeral.

They had lived for years in the village without speaking to each other. On my father's part it was a settled, and not unjustified, resolution. The irony of it was that it was he who suffered, not his dare-devil brothers. They certainly enjoyed life a good deal more than he did.

I now perceive, as I never did in his lifetime, so close was he on the subject of that early family life, that his character was formed by re-action from it. Like the miners they were, they were all given to drink; there was never any drink in our house, except a bottle of port at Christmas and a little brandy as medicine. He did not smoke until, fairly late in life, he took to an occasional cigarette. They were a foul-mouthed lot; my father was singularly delicate in matters of speech: he very rarely swore, impatient and hot-tempered as he was, and I never heard an improper word or joke cross his lips. Some of his brothers were not monogamous, one or two were wife-beaters, whereas my father's married life was exemplary and happy: I never remember angry words pass between him and my mother, though both were fiery-tempered. You would say that all this adds up to a portrait of a Puritan, and that my father's character was that of a Non-conformist who had seen the light of conversion. Nothing could be further from the facts. He was not in the least religious. He was of a rather cynical humour; any joke he made or appreciated was apt to be of a sardonic character. He was very much of this world, and would say in his cynical, sensible way: 'It's always the Bible-thumpers who are the greatest hypocrites.' In his youth, I gather, he used to go to chapel along with his sister Annie: they went to the Bible Christian Chapel in the town, and here he and my mother used to attend when they first married. It did not last very long, for my mother preferred to go to church and I was brought up there. But I remember once, at least, being taken by my father to the Bible Christian Chapel at the age of three or four, and being much impressed by a venerable old patriarch with the flowing beard of Michelangelo's Moses in the Church of St. Pietro in Vincoli, who ejaculated 'Hallelujah!' and 'Praised Be!' in the course of the preacher's discourse. With the imitative faculty strongly developed in me, I said 'Hallelujah', too, after the old boy, until checked by my father.

No such respectability marked the Sundays of my father's profane brothers. They went to the pub on Sunday mornings, as they had done the previous night; their mother sat down to Sunday dinner with my father and his sister, and then they would roll home more or less tipsy about three in the afternoon, sleep it off and to the pub again in the evening, or else sit outside the house playing the instruments of which the house was full. Each of them had his own, some of them could play on two or three, and together they constituted a little band which entertained and amused the village and led all its frolics. Even my father took part in the music which was the best part of their activities and which reached its high point with Christmas time, New Year and Twelfth Night. My father's instrument was a bass-viol — which mother did not like as it woke up the baby, my sister Hilda; so he sold it and bought a harmonium, which was exchanged for a piano when she grew into girlhood — a nice example of change of taste and a degree of economic improvement. But he always had a concertina, too, right up into my boyhood, though by then he didn't play it much, and there was a banjo and a tambourine, I remember, among other instruments stowed away in the cupboard under the stairs. When I was a small child and he was not so deaf and morose as he became, he used to take me up on his knee, marking time with his foot, playing the banjo and singing:

> Nobody in the house but Dinah,
> Nobody in the house I know;
> Nobody in the house but Dinah,
> Playing on the old banjo.

I used to find that curiously affecting; I wondered who the mysterious Dinah was: she was an occupant of my world, indeed a well-known figure in the landscape, though I had never seen her. I suppose in fact she was an American nigger-woman, and this song, about which I know nothing, may have been picked up by his mining brothers in America or Africa — one or other of them was always going to and fro.

There was another one he would still sing to me with a more active, less plaintive rhythm:

> Murder in the shoe-box, fire in the spence
> I had a little donkey and I haven't seen'n sence.
> Give'n a little oats, give'n a little straw,
> Gee up, donkey! and away she go.

These and a few other snatches were the remains into my childhood of the vast repertory the brothers' orchestra must have had. Imagine the noise when you consider that there were nine of them! They were known far beyond the bounds of the village, to the hundreds of people from higher up who passed through on their way into town and who stopped outside to listen to the minstrelsy provided them gratis. The youngest brother, Edwin — called Cheelie by everybody, because he was the 'cheel' of the family, the baby — had a violin, a guitar, an accordeon, several mouth-organs, and a 'dancing doll', a kind of marionette which he had fixed up with a string at the back and which kept time with the music. George had a harp, Joe a tin-whistle, Harry a concertina and later strummed and vamped on the piano; others had other instruments, I cannot now find out what. But, all told, they were a gay, merry, music-making lot. And who can blame them when they spent most of their young days underground?

The whole family went by their nicknames, as was fairly usual in our villages, but universally the rule with the miners. It is extraordinarily like what Carew and others tell us about Elizabethan Cornwall three hundred years before: it had not changed much, except that the old language had died out; even then many of its words remained alive in our dialect. Beare, a surveyor of the Stannaries at the end of Elizabeth's reign, tells us of the special terms employed in tinners' language — an owl was a 'braced farcer', a cat a 'rooker', etc. — and the forfeit you paid if you named one of them wrongly. Carew tells us of terms which were wanting in Cornish and that they were 'fain to borrow of the English', and adds: 'Marry, this want is relieved with a flood of most bitter curses and spiteful nick-names.' So, among the brothers, Will was known as Willsham, Joe — Crewey, Jack — Bodgy, Jim — Loppin; George was Georgie Wo-pig, my father Dickless, Edwin — Cheelie. One can see the rationale of most of these names: often they were descriptive of physical characteristics, or some joke that had attached itself mercilessly to the person; or others were purely verbal, sound-associations. But almost everybody had his name. My father's chief friend in those days, Bill Hancock, was known as Bill Wit, his father Old Man Wit; Jack Hancock was Jack Bunker, his father Dick Punk, his brother Bill Punk. (These all come from notes I took down from my father, for these men are all long since dead and I never knew them.)

Of the brothers, the eldest, Tom, who was very dark and easy-going like his father, spent his life abroad in the mines on the Rand, dying there early of phthisis and drink, and is buried in Johannesburg. There is something very pathetic and moving in that close connection between our Cornish villages and South Africa. All those lads, faced with the closing down of the mines at home, flocking off to that distant land which became so familiar to so many Cornishmen; the crowded trains leaving our little stations, all their relations to see them off; the Union Castle boats to Durban, all the music and merriment on board; the arrival and the long railway journey in cattle-trucks up through the veldt to that teeming ant-heap of the Rand in the early days of the gold-rush. There were the saloons, the raw horror of Jo'burg, as they familiarly called it, the spirits and the cash freely flowing, the gold-dust in the lungs, and, too often, their home saw them no more. Or sometimes they came home, having made their little bit, and bought themselves or built a house; one saw them about the place, gaunt-visaged men, yellow-faced and with that far-away look in their eyes, while they gasped out their breath, at least along the green lanes, in the little gardens of home. As a boy I knew several of those men, and glimpsed, from the outside, something of their lives. They were regular figures in the social landscape of Cornwall whom one took for granted.

It is only now that that strange episode which linked us so closely with South Africa is over that I realize the full tragedy of their lives, the price they paid. But it is no use sentimentalizing over it. Like so much of human action it was half tragedy, half comedy; there was a great deal of *joie-de-vivre* about it as well as much heroism; if it meant aching hearts at home, many separations and much grief, there was also much fun, the enjoyment of cameraderie, the sticking together of the Cornish folk, Cousin Jacks, out there. There were fights and quarrels and jealousies; but there was also the helping hand, the close-knit ties of friendship in a strange country. There was much coming to and fro between South Africa and home. Out there, there were in time Cornish Societies and Associations which welcomed the new-comers. (These still exist, and a good many contacts continue though the flow of emigration has stopped.) At home people knew what was going on in South Africa often rather better than what was happening 'up the country': the journey across the seas to another continent was more familiar than going very far 'up the country', say as far as London. There were all the letters going to and fro between Cornwall and Cape Town and Durban; the weekly newspapers sent out to keep them in touch with doings at home, the South African papers and journals and illustrated books that came back. (One of the first papers which I read regularly for a time, later on when I was a schoolboy, was the *Cape Times*, which Charlie Courtenay sent to his wife and which she used to lend me.) One of our few books, I remember, was a book of views — Table Mountain, the long main street of Cape Town, the beaches of Durban, the Drakensberg, the tall new buildings of Johannesburg, the rickshaws, the natives. Then there were the photographs sent back: groups of Cornish miners with their native boys. A photograph of a native drawing a rickshaw hung in my father and mother's bedroom and fascinated my early attention. In the sitting-room was a photograph of my Uncle Edwin, with the inevitable musical instrument, along with a group of other miners and native boys. Friendships were made out there which would otherwise never have been: at Maritzburg or Kimberley you met Camborne or Redruth folk whom you would never have got to know in a lifetime in Cornwall. These friendships were often life-long, and when people came home on a visit there would be much linking-up of acquaintances made in South Africa. Sometimes families would be sent for, or wives would go out and keep their husbands company for a time. But usually they stayed behind, keeping the home going, looking after their children, bringing them up alone, hoping, longing for the day when their fathers would come home again — as, often, they never did.

Of my father's brothers, Tom and Edwin, the eldest and the youngest, did not return. They are buried in the same grave, or side by side, in the same cemetery in Johannesburg.

As I write, in this summer garden full of the memories of miners, the soft sea-wind but stirring the leaves of the beeches, an occasional seagull passing over, or a cruising rook, the sun making its quiet patterns on the marl, the mines that they worked in all round, green now with the ivy that has overgrown them, the slopes up towards Carclaze which were so familiar to them glimmering in the heat-haze — my eyes fill with tears for all that vanished life of which I was never a part, all those men-folk of my family whom I never knew, who never knew me, and yet will only be remembered in and through me, in so far as I celebrate them. It is a strange sensation which I cannot fully explain; I can only hope that others know what it is and share it — this nostalgia for life which catches one by the throat in the moment as it passes. But as I write I see the blue summer sea curling round the ships of those emigrant miners, the water nostrilling the stem; the palms of Cape Town; the gin-palaces and the saloons of Johannesburg; the drinking, the quarrels, the queer sex-life of the miners; the singing, the tambourines, the mingled bravery and squalor of it all. And somehow this is more affecting than the quiet gunfire which has gone on all the afternoon in the distance towards Falmouth, the rushing up and down the road of army lorries, the rumour of planes somewhere in the sky all day this Sunday of late summer.

Tom had a heart of gold: he was the best-natured man in the world, and my father always spoke of him with affection. I know nothing of him except that, like all the Rowses, he was short and thickset, muscular, strong. One other thing I heard of him once from his son, Will Rowse of Charlestown: when Edwin was killed, through the carelessness of an engine-driver, who was drunk at the time and let go the skip which crashed to the bottom of the shaft, Tom, who was devoted, as they all were, to Cheelie, swore that he would shoot the man who was responsible. And he would have done, he was 'that mad' at Cheelie's death, so Will said, if only he had been able to lay hands on him. But I suppose the engine-driver was placed under arrest; certainly the mine paid a heavy sum in compensation. As if anything could ever compensate for the loss of Cheelie's irreplaceable personality, his gaiety and spirits, to them all! One other reminiscence of Will Rowse's — the Jameson Raid, the night he and Uncle Tom and the others spent waiting for the word to go, the rifles and the whisky-bottles and the word that never came.

Cheelie was a regular card, and to judge from the stories told of him and the impression he made on all who knew him — there are still people about who remember him — he was a born actor. He was 'so full o' fun as ever 'ee could be', says my mother, 'up to any wickedness'.

After the day's work was over he would change, 'take his music and go over to the village, playin' as he went'. He was a great hand at dressing up and frightening people and all the regular amusements of the village — only he was the ringleader and chief performer in them all. 'Now look 'ere', said my mother, who used not to encourage him, 'you ent goin' to 'ave my things to put up, so go on.' But nothing daunted him, nothing would stop him. Old Betsy Hicks, who lived in a cottage at the top of Back Lane, was a preordained victim for his games and pranks. My father used to tell how one dark winter's night Cheelie made a turnip-lantern, placed a lighted candle in it, fixed it on to a clothes-post and bobbed it up and down outside Betsy's bedroom window. Betsy had gone to bed by eight o'clock and, wakened by these unwonted flickering gleams, could be heard trying to rouse her sleeping partner: 'Cusn't tha see the lightnin'?' But Mary Jane had her head safe under the bedclothes. All to Cheelie's great glee outside and for ever after. The question, 'Cusn't tha see the lightnin'?' would bring a flicker of amusement into my father's grey eyes years afterwards — and perhaps something else: the memory of that gay, unquenchable spirit, the perpetrator of those harmless little jokes.

Little enough as I have in common with the old village folk, I do share their quite irrational pleasure in this kind of simple joke, playing a prank on people, some turn or other, giving them a fright, keeping up All Fools' Day.

Cheelie was very devoted to children, himself remaining always a child at heart. He won my mother's favour, when she was apt to look on father's family with no very friendly eye, by his devotion to the baby, Hilda. She was a querulous infant, always ready to cry, but was seduced by Cheelie's attentions. He would dandle her up and down on his knee singing:

> Daisy, Daisy, give me your answer, do;
> I'm half crazy all for the love of you.

This was well received. He was very good at minding the baby. Once when mother wanted to go to Charlestown Church — it was harvest festival, and father could never get away from Sunday work: he had to milk the cows — Cheelie looked after this difficult infant the whole evening, took her out to show her proudly round the village, brought her back, gave her her bottle of milk and put her off to sleep in her cradle. This was counted unto him for righteousness, as against his 'wickednesses', by the womenfolk. He had, for instance, a way of making up songs about people he did not like, and then singing them, performing them to the village. There was one about 'Ole Rebecca Rhubarb an' Ole Joe Oogly', two sour-faced, prim persons of the next village, Lane End: very much appreciated by our village.

Then Tom sent for him to come out to South Africa. For three weeks before going he stayed with my father; mother had the job of putting his clothes in order, making green-baize cases for the beloved musical instruments he was taking with him. One day he said to her: 'By the time I come home again there'll be a cheel lookin' out of every one of they bars', pointing to the staircase. 'Iss, I reckon', said she. During the seven months he was out there he was doing well, 'poor l'il fellow' — so she told me to-night, nearly fifty years after. He made enough money to pay back Tom's wife the advance she made him for his fare, some £20, and sent home £40 for her to bank for him. My father, after an unfortunate experience with his brother Bill, refused to have anything to do with the money side of their affairs. Cheelie wanted him to look after his money for him. My father said, with his strict sense of justice: 'The one that trust you, you must trust they. I'm not havin' anything to do with it.'

During the weeks Cheelie was at home, he was forever fiddling with an old worn-out clock that had stopped working, yet hung in the kitchen over the table. One morning about eight o'clock, some months after he had gone away, while mother and father were sitting at breakfast, the clock suddenly struck 'one' out loud. 'That's funny', said my father, 'there must be a mouse in'n.' He got up and looked; there was no mouse there. Three weeks later they got the news that Cheelie had been killed on that day, about that time. They ever afterwards took it as a 'token', a signal of his death: there are many such stories in Cornish families. When the poor boy was brought up to the surface dying — he was almost cut in two by the crashed skip — he said these last words: 'I've neither father nor mother to grieve for me, so it's all right.' I have always taken those last words of an unknown Cornish lad as equal to any of the famous last words uttered by the great. He was a brave spirit, Cheelie, and has left a fragrant and beautiful memory in my family and among all that knew him. My father didn't trust himself to talk about him much, and I have noticed that there came a little pause, a silence upon the lips of these simple folk after a while, when they talked about him. I suppose they saw a glimpse in the mind's eye of that gay, dancing personality, the years roll away from them and themselves young again with him, who was for ever young. He must have been about twenty-two when he died. To think that he would have been seventy now if he were alive! Though he was dead long before I was born, I have often thought of him about the fields at Tregonissey, roaming about the village in the evening, the day's work over; but it is only to-night that I see myself in his words as one of the children 'lookin' out of they bars' by the time Cheelie came home again.

A great contrast with Tom and Cheelie was the second oldest of the brothers, Bill; for he was a bully and a ruffian — it is not too much to say a rogue and a cheat — and my father's experience with him made a marked impression upon him. It was another of the things that had hurt him when young. He never mentioned it, and never spoke of his brother Bill. It was a pity: the hurt rankled and his own case went by default. It is only quite recently that I have discovered how right he was about his brother. It seems that when my father went, like all the rest, to South Africa, Bill advanced him the money and took an IOU from him. My father went out, but only stayed there three months. He never referred to this failure: perhaps it was a failure of nerve, for it seems clear that he was not as tough as his daredevil brothers; but I gather that he was blinded temporarily by the sand-storms and dazzle of the Rand and unable to work. So, like a sensible man, he came home and, I believe, paid his brother back, but never got his IOU cancelled. Bill, like the rascal he was, presented the IOU for payment again and, when my father refused, put him in court. My father had nothing to show and was made to pay it again. His bitterness and resentment against a brother who could do such a thing knew no bounds; and there was added to it all the humiliation of defeat and of being put through a court. There was nothing to be done about it, and I think he feared his brother, who was altogether stronger and utterly unscrupulous. The only remedy was never again to speak to him, and to close his doors to Bill and his. For the rest, he kept silent. The result was that I, when I learned the mere outline of the story from someone else many years later, was convinced that he was in the wrong. In fact he was in the right, and said nothing to justify himself.

That Bill was a rogue there is not a shadow of doubt. Everybody knew it, yet the old buccaneer was never caught. He was much the cleverest and most successful member of the family. He went to America when he was young and came back with a good deal more money than he could ever have honestly earned. He was a fighter by nature. I daresay he despised my father, who was not. My father said of him: 'He'd rather fight than eat meat.' Back from America, he built the two largest houses in the village, on ground scrounged from my grandmother's holding. Then he set up as a butcher and married a butcher's daughter, Mary Stephens, sister of Dick Stephens of Trevissick, who wrestled the bear in St. Austell—a splendid dialect-story which I broadcast some time ago exactly as Dick told it me in his own words.[1] Mary, like all the Stephenses, was a fine person; fortunately she was big and strong, for she had much to put up with from Bill, who would have beaten her, had she shown the slightest sign of being cowed by him. As it was, he would hit her, and she would throw whatever was handy at him.

All the odds and ends which he couldn't sell in his shop, pig's face and trotters and belly, he would bring up to his mother and make her pay for them. She was afraid of him, or, unwilling to make a fuss, paid what he asked. One day Tom's wife, who saw the rubbish he brought in to his mother and the price he asked, protested. My father said that he would 'rob the shif' off his mother's back'. Dick Stephens used to tell the story of being in his shop one day when a man came in with a carcass, a pig or something, which Bill weighed and made out to be so many pounds weight. 'That's a funny thing,' said the man, 'I weighed'n just before comin' in and 'ee was then so many more pounds in weight. There idn' anything wrong with your scales, I suppose?' 'No, certainly not', said Bill. When the man began looking around underneath the balances, he found just so many weights as made the difference fixed under the other scale. Without turning a hair,

[1] Printed in *The Listener*, April 10th, 1941.

Bill shouted in to his wife, very indignant: 'Mary, they damned children have been 'ere playin' with the scales again. Nearly made me give Mr. So-and-so wrong weight for his pig.'

With these and other means he built up a little fortune, and was able to retire from butchering to devote himself to his favourite interests, speculation, boxing, wrestling, drinking, quarrelling with his family and making life a hell for them. He enjoyed all of these interests very much. He built himself houses, was a great fancier of boxing and wrestling. He was related to, and no doubt a backer of, Dick Allen, the Cornish boxer; and in his last years he was very proud of his acquaintance with Len Harvey. He was what is called a sportsman, and was so described by the local papers when he died. He made his wife and daughters miserable. He made my father miserable, whenever the latter thought of Bill's success and his own ill-success in life. It was poor consolation to take refuge in one's own virtue and say ' 'ee maade *'is* money by cheatin' other people'. For the old rogue certainly amassed some thousands. He was very sharp. But in his last years he had some sharp reverses. Someone told me that in one of them he had lost £7,000 on Japanese bonds, so that he must have had a fair amount to lose.

One day, many years ago, he saw my brother in the Market-house, and some odd turn of conscience made him say: 'You're Dick's boy, aren't 'ee? Here's a penny for 'ee': of which my brother was oddly proud. He might have made it the £20 of which he robbed father. He would certainly not have succeeded in giving me a penny. I knew him well enough by sight – he was the very spit of my father: but I never spoke to him in my life, and in his latter years, when he would gladly have been spoken to – for his family life was miserable and he lost both his daughters in young middle-age – I ignored him. I think he knew who I was, and I was told that in late years, the old man was proud of his connection with me; it was suggested that he would very much like to see me and wouldn't I go and talk to him? It never even occurred to me to do so, so deep-rooted was the ostracism with which he had been treated in our family from years before my birth.

When at length the old man died – he had, of course, outlived father, was proud of being the only one of the Rowses to reach eighty –

his death was noticed in the papers as that of my uncle. For a moment in Oxford, away from the family background, the environment of that old feud, I regretted that I had never had a talk with him: he must have had so many interesting memories. He, better than anybody alive, could have told me about the 'old days at Tregonissey', which I so much wanted to know about. He had had a variegated, interesting life — in America, in South Africa, on board ship, through his passion for and contacts with sport. He was so much cleverer and shrewder than father, with so much more to tell me. He had wanted to see me before he died. Of course, he did not hold with my political views; he used, I gather, to 'go on' against them. He didn't hold with my being Labour. He was a diehard Tory, and a pillar, if that is the word, of the Conservative and Constitutional Club in the town. He must have voted against me in the elections of 1931 and 1935.

When I reflect on what he was, and what he might have had to tell me that most interests me, if he were dying and asked me urgently to come, still I would not have gone. My father in me would have won that last round of the long contest between them — as he certainly wins it now!

'To weave on our former web', as Carew says — from notes I took down from father. Such schooling as he had was at a dame's school in the house which subsequently became our shop, where I was born: at that time it was just two little cottages, which Uncle Rowe must have converted when he married and set up in business. In the downstairs room which became our sitting-room Granny Collins carried on her dame's school, which she combined with a sweetshop; so that when her back was turned (she hobbled about on a crutch) her pupils helped themselves to lollipops and bull's-eyes. But when it came to tea-treat and Sunday-school outing, she did not forget to put a few sweets into the hand of each of her pupils. The little boys and girls used to sit on forms on either side of the table, with Granny Collins at the head; she had a cane which would reach any of them, and also a custiss — this had a round, flat end for hitting the palm of the hand. There were two classes: the 'ABC' class and the 'G-O, go' class. Later she moved out and up Back Lane, I suppose on Uncle's accession. This must have been at the end of the sixties. Father went then to a dame's school at the corner of Polketh, near the little old chapel which I remember as a stable — now demolished to make way for council houses. Thence, after the Education Act of 1870 (he would be seven), he went to the National School, which later became the Church School we children attended on Sundays. The girls sat on one side, the boys on the other. The master was a brute. One of the younger teachers was H. I. Hugh, who was subsequently my headmaster at the elementary school at Carclaze.

There they learned reading, writing and sums. Father was taken away when he was in Standard II at the age of eight or nine, and for a few weeks went to Mount Charles School while carrying dinners to the mine, Wheal Eliza or Bucklers, where his father and brothers were working. Then he was taken on by Uncle Rowe to go on his rounds with him, collecting rags and selling china. Mitchell, the whipper-in, coming into the shop to ask how old he was, for children had to go to school till they were thirteen, 'Thirteen', answered father, as Uncle had told him to. That ended his schooling.

The consequence was that he was a very poor scholar — though rather better than mother, whose schooling was after the same pattern, though even more exiguous. He could read sufficiently for his purposes, which meant the newspaper; he never read a book: I doubt if he ever read a book in his life, not even the Bible, which so many of the old-stagers, like my maternal grandmother, read in a great deal. He wrote with difficulty, and very little; though in the last months of his life, shut up in a nursing-home and hospital, he wrote to me at Oxford and in London a flood of letters, every one of which I kept. They were simple and direct, moving in their way, with a gleam of self-deprecatory humour, though he was frequently in pain. I think he must have found, to his surprise, the pleasure of self-expression, that same pleasure which dawned upon me as a child, very lonely and left to my own devices. Busy as I was then at the University and with my research, and ill off and on all those years with a duodenal ulcer, I could hardly keep pace in my replies. But I kept his letters. For some years I had had the idea that one day I would write his life, a life without interest, without incident, but of which that would be the very point — the life of a plain working man. After all, Prime Ministers and famous persons had their lives written, and I was determined that he should have his. It would be much more rare; and because of its rarity, and because at the same time it was of a type, it would be all the more significant. But it would be more difficult, because of his reserve, his essential inhibitedness. He knew that I had this in mind, and that I had an exercise book inscribed *The Life of Richard Rowse*, into which I would write such memories as with difficulty I could persuade him to tell me. I do not think he took it very seriously, or much liked the idea. Immured within the walls of reserve, disappointment and deafness, he was too dissatisfied with his life and its lack of achievement. But I still held to my idea of writing his life, in spite of its difficulties — the silences, the lacunae — the more firmly in the months after he died, and I thought that I would publish his letters with it, as a faithful portrait of a working man, who had had no education or opportunity in life, but was of the salt of the earth. They would, after all, I thought, be more worth having than the letters of most English dukes.

So father, his schooling finished at the age of nine, would be heaved up on Uncle's cart packed with cloam (i.e. china), cramped down in front. All over the district Uncle was known, Mr. Rawe the ragman — a title which Auntie could not bear to hear. They went as far as Roche in one direction, where they used to have a cup of cocoa, and as far as Goran Haven the other way. At St. Blazey Uncle would do the whole place, finishing up at four o'clock in the afternoon at Aunt Mary's, who always got him a cup of tea and a red herring, while father looked after the horse and afterwards had his share. If everything was going all right and he was taking money, Uncle would be as 'plaised as puss'; but if he saw a magpie he would say: 'Damn that bird! No luck to-day.' If he saw two magpies, he would say:

> One for sorrow, two for mirth;
> Three for a wedding, four for a birth.

If he went into a shop where Burton, his professional rival, had just been and delivered a load: 'Aw, my Gore! He'd swear like anything!'

But in general, as he was prospering and enjoyed life enormously, Uncle was in a good humour and used to spend much of his time out on the road singing loudly in that clear, bell-like voice, with the fruity tremolo for affecting passages and songs, of which he was very proud. Going out any distance, to Penwithick or Tywardreath, he would sing 'Beautiful Isle of the Sea':

> Round her splendid form
> I drew a magic circle:
> I kissed her and called her a pretty girl.

After fifty years, father was not very sure of the words; there was one with the refrain:

> Don't sob and cry,
> That was the words the poor mother said,
> Cheer up my darlings.

'You knaw the top of th' 'ill, that's where 'ee used to sing: sing like a bird up there, and coming down over th' 'ill.'

I can bear that out from my own experience forty years later, for as father was in at the beginning of Uncle's business career, so was I at the end of it. I do not remember going any other than the Penwithick trip — my brother went about much more with him. But that had one great excitement for me. There was first the long steep pull up Carclaze Hill, up which we crawled, Uncle flicking his whip and scolding the horse, with an occasional rattle of china in the rear of the trap. When we had got on the high flat table-land of the Higher Quarter, with the view over all the bay behind us and over the moors to Helman Tors and Brown Willy and Rowtor on the skyline, and with that lovely pure moorland air with all the scents of the moor in it, Uncle would fill his lungs and burst into song. And no wonder! I think his favourite song in my time was

> O where is my wandering boy to-night?
> O where is my boy to-night?

I found that, at the age of five, very affecting; and so did Uncle, who was easily moved by his own emotions; there was a sob in his voice as he sang it. And Auntie (good soul) never failed to be moved to tears by his rendering of it, as he stood before the kitchen fire in the new house he had built to retire to at Hillside. Like Mr. Gladstone singing together with Mrs. Gladstone on the Victorian hearth. This was Uncle's talent which was death to hide, though not his only one; and he enjoyed his success in this as in other spheres. There were other songs, too, which he carolled or quavered, as the case demanded, along that delectable bit of road.

As for me, the great excitement of it was that, on the left-hand side, opposite the deep gash in the soil, Carclaze Pit, where father worked in later years, there was a large pool dammed up for use in connection with the pit. Sometimes after rain the water came right up to the roadside, where it was shallow, and Uncle would drive the horse a little way in, to do his fetlocks good (I suppose) and let him drink. It was a regular ritual here and one which I looked forward to not without a tremulous excitement, for I was a timorous and easily-frightened child. But I loved it all the same: as you looked out over the front of the trap where you were stowed away safely, there was nothing but a waste of waters before you. I believed it was a lake; it was my Lake Superior or Victoria Nyanza. There was the delicious sucking noise of the horse drinking; perhaps a lark singing (there was always a lark singing up there); for the rest, silence: Uncle did not resume until we were well on the road again; the tufts of grass and rushes lifted their heads above the water; there was nothing but water so far as the eye could see, away from the road: I was careful to look only that way. I knew that further in it must be unfathomably deep; I hugged myself with the thought of the danger in going further in. At the same time I trusted Uncle, and we never did go further in than the edge. Yet it was always with a pang of disappointment that I watched him tug the horse's reins and drive away once more from the margins of enchantment and the lake to resume our jog-trot along the prosaic road to Mr. Sturtridge's at Penwithick.

The truth was that Uncle and Auntie — they were Uncle and Auntie *sans phrase* or qualification to us, for they were the dominating figures in the background — were real characters and in themselves the most interesting members of the family. When they lived in the village, a time which I don't remember, for I was born a year or two after we took their place at the shop, they reigned undisputed — as somebody called them, King and Queen of Tregonissey. And so they well deserved to be, for they had more intelligence, business-sense, character, energy and general liveliness than anybody else in the village. They had a tremendous sense of fun and bubbled over with enjoyment of life. They were great hands at laughing — laughing in a way one never sees now. 'Laugh? he'd laugh like a pisky', was the usual phrase about Uncle: it meant that he would go off into a paroxysm of laughter — he was a very Dickensian figure — shut his eyes and hold his shaking sides. They were both of them completely unselfconscious, unrestrained, unrepressed. They were successful and prosperous; there was no one in the village or anywhere else to say them nay. They were a good-hearted old couple, who made a wonderful life together. I think the clue to it was their happiness in each other, their happy comradeship; they were lovers all their life long. And when Auntie died, life had nothing more, had no goodness or savour whatsoever for Uncle; he lingered for a year or two, a miserable shadow of his former self, longing to join her whom he thought about all day and all night. I think he was the only man I have ever known who really did die of a broken heart.

But this was in the far future at the time I am writing of. Auntie had had a small competence of her own, and that had been the making of Uncle in marrying her. Her mother — by name Hore — had kept a shop at Mount Charles; her brother had gone away to America when young, and they never heard of him again. What became of him they never knew — whether he was killed or what. 'Ma used to grieve terrible about him', Auntie once told mother. That kind of tragedy was not unusual in Cornish families of those days. I remember her telling me that as a girl she had seen the first railway train pass through Mount Charles: they all went over to the bridge over the railway-cutting to look down on the great event.

Anyway, their marriage was blissfully happy, and everything prospered with them. The only thing that wanted to make it perfect was children. And as is the way, it seemed, with childless couples, they were both devoted to children, especially Auntie, though Uncle was no less good with them. They had never had any — though perfectly fit physically. Auntie was a little, fat round woman, with the red, healthy complexion of a dried apple, sparkling blue eyes always ready to laugh, short, crisp, dark hair. Uncle was made on a larger scale, with fine large nose and hands and drooping walrus moustache: mischievous, merry blue eyes. However, they didn't take their childlessness tragically; they just did the next best thing and made what they could of us. They were particularly fond of us two boys, though especially, I think, of my brother, who was called (hopefully) George, after Uncle. When he was a little boy Auntie used to have him up to stay with her for weeks on end. By the time I came — I do not remember that she was particularly fond of me — our place was filled.

One of my father's good-for-nothing brothers lost his wife, whom in life he had maltreated; she left him with a family of small children, who were pitifully neglected, and what was to be done with them? Father wanted to adopt one of them, but was not allowed to by my mother; he persuaded Auntie and Uncle to take the little girl instead — a regular Rowse she was, spirited and independent. It was a very foolish move. Auntie and Uncle adopted the child and brought her up as their own. Father had always been promised that he should have the house we lived in, as Harry was to have his. There was also a row of new houses which Uncle had built at the top of the hill, beside his own larger house to which they retired from the shop. Anybody could have foreseen what would happen. After Auntie's death, Uncle went away to live with his adopted daughter, now married, and not un-naturally made a new will, leaving all his property, including the house we lived in, to her. A short while after — it was just after the last war — she exchanged the whole lot for a packet of shipping shares with one of her husband's relations. The shares soon became worthless, and there was all Uncle's property in the hands of strangers. My father had been a fool; an honest, upright, but unmistakable fool. He never forgave himself or Uncle. It became the King Charles's head of his later years.

Auntie and Uncle, living in their grand house, with two bow-windows, on the hill above us, represented to us the very idea of opulence. They were, compared with our working-class standards, well-to-do. They had, as I now see, risen from the level of working people into that of the lower middle-class. They had made their little pile; they were property-owners living mainly on the proceeds. In their new house they lived in what was grandeur to us — the grandeur of the small rentier, with superior furniture and piano, a dining-room furnished in red plush, as well as a drawing-room in which they reposed on Sunday afternoons, snoring one each side of the bright fire leaping up in winter. They had gone up in the world, but I am sure they missed the fun and frolics of the village in which they had led. Indeed, Auntie said to my mother many and many a time: 'If I had known how lonely I was going to be coming away from the village I would never have left the shop, Aunt Annie.' (Mother, I am afraid, did not sympathize with this, but went through exactly the same experience when her turn came to leave village and shop twenty years later.)

In those earlier days, according to my father, they always used to be dressing up in the village, frightening each other, taking each other in. The great point was to 'have' somebody, never to be 'had' yourself. Uncle, as the cleverest of them, used to manage to 'have' them all; but was occasionally caught out himself and then got 'vex'. One night he put a sheet all round himself and rode up through the village on a donkey, frightening everybody: they were all very prone to seeing ghosts and took them seriously. Another night, 'there was donkeys down eatin' 'is flowers — 'ee used to worship 'is flowers, you knaw —, an' 'ee got out, an' put 'is slippers on an' run through the village with nothin' on but 'is shirt. Ole Mrs. Johns 'eard somethin' an' looked out o' window, an' saw this figure runnin' through the village. She was frightened to death, thot she see'd a ghost. In the mornin' she come over to Auntie in the shop, an' said: "Aw, my dear life! I see'd a ghost runnin' through the village in the night. Ess, I did, sure 'nough, an' no mistaake 'bout et." "Where did a go?" said Aunt Rawe, all solemn-like. "'E went through the village and run down town way." I suppawse Mrs. Johns never knawed to this day 'oo 'twas. Aunt Rawe wudn' the one to tell 'er.'

Mother's comment on this: 'There used to be some fun op there with 'em. Awful ole plaace w'en I went op there first, nearly forty years ago. Aunt Rawe used to laff till 'er sides fairly shaaked.'

Next door to my grandmother lived an old couple called Bray. Mrs. Bray rejoiced in the name of Lavinia; they had three daughters, Maria, Selina, Triphena, who was always referred to as Tite or Titey. (Cf. constructions such as 'God damn tha, Tite, if tha dusna be quite, I'll knock tha over th'ead with the cracket.' Cracket=three-legged stool.) Mr. Bray was an odd old man with a wooden leg, and very mean. To play on that characteristic was the point of Uncle's turn, for Mrs. Bray *per contra* was generous and would give away anything. One Christmas night — it was a downpour of rain — 'Uncle dressed up like

49

Mr. Craddick op Trewoon: they used to call 'ee ole Figger Jerk. 'Ee went for to the door — 'twas rainin' an' the wind was blawin', an' 'ee knocked to the door an' said:

"If you plaise, 'ave 'ee got an umbrella you cud lend me? I've got a long way to go. I'm Mr. Craddick op Trewoon."

"Iss", said Mrs. Bray to once; "I've got an' ole wan you can 'ave" —

she was always willin' to give or lend anythin'. ('Course Uncle knaw'd that an' went there purpose for a bit o' fun.) But ole Mr. Bray 'olla'd out an' said:

"No, you went lend 'ee no umbrella. Thees'll never 'ave'n no more. I knaw'n. Tha's ole Figger Jerk, live op Trewoon. Thee's went 'av'n." '

The point of these turns was never to be discovered at the time, but to have the laugh of your neighbours afterwards. But sometimes the joke was on Uncle, as when a boy called Harvey Dick 'tiptooed into Auntie's shop and saw Uncle takin' the bee stingle out of Auntie's backside'. Uncle was furious at this impertinence: the best one in the village at 'having on' others, he could not bear to be 'had on' himself. All the same he was highly tickled at a valentine he once received, a picture of a chamber-pot with the inscription 'George Rawe, Piss-pot Dealer'. After all he sold them, and was not ashamed to hang the valentine up in his china-shop *pour encourager les autres*. Auntie tried to discourage this and deprecated it, but with no depth of conviction; she was too much amused herself, as he very well knew, and that only tickled him the more. There was a healthy eighteenth-century broadness about all this side of life, though with regard to sex they were very prudish— Victorian of the Victorians.

The ritual of life provided them with other amusements; for example, they sang together a lot. Every Christmas morning Uncle would sing the old Cornish carol:

As I sat on a sunny bank, a sunny bank,
On Christmas Day in the morning,
I spied three ships come sailing by, sailing by,
On Christmas Day in the morning:

Who was on those three ships
        but Joseph and his fair lady?
He did whistle and she did sing
And all the bells on earth did ring.

Auntie would chime in with the chorus. Then they would sing in duet the famous old carol:

I can sing you one-O.
What is your one-O?
One of them's a lily-white babe
Clothed all in green-O.

And so on right up to the Twelve Apostles. It took a jolly long time. But these old people had plenty of time on their hands: no cinemas, no wireless, no gadding about by bus and car. They had to provide their own amusements, and this they did heartily and with vivacity and inventiveness. I daresay they were the last generation in which the fullness of old Cornish customs and ways was maintained. For all these same songs were sung by my mother's parents, Granny and Grandfather Vanson; while the next generation, their children, were incapable of singing them. There was an unconscious change of taste and habit going on which let these old things die, so that by the next generation again, mine, they had practically completely gone and we never heard them.

So with the games and dressing-up and practical jokes, we did not find them so funny as they had: they derived amusement from them over years and would laugh till tears ran from their eyes when the old folk who remembered them got together and recalled the 'old days'. But then we had never taken part in them, and, I suppose, were affected unconsciously by the change of taste. The jokes were very elementary; we did not find them so amusing. But I have no doubt now that there was infinitely greater value, more character, variety and fun in the amusement which they provided for themselves and of their own inventiveness — genuine folk-creativeness in its own way — than in all the passive, provided amusements of cinemas, jazz-dancing, swing-music, theatre-organs (the most horrible invention of the human mind), in our own doped, decadent and rather despicable age.

One respect in which Auntie and Uncle were obviously superior, socially, to us was that they had been to London — a great test — not once only, but several times. They did not talk a great deal about it, but there it was all the same in the background. Nobody else in the village had been to London. The very names which sometimes appeared in their conversation and indicated their acquaintance with the great world were symbols of mystery and excitement to me. There was the Tower of London, the instruments of torture, the block, the axe, which most stirred my imagination. With them it was undeniably Madame Tussaud's (I saw her as an exotic, rather sinister figure, like a circus-lady, raking in the cash) which made the greatest and most lasting impression upon their country minds. Auntie had turned to the policeman at the foot of the stairs and asked the usual question: 'Can you tell me, is this the way up?' He was part of the waxworks: great joke. It was then that Auntie first tasted ice-cream. Mrs. Lake, her companion on several visits to London — the Lakes owned the earthenware store at St. Austell and Uncle dealt with them — Mrs. Lake protested: 'I can't eat this, Kate. I must take it home and warm it up before I can eat it.' Auntie was tickled to death. She and Uncle went to hear Spurgeon, who was ever afterwards a great hero of theirs. They were devoted readers of *The Christian Herald*: I don't know if that was one of the many sources of profit which enabled Spurgeon to keep up his opulent establishment, country-house, coach and all. What a typical Victorian capitalist he was, the nasty type, his stocks and shares people's hopes of the next world and sensational thrills in this! Auntie and Uncle were fairly regular chapel-goers — especially Auntie, whose own uncle had been for years the Bible Christian minister at St. Austell, and there she attended and I suppose had a pew. Father and mother gradually dropped off completely, what with the shop and the children and housework to attend to, and when mother re-emerged as a church-goer, like the phoenix, it it was to church she went.

The second respect in which these two old Victorians were undoubtedly superior to the next generation was in their reading. Father and mother seem hardly ever to have read a book — father not at all, mother only one or two when in service: *Molly Bawn*, a popular Victorian novelette, did much duty on her lips when reading was in question. But Auntie and Uncle had read a number of books, and Dickens was their great favourite. They read aloud to each other in the evenings; usually she read, till Uncle fell into a slumber punctuated by snores in a gathering crescendo which broke and woke him up, when he attended again until the next attack of somnolence. 'Go's home, co, Rawe', she would say affectionately, but all the same a little put out by his inability to keep awake after the day in the open air. But they knew their favourite books of Dickens well: they shed tears together over the sorrows of Little Nell and the graveyard scene in *Bleak House*. There was one of the stories the point of which they would not divulge to me — it must have been about some girl having a baby — but the thought of which brought the ready tears to their eyes.

Reading Dickens was a great experience they had in common; they cried and laughed (chiefly cried) over him together. It meant a great deal to them — their contact with the great world of literature, a closed book to my practically illiterate parents. What a wizard Dickens was! To think of him writing away there in Gadshill, and pulling the heart-strings of this old couple far away in remote Victorian Cornwall. We may take their emotional response as so much evidence of what appealed most widely in Dickens to his contemporary public — the very parts we most deplore. Shakespeare, too, meant something to them, chiefly opportunities for Uncle to declaim: he would stand up, invariably stick his right hand into his waistcoat, a gesture he must have caught from some actor, and then say with a very special voice, trembling with falsetto emotion:

Who steals my purse steals trash;

(a sentiment he was very far from entertaining in life)

'tis something, nothing;
'Twas mine, 'tis his, and has been slave to thousands;
But he that filches from me my good name
Robs me of that which not enriches him,
And makes me poor indeed.

('Slave to thousands': what did that mean, I used to wonder? I understood the first line best: WHO STEALS MY PURSE STEALS TRASH: the way Uncle brought out 'trash' and ''tis something, nothing; 'Twas mine, 'tis his', was thrilling.) I doubt if my parents had so much as heard the name of Shakespeare; nor were there any books in our house. (If you were to look at the present state of affairs, either at home or in my rooms at Oxford, a study full of books, two book-rooms, books in the bedrooms, books on the stairs, books on the floor, everywhere, even in the pantry, you would see that I have subsequently rather rectified this — perhaps over-compensated it, as the psychologists say.)

I am afraid that Uncle, with all his laughing and singing, was a bit of a *faux-bonhomme*. It did not mean that he had a really generous disposition — it was Auntie who had that, the kindest, truest of hearts: he just amused himself and enjoyed the success and applause his stories and singing and turns brought him. He had no real disposition to help others. Sometimes his *jeux d'esprit* were returned on him by the innocent or the more sophisticated. There was an old reprobate, Frankie Dewlaps, who used to vary bouts of a week or more off at Plymouth, in which he spent all his money on drink and women, with being washed in the blood of the Lamb and being eternally saved: this old boy had a terrifying appearance which betrayed his pleasures to the knowing eye and with which he used regularly to frighten me as a child. Uncle, who had a name for everybody, used to call him Ole Leatherlips. A Falmouth cousin of mine who used to stay with us and liked being about with Uncle, went into the shop one day in front of Frankie and said loudly: 'Uncle, Ole Leatherlips is here.' He thought that that was his name. Afterwards Uncle had to tell him: 'You mustn't call him that to his face; I only call him that behind his back.'

He received a lesson in his later years in his decline — after Auntie died he deteriorated apace, into miserliness and careless apathy — from a pompous auctioneer who came into our district with a pompous name and who aped the manners of the gentry. This ass was putting up for the urban council. For weeks before the election Uncle, who was a considerable ratepayer, was the recipient of a careful 'Good morning, Mr. Rowe' from the gent who had never deigned to recognize him before. Uncle, in his innocence, was very pleased and looked out every morning for this honour as welcome as the rising sun. One morning after the election was over — Uncle had probably forgotten to vote — when he looked out for the passing auctioneer in his glory, the newly-elected turned his head in the other direction. Uncle was furious, and, to his credit, saw the explanation in a moment. From that minute the auctioneer was always referred to as Vinegar-Chaks (='cheeks), apposite enough to that soured expression.

It goes to show how utterly innocent Uncle was, who was shrewd enough in other spheres, how at a loss in the realm of politics. The same was true of my father and of all the village folk. Of all the talk that went on around me in all those years, I never heard a word of politics. My father voted Liberal — I remember the red and yellow rosette of Tommy Agar-Robartes stuck on the pincushion by the stove in the elections of 1910 — as all the other china-clay workers voted Liberal, because the china-clay captains were Liberals. My grandfather Vanson voted Liberal, because the Carlyons on whose estate he was employed were — strange as it may seem — Liberals. My mother was a member of the Primrose League, because she went to church: not that it meant anything to her, or she had the remotest conception of its purpose; I think my Aunt Rowe was a member, too, and together they went for pleasant outings to Carhayes Castle and such places. My father and mother were never Labour, until after the War, just before going to Oxford, I began to take an interest in politics and got them to vote Labour. It didn't matter to them, or to anybody else in the village, which way they voted: they hadn't the faintest idea what it was all about or the slightest interest in learning. A Labour man myself, the son of the working people, when my middle-class friends of the intellectual Left assume the political capacity of the people, their rationality and responsibility about public affairs, I know to the roots of my being what nonsense they are talking, and how right the Conservative view of human nature is, its congealed stupidity, childishness, credulity, liability to panic — in a word, its political foolery.

Intellectuals, Liberals, are profoundly wrong, precisely because they are not like ordinary human beings themselves and would make mankind in their own image — reasonable, or rather rational, not to say rationalist, intelligent, public-spirited, responsible, political. They idealize the people because they do not know what they are really like; they see them from the outside, rather patronizingly, hopefully, as a schoolmaster, if young and optimistic, sees his pupils — growing daily more and more like himself. Because I belong to the people, born and bred among them, and have never lost contact with them, I have no such illusions.

CHAPTER III

FAMILY

SUCH was the environment into which I was born.

I have said nothing yet of my mother's family, from which I get all my inherited characteristics, temperament, emotional disposition, and so on. If I get anything from the Rowses (I do not take after them physically) it is only a certain pugnacity, for they were excessively pugnacious, impatience, shortness of temper, a gift for music: a deep love of it which, had it been given a chance, might have determined my life for me in quite a different direction, for nothing carries me away as music does — not poetry, not painting, nor religion, nor politics (that is on an altogether lower level: the public, as opposed to the private, life), not even love or friendship, nothing. I think I would rather have been a great musician, or just a pianist, than anything, as certainly it is the life and work of a great composer, a Beethoven or Bach, Mozart or Schubert, a Brahms or Debussy — but, most of all, Beethoven — that I admire above all human kind. In default, perhaps, of that, there is something frustrated about my life and its modes of self-expression. I have thought sometimes that it was for want of the religious life:

> opening the casements
> upon what inner kingdoms,
> what peace forgotten,
> save in the unquiet tongues of bells
> ringing to church on Christmas Eve . . .

as I have written in my poem in memory of Charles Henderson. Even there it is to be noticed that that mood is induced by the sound of bells ringing, for with me music and religion are inseparably entwined. But I know which is fundamental.

There could hardly be a greater contrast than between my father's family and my mother's. The Rowses were a family of men, the Vansons were mainly women; and certainly where masculine traits almost exclusively characterized the one, in the other the feminine element was markedly dominant (even in the men, I think). There was a regular Rowse physical type: short, thickset, muscular, energetic, inclining to be stout, round-headed, and many of them — Bill, my father, Harry, Edwin — were sandy-haired and blue-eyed. My mother's family were all tall, long-headed and dark: Mediterranean type (Atlantic extension), and I should add that they were distinctly good-looking, which the Rowses were not. In character there was as great a contrast; where the one was fiery, fighting and rather dare-devil, miners' stock, the other was passive, well-mannered, emotional, cautious, inclined to make its way by a distinct strain of obsequiousness and flattery. In short, it looks very much like my contrast between the men of the 'Higher Quarter' and those of the coastal plain, the miners as opposed to the men on the arable land.

Yet there are exceptions to this, for my grandmother, who was the dominant force in her large Victorian family, from whom nearly all my recognizable characteristics come, was anything but submissive or obsequious, and flattered nobody. Indeed, she was liable to make life difficult for herself and her pacific husband by her unbridled tongue; but such was her force of character that she managed to compensate the damage she did in one direction by her conquests in another. She was not a Vanson, but a Goynes, and overwhelmingly the most interesting personality of the whole lot.

You may notice that both these names are uncommon, and it may be that they are French. In my grandfather's family there is a tradition, which I have now heard of from two sources, that they came over from France at the time of the Revolution and landed at Polkerris — that delicious little cove which I can almost see from these windows (if it were not for the bluff on which stands Appletree Mine), some way along the Gribbin peninsula: a tiny fishing village, now almost deserted by its fishermen, with its pier and a few nets and crab-pots lying in the sun, the air filled with the thick scent of honeysuckles and fuchsias and veronicas in summer, a dog or two scratching themselves lazily in the one little street. An almost Italian scene, facing the eye of the western sun. There the Vansons came in, and there their family lived. It seems that they had no friends or relations, and theirs is the only name of that kind we know of. I have subsequently wondered whether it may not represent the French pronunciation of Vincent.

My grandfather, Edward Vanson, was one of five sons and one daughter. Two of the boys went to sea, one of them, Christopher, being drowned young, the other living out his life as a sailor. Harry went to America. Grandfather, from the time that I remember him, was a noble-looking, beautiful old man. He had a very fine profile, a well-shaped Norman nose, clean, tall forehead, deep blue eyes and white beard, fairly full but kept trim. A slight stroke had drawn down one of his eyes; it did not disfigure his good looks, but gave further character to his appearance. He was extremely gentle and patient and courteous — I never heard him say a rough word in his life, though he had a good deal to put up with from grandmother, whom he was completely under the thumb of, and for the rest adored. He had a wonderful way with animals, so gentle and instinctively understanding; after all, he passed so much of his life among them. But it was a marked contrast to my father, who had also had a good deal to do with them, but was impatient and fussy and often ill-tempered — my grandfather, never. And then he had such a wonderful voice for dealing with them: however restive the pony or donkey — we had a succession of ponies and ended up with an excellent donkey, which we had for years — however restive with the long wait at the lodge-gates at Tregrehan, bitten by the summer flies under the trees, grandfather could do what he liked with his golden-toned, long 'Whoa, my beauty' and patient, discerning hand. When mother was a little girl at home on the farm at Quintrells, among the dark pine-woods of Crinnis, she used to follow him at the plough driving his team of oxen, and would listen to him saying: 'Whoa there, Neat and Comely, Spark and Beauty'. And years later, when I was a lad and he an old man, I used to get him to say 'Whoa there' — he said it so beautifully.

Apparently, long before my mother married into his family, Uncle Rowe, out on his St. Blazey round, used to notice how good-looking grandfather was — he was especially struck by his fresh pink and white complexion, his blue eyes — and would come home and say to Auntie: 'There's a 'ansome lookin' man that do work in the fields to Tregrehan.' Later he used to tell mother: 'Your father is too good-lookin' a man to be ploughin' the fields' — the point of view of a *petit-bourgeois* who had risen a bit above the level of the working people, which my Uncle was. But grandfather was quite contented to be ploughing, as he was with his life all through: never the discontent of my father, who felt all the time — it gave an edge to his temper — that he hadn't done justice to himself. Nor had he. Grandfather was happily married: he adored his wife, 'Elizabeth' as he always said in full, with deference, as if he were talking of Queen Elizabeth. And she was his Queen Elizabeth. Mother to me: ''Ee was s'aisy as n'ole duck with mother, you knaw 'ee was: dearly loved 'er.'

Whether this worship and all the deference she received from a numerous family — nobody dared to answer her back — was good for her is another question. She certainly was spoiled by her husband — Edward, as she called him grandly, where others called him Ned. There was a remarkable degree of mutual courtesy between this simple couple, an old-fashioned respect which was even a little formal, something a little Spanish in our eyes. There were things that grandmother would not think of doing before her husband — such as giving vent to an unfortunate sound, to use Strachey's elegant periphrasis. And, of course, *a fortiori* — if I am not thought guilty of a pun — for grandfather in her presence.

She was a farmer's daughter, born, I believe, in the parish of Duloe. Her mother died young, her father married again, and then the three daughters of the first marriage were 'not wanted at home'; their father sent them down to Tywardreath, where they were brought up by their aunt. But her earliest memories, and her relations, were all of those delightful places in the lovely Looe Valley: Morval and Morval Church which they went to in childhood, Sandplace and Widegates and Hessenford, that pretty village in the hollow with the little River Seaton running clear through it. Such were the names that appeared in her conversation, and there she would occasionally visit her relations in later life. Her family name was Goynes, another rare name with a French sound to me. It certainly is not a Cornish name. Might it not be some French name such as Guynes?

These coastal districts of Cornwall have historically had a considerable infusion of foreign blood, mainly French and Breton. For example, Q.'s descent from Quillers of Polperro — and thereby hangs a fascinating story. It is curious that I, who have been used to considering myself 100 per cent Cornish — Cornish on both sides of my family — really go back to this Goynes strain for my characteristics, and that is probably French. My grandmother had the looks of a dark handsome old Frenchwoman. And then there is, too, the probable enough story of the French origin of the Vansons. It may partly account for the deep French sympathies I remark in myself. I have nothing but loathing for Teutonism and Teutonic characteristics; even their very virtues I hate and despise. I regard them as barbarians — culturally inferior: which, indeed, to do them justice, they know they are. So much of German reflection on the subject, their literature and deplorable record of self-assertiveness, springs from their deep, and justified, sense of inferiority to the West, the centre of European civilization. So many of the greatest Germans have felt that: look at Rilke.

It may account, too, for the extreme pleasure I took as a schoolboy in learning French — I would rather speak French perfectly than any other European language — and the distaste I had as a young Fellow of All Souls for learning German.

So, too, with my feelings for Paris. Paris was the first great city in which I ever spent so much as a month. A feeling for London did not come until much later — till I had a little flat of my own and lived there. But as soon as ever I had any money to go abroad, which was not until I became a Fellow of All Souls, I went straight to Paris, and fell for the place as for nowhere else. Something in it — not merely its appearance, lovely as that is, nor entirely its history and associations, incomparable as they have been — but something in its personality as a whole, some gift of grace, appealed to something deep in me. I felt about Paris as Daudet felt ('Nostalgie de Caserne'), as Baudelaire and Verlaine felt, and Renoir and Manet, and Matthew Arnold and Joyce and Rilke, or as the English medievals must have felt when they thronged the lecture-rooms of Abélard and William of Champeaux, jostled in the Rue du Cloître or the Rue de la Chanoine or fought in the Pré aux Clercs. As I write, I remember the little Prince Impérial in exile sighing: 'If only I might see the bus from Grenelle for the Buttes-Montmartre debouching from the Rue du Bac.' And I think of the Fontaine de Médicis in the Luxembourg Gardens, the children playing paper-boats on the ponds, the bookstalls in the arcades of the Odéon, the solemn-faced, lively-eyed, grey-bearded old Frenchmen making their discriminating rounds. Or it is the Tuileries Garden upon which my room in the Hôtel du Quai Voltaire looked: it pleased me to find later that Rilke and the English poets of the nineties always stayed there. I had a name of my own for those gardens winking with their myriad lights under the trees: the Champs des Lumières. There was the thought of that hurried retreat of Eugénie from the Tuileries all down the long galleries of the Louvre to the fiacre of the American dentist waiting to take her away to safety. My earliest stay in Paris was at a little pension off the Place St. Sulpice, in a tiny street, the Rue Honoré Chevalier. And all that neighbourhood was filled for me with the thought of Renan and the Séminaire de St. Sulpice just across the street, now occupied by a barracks. How intolerable it is to think of Paris under the heel of the Germans, of all European peoples the least civilized: that city which has been for so long the centre of European civilization!

All this is a far cry from my grandparents who, I believe, had never been as far as Plymouth in their lives. But it at least serves to explain something that is rather un-Cornish in my cast of mind, in spite of Cornish ancestry on both sides, and a wholly Cornish temperament. It accounts for my sympathy with French realism of outlook, the point of view of Latin peoples and their culture; a certain distaste for the kind of Puritan idealism which is apt to shade off into smugness and from that into hypocrisy.

People do not realize that to be Cornish is a very different thing from being English. It means having quite a different temperament for one thing. In a way, the English do not go in much for temperament; they certainly don't approve of giving way to it, as Celts are apt to do. Intellectually I share the English point of view about that; I am sure they are right: the world would be a much easier place if only people would subdue their temperaments a bit. That may be the ideal, but I can't live up to it. I find life in the English environment one long struggle with one's temperament: so many things you must not do or say, or perhaps even think, such sedateness, such sobriety and self-control, the comfortable and instinctive adherence to correctness and convention. The old dears, how I admire them for it — but how very unlike them I am!

But then we Cornish are very different. William Saroyan is proud of belonging to his very elect community of — what is it? — only a hundred thousand Assyrians. Well, we Cornish are a very interesting small people with our own character and contribution to make. Perhaps not much more than half a million all told, certainly not more than three-quarters of a million — it would be interesting to know how many. And of them the majority must live outside of Cornwall, many of them across the seven seas: little Cornish mining communities in Australia, South Africa, Canada, in U.S.A. — there are several communities of them in Montana, Michigan, Detroit, New York.

What the Cornish temperament is I cannot go into here and perhaps I do not need to: this book itself must be a revelation of it. But what chiefly marks me off from my fellow-Cornishmen is not having been brought up a Nonconformist. That has its advantages.

Back to Grandmother Vanson. According to mother, she was 'a great 'and for goin' to chapel'. It was a pleasure; for otherwise she was a worldly old woman. She was very proud and of a jealous disposition. Her great rival in later years was the old lady, Mrs. Bunney, all jet and black silk with a little white lace-cap, who kept the Britannia Inn. Her position in the village was superior to granny's. Yet if she went by the Lodge with a new bonnet better than granny's the latter would say, hoity-toity: 'There goes old Lady Bunney.' I remember from my childhood that old lady's proud Victorian carriage of herself, her shrewd grey eyes, the inn, a romantic place with shutters, a swing sign-board, and the plums on the wall. Grandmother was much addicted to Bible-reading in her later years; but at the last she drew no comfort from it: 'There's nothin' but the dark ole graave waitin' for me', she would say, and determined, very sensibly, to keep out of it for as long as she could. She did until she was eighty-two.

When grandfather first came to Tregrehan to work as a hind on the estate he was paid 12s. a week, with a house rent-free; then he was raised to 15s. with the same privilege; and finally, when he went to the lodge-gate, £1 a week. At the end the old couple received a pension of 10s. a week and a little house, rent-free: much better treatment than the clay-workers anyway, who received nothing at the end of years of service. As I well remember in the case of my father towards the end of his life, when his health was breaking down and he was given the worst work to do — cleaning 'leats', i.e. the china-clay streams, which involved standing in water for hours, or 'breaking burden', which meant digging the clay and china-stone out of the sides of the pits, sometimes dangerous work, for it was liable to fall away in a mass. Grandfather's last years, pensioned off from the estate on which he had worked for sixty years, were much easier: a natural, mellow decline like an overripe pear ready to fall from the tree.

But at the beginning they kept the farm at Quintrells for the estate, rearing poultry, geese and turkeys, ducks and fowls, and looking after the cattle. Here the family was born and brought up: twelve children, of whom ten survived, seven daughters and three sons, which may be in part responsible for my impression of the ascendancy of feminine characteristics in the family. All this country is seamed with mine-workings, and my mother has various reminiscences of childhood excitements in consequence: of the tennis-party being given at Crinnis House (where a younger generation of Carlyons was living at the time), in the course of which the tennis lawn collapsed, there being a shaft beneath. Then there was the neighbouring farm of Mrs. Hicks's, where they had all been to help about the hayrick which was constructed for shelter right beside the house. Next morning, when they got up, it had disappeared — also down a shaft.

The farm was quite close to Crinnis Beach, that magnificent great stretch of white, glistening sand almost a mile long, with the red-brown, tin-and-copper-stained cliffs enclosing it, about which Q., I remember, once spoke of its virginal condition in the years before the War, when he would ride over for a bathe and not a soul in sight — now the locale of a large hotel and a whole settlement of marine villas. But grandmother would never allow the children to go down on the beach for a picnic. She couldn't be there to look after them and she had that feeling of fear for the sea which so many of the old people who dwelt by it, but were not of it, had. She used to refer to it as the 'crooel' sea or the ''ungry' sea. It never had a good word said in its favour by grandmother. She never went on it, or near it, or even looked at it, if she could help it. I think she hated the sea with a personal hatred. What it was due to I don't fully know; the drowning of grandfather's brother, Christopher, may have had something to do with it; and there were other unfortunates who came by their end on that melancholy, deserted beach, including, for one, Uncle Rowe's brother, Joe, who drowned himself there; a curious and interesting story which

I never even heard of — so close they were about this sort of thing — until many years later, and then in a curious and indirect way.

One evening, not many years ago, when down here on vacation from Oxford, I had walked up as usual from the village to Carn Grey, and some old clay-worker mate of my father's was telling me about the 'old days' and how, when there was a hanging at Bodmin Gaol, people used to trek over in hundreds for the spectacle, making a regular picnic of it. And then with a sudden decision he told me the story of Joe Rowe. I could see, knowing my Cornishmen as I do, that his motives were mixed: this was a story against my family: it would bring this young man who had gone to Oxford down a peg or two, let him know that there were skeletons in his family cupboard as in everybody else's, etc. All very Cornish — as it is also very Cornish of me to have spotted the hesitation, the sudden decision, to have suspected the motive. When Cornishman meets Cornishman, there is a good deal of *sous-entendu*. What he could not have suspected was that I positively love skeletons in the cupboard. I think he was rather disappointed at the friendly and indeed grateful reception of the story — not at all what he had expected, and on its ending he vanished abruptly over the hillside. I, of course, went back and at once asked my father for corroboration. Still I remain grateful to the unknown man at Carn Grey, but for whom I should never have heard it.

Father as a boy had shared a bed with his uncle Joe Rowe. He was a quarryman, who worked at Luxulyan and all around, a great one for 'ringing the jumper'. (Quarrymen in those days had the art of making their long crowbars, i.e. jumpers, ring like a peal of bells. It must have been delightful to hear over those wind-keen hillsides. Alas, I have never heard it. My father had.) Joe was also a great fighter, a boxer and a drinker. He got out of work through it and went on drinking for a long time. His girl gave him up, and, bitterest blow of all, took to his rival instead. There was a great fight to settle it; on that depended Joe's fate. There was a crowd out at Five-Gates — nobody knows that name now: it is now the town football field. Just when they were ready to begin — you could hear a pin drop, father said — a voice was heard: 'I'm George Rowe, and I've come to see fair play.' It was Uncle, stripped to his vest, then a young unmarried man.

It was a long, hard fight. But Joe was not in condition: he had been drinking too long and too hard. He lost the fight. He was down on his luck. He went down through Holmbush, and was seen looking into the garden where she lived, and then no more. He went on to Crinnis. The white cap he was wearing when he drowned himself his mother kept always hanging up on the peg on the kitchen door, as if expecting him any time to come home and take it. And if anybody came in and touched it, she wanted to know who'd been there. She always knew.

So much my father. That must have been at the very end of the sixties or early in the seventies. It is very touching. Who was the girl, one wonders, whom he loved so much that he gave up his life when he had lost her irretrievably? Who was Joe's rival, and what sort of a man was he? Did she marry him and bring up a satisfactory family — the sort of family Joe might have had if things had been a little different? Whoever she was, she must be long dead now, like Joe, long before, and Uncle and all the old folk of the village:

> Now are their account-books all closed up:
> It has ceased to matter whether they were happy
> More than half a century ago, or whether
> In their long absence someone else did sleep
> With their wives, or if their children were another's:
> What do these things matter in the eye of death?

But to think that the cautious, acquisitive career of Uncle — 'Look after the pence and the pounds will look after themselves' was his favourite motto, which he impressed upon me in childhood — had that in the background! Never a word crossed his lips, at any rate, in front of us children. And yet, as I write, I remember a thing which I have not thought of for years, perhaps never since, and of which only now do I appreciate the the significance. One of those resplendent Christmas evenings the whole family spent up at Auntie's: the dining-room, warm with the glow of fire and the impressive bright gas-light, the rich red wallpaper, the sideboard, the dates and nuts; and suddenly the name of 'my brother Joe' dropped into the conversation, and the smallest boy at once wanting to know who he was; the 'Sh —' of the elders, as if one had committed some impropriety, such as leaving one's fly-fronts open —

a solecism I could never have committed, so extreme was my sensitiveness, my feminine delicacy in such matters.

I admit that I was exceedingly inquisitive, devoured by an insatiable desire to know and in every direction; but I was never encouraged—in our family it was as much of a solecism as the other, and far more awkward for others. So a technique of dealing with me was developed from my earliest years. My questions were unanswered; the more I asked the less satisfaction I got; I was told on every hand: 'Little boys should be seen and not heard'—the most odious of all sentences to inflict upon intelligent, clever children. There was a blank wall all round. The result was that I was very much thrown in upon myself, my head teeming with ideas and questions and comments of all sorts and kinds, which were, it seemed, never welcome and usually bitten off with: 'Little boys should be seen and not heard.' When I first heard this dreary, discouraging remark, I wondered quite what it meant: why should little boys be *seen*? Were they to be looked at as if on exhibition? And what was the point of that? And then the point that they were to be unheard — *seen* but not *heard* — sank in, and I realized that that was the point of the remark. How I resented it. I could feel a blush going down my neck, bristling the hairs on the way down. And always when cut off in the midst of some — to me — entrancing exordium, some trope of imagination, which I cannot but think intelligent grownups would have found fascinating from a small child of five and known how to deal with, but which the plain working-people in whose family I was born and brought up never showed the slightest interest in and cut short—always I remember the hot blush of shame and the confusion which overcame me when I heard: 'Little boys should be seen and not heard.'

I grant that I must have been an altogether too knowing little boy, or would have been if the questions had been answered — if they had been capable of answering them. But this process of stubbing every shoot of confidence on the part of a naturally sanguine and vivacious temperament had all sorts of unforeseen consequences, some of them detrimental to happiness. For one thing, this repressive, discouraged youth drove me in upon myself and made me excessively ambitious: not until I was thirty-five and nearly lost my life over a couple of duodenal operations did this pressure relax, and, with the possibility of enjoying life returning (for the first time since I was nineteen), there came a more natural attitude to life.

I suppose the difficulties were due to the oddity of an exceptionally sharp and sensitive lad in a very ordinary working-class home. Anyone with as feminine a sensitiveness, and without a really tough will, would, I think, have succumbed to such a discouraging atmosphere and would have dropped out. I see now that, with me, I owe what I am to the struggle. It isolated me from others, it concentrated me within the unapproachable tower of my own resolve; I was determined to do what I wanted to do; I was left sufficiently to myself, for nobody was interested, to carry on what I wanted in my own way and nourish the inner life of my own imagination. But I suffered, all the same. From the loneliness of it, from having no one for a friend, no one to encourage me (except at school: hence my devotion and passionate gratitude to it), no one to turn to for help when I wanted advice or solace for defeat: when I turned, there was nobody. It made me, already proud enough, passionately so; it made a temperament, spontaneous and exceedingly affectionate, grateful for a crumb of affection, in the end resentful; it made me contemptuous.

I now don't regret the way it was. And I see that my people, being the simple people they were, could hardly have been any other. It made me different, however; from early years I ceased, inside myself, to share their lives.

But I was speaking of my mother's childhood. With so many children to rear on 12s. a week, they were poor; indeed, it is wonderful to me now how these people managed to keep a family on what wouldn't keep me in postage stamps, let alone books. Yet they never went without food, if it was of the simplest character. Quantity, not quality, was what counted. There was frequent 'teddy' (i.e. potato) and turnip pie, and for variation potato and turnip stew; there'd be pasties and rabbit pie, and a lot of potato and heavy cake. If any of them complained, grandmother would say what about when she was a girl; in the Crimean War wheat went to such a price, they had to live on barley bread, with just a little white bread for tea on Sundays. (Two of her brothers died in the Crimean War. They were young lads. Presumably they died of frostbite, for she had a gruesome story of their toes coming off in their stockings. Uncle, I remember, had some song of the Crimean War, all about the Russian Czar in his long league-boots. It is interesting how much history, and what social changes, the span of one life contains, and to think that a really old man now (1941) can go back through what his grandparents remembered and told him into the eighteenth century.)

On Christmas Eve grandmother used to make saffron cake and a big saffron bun for each one of the children; that and a cup of cocoa each, a rarity for them, was their treat. Grandfather would sing 'Warsael! Warsael!' — as we pronounce it. And on Christmas morning he would get up and sing outside their bedroom door: 'I spied three ships come sailin' by.' He was not very good at carrying the tune, and grandmother would laugh and say, 'That edn' the tune, Edward', and sing it herself. Mother (nearly seventy years after): 'We used to 'ave fine fun 'ome there to ourselfs.'

Grandmother went into St. Austell to do her shopping. On a Monday she would walk in and come back by Mansel's van, which travelled from Truro to Fowey on Mondays and back Tuesdays. It came up again on Thursdays and went back Fridays. So that she rode in on Friday, market day, and walked back carrying all her parcels and goods, a distance of two miles and a half. She used to say: 'I'm come 'ome loaded like a millerd's 'orse.' I've heard her say in later years: 'I've often come 'ome from town loaded like a bee.' She had indeed a most vivid and poetic gift of speech; but it was not individual to herself, it was the vividness and poetry of the people she came from. This is not the place for an essay on the character and usage of Cornish dialect: suffice it to say that the traditional speech of the people reached a flower of perfection in her. In her nothing was changed; all the phrases and images and metaphors that had been used for centuries in East Cornwall, since the days when the Prayer Book and Bible had brought to an end the old Celtic language, were unspoiled and complete in her talk. And since she was naturally talkative, with a very sharp edge to her tongue, her range of images and metaphors was a very full one, much wider than the average. She always retained a flavouring of the East Cornwall dialect noticeable particularly in the 'u' sounds — words like moon and spoon tended to become 'mune' and 'spune'. The intonation with which she spoke had a rather beauti-

ful, melancholy line with drooping tones. Actually her speech is alive
and present with my mother, without its East Cornwall flavouring:
the whole range of idiom and usage remains intact with her—practically the last generation with which it is.

Having been brought up in a house where my parents spoke the
dialect unashamed and unspoiled, with no attempt, or even if they had
wished, no capacity, to improve on it, I have in consequence a very
accurate ear for it, though I ceased to speak it more and more from the
time I went to school. Like all questions of language it is a very subtle
business; and I doubt if anybody who was not brought up in a home
where Cornish dialect was regularly spoken could be relied on to get
it absolutely right. Bernard Walke, for instance, in his well-known
broadcast plays, doesn't get it quite right; it is observed from the outside, and as such, is very good. But that is not the same thing as knowing
it from the inside. Hardy in *A Pair of Blue Eyes* makes his North
Cornwall villagers talk unashamed Dorset dialect; perhaps it is just as
well, he would have made an awful hash if he had tried his hand at
Cornish. The outsider who has come nearest to getting it right is
Charles Lee in his *Cornish Tales*: it is very remarkable, there is hardly a
thing that one could question in his usage. Q., of course, gets it
absolutely right; but then, he belongs.

When grandmother and grandfather were promoted to keep the
lodge-gate at Tregrehan — 'The Lodge' or 'to th' Lodge' it was
referred to respectfully by the family — I think the old lady felt that
she had gone up in the world. No more 'ole farmplaace with nobody
and nothin' to look at year in, year out, and nobody to come fore to the
door, you 'ad to get everything for yourself.' There at the Lodge she was
entrenched upon the main road, with a view of everything going up
and down, but at the same time a little withdrawn within the defences
of the park. 'Entrenched' is the word; for grandmother thought as
much of herself as the lady at the big house. She wasn't going to open
and shut the gates for them as they went in or out: the gates should be
opened and remain open, or they should be shut and they could open
them themselves! It was a good thing for her that the family was
absent through all these years, or she would perhaps not have been
there long. As it was she had the place to herself. The Carlyons were

away in New Zealand, and then the young heir was in the War, in which he was very badly wounded; the great house was shut up and in the hands of an old butler-housekeeper, Mr. Pope, with mutton-chop whiskers and silver hair, and silvery, obsequious voice and manner.

The place opened a window in my imagination as a boy. On Thursday afternoons when the shop was shut, in the summer during the school holidays, mother and I used to drive out in the donkey-and-jingle to Tregrehan. I used to wander about the park by myself, the place full of memories of the family that had lived there — for we knew all the servants' gossip about the gentry and their strange, exotic life: how many horses the Major had kept in his heyday, when the royalties were pouring in from the mines round about, Wheal Eliza, Wheal Buckler and the rest, and it seemed that their prosperity would never come to an end; how many servants there were in the house, the grand lady that was the housekeeper, with a housemaid all to herself to wait on her in the housekeeper's room; the Major coming home from abroad on his last illness, a neat dapper little man with red complexion and black beard, elegant small feet and hands; stories of Ann Bone, the cook (still alive, good soul, a tiny little woman of between eighty and ninety, whom I went to see in her cottage at Tregrehan Mills a year or two ago, out of nostalgia for these memories which were never mine); the coming to and fro between Tregrehan and the Major's town-house in Mayfair; the shooting-parties, the mass of meat-pasties that would be made in the kitchen, for my mother had her start in service in that great stone-kitchen with the slate passages.

Sometimes, rather timorously, I wandered on up the drive or across the park under the fine beeches that remembered other days, and round the curve with the steep banks of grass (they seemed high then) to the gate and looked, greatly daring, into that sacred preserve: the melancholy, green gloom around the house, the long pillared portico to the front door, the big lion couchant on the grass that seemed very much on guard against small boys trespassing in those dedicated precincts. Sometimes when I thought nobody was about, the great house silently eyeing me with all its shuttered windows, I have stolen by that knowing lion, made for the path between the thick shrubs that led to a more remote paradise where I felt for a moment secure in the angle of those box-hedges. There was the sunk Italian garden, with its formal flowerbeds and box-borders, the raised terraces all round with the figures of Spring, Summer, Autumn, Winter (an old man, I remember, bent beneath his burden of sticks) in white marble at the corners; the long colonnade of the south front looking down upon that empty, waiting scene with one small boy moonstruck in his nook. Silence, save for the rustle of leaves, a sigh along the nearer trees outside in the park — or was it the silk skirt of some long-dead lady, wife of the Admiral or the Major, upon the terrace? — silence and waiting accentuated by the tinkle of the fountain plashing patiently among the water-lilies of the decorated basin. When later I read

> Now sleeps the crimson petal, now the white;
> Nor waves the cypress in the palace walk;
> Nor winks the gold fin in the porphyry font . . .
>
> Now folds the lily all her sweetness up,

it was the deserted Italian garden at Tregrehan that was always present in the back of my mind.

Once or twice I wandered a little farther, keeping carefully to the farthest walk from the house, and found my way into the deep gloom of the cedar-walk, a vista which ended with a figure of a dog agonizing on his pedestal: I assumed that it must be the grave of a favourite dog. Stealing back along the path, soft and plumb with accumulated moss, I returned by way of the sunk garden, catching sight as I passed of a shadowy figure in an upper window moving forward to shut the shutters: the ancient ritual of the venerable old retainer, as slow, deliberate, formal as some devotee in the temple of a vanished religion.

Once, and once only, I was admitted within, with full, polite honours rendered by the old gentleman, with his perfect silvery manner, no doubt tinged with amusement behind the reserve of his silver-rimmed spectacles. I had won a scholarship and was now going to the secondary school; I think this visit, which had been carefully arranged for me as if I were a personage paying my respects to a museum of the family pieties, was in some sense a reward, tribute to my enhanced status. Mr. Pope received me at the front door and showed me all over the house, which had been for so long a temple of mystery and imagination for me. It did not cease to be, as the result of my visit: perhaps the best tribute one could pay it. There were the cabinets full of old china, the long mahogany sideboard which had been bought in the Great Exhibition of 1861, the heavy mahogany doors which had been put in by the Admiral at the beginning of the century—no doubt treasure-trove from his voyages to the West Indies. There were the heavy, old-fashioned footbaths of china in the bedrooms. Mr. Pope explained to me the history of the house: the old nucleus of red sandstone of the reign of William and Mary; when they must have married some heiress, a Trewbody or a Spry, with whom there came such-and-such a property, Boscundle or Pennance; the colonnade and south front in which were library and drawing-room, the latter never furnished.

I was awestruck by the splendour of the library, fascinated and faintly alarmed by the closing door which continued the rows of books so that you could not tell where to get out. I was left by myself for a moment, and was relieved when Mr. Pope came back to show me the Treacle Bible. I turned over the pages of a book on the round table: there was the book-plate, Thomas Tristram Carlyon. What a curiously moving name, Tristram, I thought. What sadness had brought him into the world, and left him now, only a name-plate in a book? It sent melancholy echoes faintly sounding down the corridors of my mind. Who was this unknown young man? for I saw him as young and yet lost for ever to this deserted, waiting house. Behind the library, looking out upon what had been once the cockpit, was the gloomy, masculine, leather-furnished smoking-room, with its memory of the last occupant of the house, a melancholy bachelor, who, they said, had been crossed in love and lost heart and died. There were the books he read: the popular Victorian novels in their green-and-yellow paper bindings (I thought of *Molly Bawn*, and now after so many years I half-believe I saw it there on the shelves). One or two of them Mr. Pope took down to show me what their owner had written at the end. 'Do you know what that word means?' he said in that quiet voice. It was the word *Nihil*. 'Yes, "nothing",' I said. It filled me with a sense of unutterable weariness, as if I had looked into the marrow of someone else's life who found no savour in it.

My tour of the house, my glimpse into that unknown way of life, even then over and done with though preserved by absence as if the clock had stopped some time in the late nineties and all was sealed and waiting for the recall to life and change — my visit was over. I said good-bye to Mr. Pope at the front door. Upon the doorstep we exchanged a word about Queen Victoria. 'Ah,' he said with a remote look, 'you see I lived so many years of my life in her reign that when she died it seemed as if the world was coming to an end.'

It was understood that I should write an essay for Mr. Pope upon the house and its history. This I did, after the usual schoolboy delays and some reminding. The essay was delivered to the old gentleman, whose only comment was, I gathered, that it was all right save for one or two mistakes he could have corrected in it. I do not think I ever saw him again. I wonder what has become of that youthful work? It must have been my first essay in that genre.

So there my grandparents were installed at the Lodge during all those years of the family's absence. Sometimes there was a rumour that the young Captain would come home to the house of his ancestors and settle down; but the expectation, after so many years of waiting, failed to arouse conviction. Occasionally the great Mrs. Meinertzhagen, an improbable name for a Carlyon, which she was, would descend upon Tregrehan from her house in Cheyne Walk, and for a week or so the dust-sheets would be removed from a few rooms. These visits were not relished by grandmother, who had the dislike of one dominating woman for another. 'Mrs. Mannisorgan', as the name was rendered, — it fascinated me by its strangeness — apparently entertained the same sentiment for Mrs. Vanson: she probably well recognized her for an old tartar, but hardly worth a fuss when grandfather was such a quiet old soul and faithful, reliable servant. (He had carried three generations of Carlyons to their graves in the family vault at St. Blazey, from which parish they sprang: there was the Colonel, the Major's father, the Major himself, and his nephew and successor, the melancholy bachelor.)

How often I have recalled those pleasant Thursday afternoon jog-trots along the road down through Holmbush, under the shade of the great beeches planted by previous generations of Carlyons. War-time, the War of 1914, and the roads free of traffic, the only excitement was going under Holmbush railway-bridge, for Neddy was a spirited and well-fed donkey who went like a pony, and the competition of a train made him try to run away. How smartly, too, he would run up around the corner to the Lodge, well knowing what a good feed of fresh grass there was awaiting him at his destination. There was the great copper-beech, and the Lodge itself under the trees: a pretty Gothic house of the eighteen-fifties, which might have been an illustration to Trollope, with its lattice-windows and diamond panes, its tall, decorated chimneys and gables, all of the local red sandstone. Within, it was always cool in the hottest summer weather. Grandmother, who complained of every-thing, complained of the trees which shut out the light. I loved them, and loved the way the late evening sun would strike richly across the park under the branches to throw fingers of light into the big stone-floored kitchen where we sat. There was a curious smell about the house, an unmistakeable, undefinable odour of old age, and perhaps damp. On the little table before the window there were a few books which always intrigued me, but which I found uninviting when I opened them. One was Cary's translation of Dante; another was a Shakespeare; and of course there was grandmother's Bible. The pre-siding presence of the place was grandmother, sitting quavering by the fireplace; ageing now, but still quick of mind, sharp of retort and as wilful as an old woman as she had been through youth and middle-age, the undisputed authority in her now almost tribal family. (She is the 'Old Cornishwoman by the Fire' whose portrait is drawn in one of the earlier poems of my *Poems of a Decade*.)

Or, again, I wandered about by myself in the park, into the corner farther from the Lodge which I knew had been the deer-park once; or went over the road to see my aunts and uncles and cousins who were strung out in a string of houses backing into the woods; or went mooning alone down the straight avenue that led to Crinnis Beach. The woods were everywhere here; one recognized, only half aware, the difference of the woodland sounds, the squawk of pheasants (which one never heard at Tregonissey), the whirr of partridges' wings, the echoes of voices in the woodland valleys, the felling of a tree in a distant plantation. When I was a child of five to seven or eight, I used to go for my summer holiday to stay with my Aunt Emily, across the road from Britannia. Then these woodland scents and sounds and smells struck me with all the force of their difference. In their garden under the trees there were innumerable dragon-flies in summer, blue and gold and red and green. I was terrified of them, and at the same time fascinated. I have never seen such dragon-flies since. What has happened to them? When autumn came on there would be the smoke of wood-fires rising in the openings in the woods. As you approached Tregrehan from St. Austell it looked surrounded by woods: the main road narrowed until between the great firs and pines you could just see the expanse of roof of the Britannia Inn. I never saw it without a pulse of pleasure at heart; and I never left it for home without that desolating sense of nostalgia for what I am leaving and where I have been happy which was a constantly recurring and acute sensation right through childhood and youth and early manhood — until the thirties brought either a hardening of fibre or an increase of rationality, certainly a less romantic and more common-sense attitude to experience.

Tregrehan, and the suspended, waiting life of the place, provided another element, and a contrasting one, to the background in which I grew up, and in my imagination it occupied a place apart. When years later at Oxford I read Hardy's *Woodlanders*, the scene in which it all took place at the back of my mind was the woods about Tregrehan.

CHAPTER IV

EARLY YEARS

My father and mother were married at Charlestown Church (a pretty little Victorian Gothic building, all Early English lancet windows and pitch-pine pews, very G. S. Street, very Betjeman: which, it is pleasant to me to think, is not much more than a stone's throw away from this house, across the fields, among the trees to the left from my window) on a February day in the year 1893 — ten years from my arrival. Cheelie, as was to be expected, was the chief turn at the wedding feast: he sang, played the concertina, made his dancing doll perform and ended up by dancing over the broomstick. This pleased everybody and won the heart of even grandmother, who had not regarded the match at first with any favour. 'I *'ear* that you are goin' to marry an ole 'orse-jockey', she had said with her unfailing flair for hitting the nail on the head, her incomparable gift for the *mot juste*. For my father was at this time, and for eleven years all told, groom at Dr. Stephens's in the town. Doctor, as he was to all the family, for the rest a great character, was well-off and addicted to horses: father's job, among other things, was to break them in.

Only the other day at Porthpean, Axford told me the story, which I had heard first years ago, of how he saved father from being drowned. He was exercising one of the Doctor's horses on the beach, riding him along the edge of the water, when suddenly the beast took to sea. Father couldn't swim and had difficulty in extricating himself from the stirrups; by the time he had, he was well out of his depth, fully dressed and with heavy boots and leggings on. He would infallibly have drowned if it had not been for Axford, who swam out and brought him in. Apparently the best thing would have been to stay on the horse, give him his head and gently turn him back to land. Or so father said, years after. All I can say is that I wouldn't have risked it, and it would have demanded a cool collectedness father did not possess. The horse went a long way out, almost to the Gull Rock, before he turned back and came in again.

These two, Richard Rowse and Ann Vanson, though born and brought up within a few miles of each other, had each come a long and devious route before they reached this meeting-point in Charlestown Church which fixed their lives for over forty years together. Granny Rowse, brave little woman, had died in the previous October. Mother: 'She was 'nother such woman as Uncle — full o' fun.' She was always cheerful and lively, and father was devoted to her. 'That edn' 'ow mother used to do it', he would say in early married life. On her death-bed she had given him a good testimonial: 'Dick's the best boy of the lot and do deserve a good wife.' She was glad he was going to have somebody to look after him. She was not old when she died — in the sixties. A blow on her breast brought out a bruise. When she went to Doctor, he said: 'Now look here, Fanny; you have your breast off and you'll be a new woman.' She wouldn't have it done — 'rather die, she said, than 'ave a knife in her'. It was cancer, and she did. (It is curious this primitive hatred among simple folk of 'having a knife in them' — incomprehensible to me, who have had so many, of one sort or another.)

Father had been to South Africa and back; mother's course had taken her from Tregrehan to St. Michael's Mount, and thence to the middle-class comfort and friendliness of the Doctor's, where she was treated almost as one of the family and slept with Miss Milly, Doctor's daughter, too nervous and spoiled to sleep by herself. In the background was that experience of the Mount, most romantic in its associations and memories of all places in Cornish history, the most sensationally beautiful of them all. One thinks of the pilgrims' way worn in the living rock by the footsteps of innumerable devotees all through the Middle Ages going up to pray at the shrine of the Archangel at the top (the same trodden by their successors, the modern tourists). Or one thinks of the Earl of Oxford, last hope of the Lancastrian cause, holding out here against Edward IV; Sir John Arundell of Trerice slain on the sands below; the ruse that finally took the stronghold. One thinks of the succession of Captains of the Mount, Millitons, Harrises, successors of the archpriests who kept watch against the Spaniards and tended the beacon:

> High on St. Michael's Mount it shone,
> It shone on Beachy Head . . .

Then the succession of owners of the Mount: for a brief space, the great Robert Cecil, Earl of Salisbury (which is why the Cartulary is now at Hatfield), Bassets, St. Aubyns. Or further back in time, before the medieval dedication to St. Michael and its gift to the greater, though not more beautiful, Mont St. Michel across the Channel, to the Celtic legends of Carrick Loose en Coose, the Grey Rock in the Wood, the submerged forest around it, the bells of drowned churches that the fishermen hear ringing under the tides.

Not much of all this, it may be supposed, entered the head of a very young, very lovely housemaid, with those wonderful dark eyes and perfect features, the exquisite line of mouth and nose, the small ears under wavy black hair, drawn straight back. A *bonne bouche*, a discerning eye would decide. Age: twenty. The reaction on her part, in terms of how many bedrooms (so much larger than Tregrehan), so many stairs and tunnels and passages in the rock; here you had to go downstairs to go to bed; you were for ever losing your way in such a large place. Here, too, the sacrosanct, mysterious routine of the gentry, on an even grander scale: at the apex of it the remote, the unseen figure of 'his lordship'; the strangeness of a house upon an island in the sea, going to and fro to Marazion by boat, or, when the tide was low, over the causeway; the gale of wind blowing against those high, defensive walls. (And always against that background, the interminable passages, the Chevy Chase Room, the Chapel with its family memorials, the figure of the young Captain, invalided home from the East. Only a few years ago, with strange emotion, I saw his memorial, dead a year or two after that brief time, there along with the rest.)

From that overwhelming experience to the comfortable, middle-class background of 'Doctor's' in High Cross Street was security indeed. Life was cheerful and kindly. There was Mrs. Doctor, good soul, easy-going, generous, with her liking for green tea, her difficult determination to cut a good figure in the tight-laced corsets, fashionable in those days, the despair of the Doctor; 'Doctor' himself, red-faced, choleric, good-hearted, with his intimate knowledge of the family on both sides, his presence at lyings-in and passings-out, his well-known mannerisms — 'See-see-see, Vanson' or 'See-see-see, Rowse', as the case might be. There were the servants, Budd the cook and the merry-making among the girls in the kitchen: putting the white of an egg in a glass of water to stand outside on Midsummer's Day to see the shape of your future husband; Budd declaring that hers would be a sailor — she could see the riggings. (Did she marry a sailor, I wonder?) Then there was the excitement of the Great Blizzard, when the snow came up over the steps of the house, and there were drifts as high as the hedges at Tregonissey, and snow lay upon Campdowns from March till June. I see it all as vividly through their eyes as if I were there myself, among the girls looking out through the dining-room window, the fire burning up brightly within, men clearing away the snow in the street outside.

Then marriage and the births of the children: my sister Hilda born at the end of the year, followed five years later by my brother George. Auntie and Uncle made way at the shop for the growing family. This infuriated Harry's wife, Polly, a bitter shrew of a woman, not quite right in the head, blinded by jealousy, but brave. She refused to buy a thing from her brother-in-law; when Auntie suggested, 'You needn't go all the way out Lane End, Polly, to buy lamp-oil; Dick have got lamp-oil to sell'; 'Yes, I'll buy a quart of lamp-oil from Dickless, and set fire to 'n,' she said. And the point was that for two pins she would have done it. Her next move was to join the Co-operative Society; she then went all round the village to try and persuade everybody to join it. I, as a Labour man, have nothing against Co-operative Societies; on general grounds I am rather in favour. I only mention this as an example of the sort of motives that operate with the people.

Much later on, at the end of her life, having tried to be friendly to her and to do her a kindness, I found how impossible she was, and was bitten myself for my pains. All the same, she had great spirit and courage; for years Harry never worked, and she kept him and herself by her sewing. She was a wonderful needlewoman, but it must have taken some doing. Her only child, a little girl, died young. Everything had gone wrong with her: no wonder she had that soured, yellow look. When we were small children she never looked at us passing in the village, save to grin like a dog or show her teeth. Everybody who knows the people will know how true that is: irrational, instinctive lives led purely by emotion and emotional reactions, uncontrolled, unhelped by reason, or even the cool common sense of the upper middle class.

So the family was already installed at the shop when five years after my brother, ten years after my sister, I made my appearance. (Those intervals were an important factor, rather an unhappy one, in my growing up.) I have never supposed since my childhood that I was wanted; later I regarded my appearance as a regrettable accident — and such, I have subsequently gathered, was the case. The one member of the family who greeted my appearance with enthusiasm was my sister, aged ten; and the second name I possess, by which I have always gone in the family, bears witness to a schoolgirl crush of hers for a young teacher — who came to his end in the Lunatic Asylum in Bodmin. Needless to say, I do not care much for the name. My father, marching into the town to register the new arrival, turned over the name in his mind — he seems to have given the matter no thought till that moment, except that he was determined not to call me Richard — reflected that 'Leslie isn't much of a name for a boy's name' and, starting the alphabet, arrived at 'A — Alfred the Great', and decided to call me after him. Where on earth he can have heard of Alfred the Great I do not know: hardly in the course of his exiguous schooling; my guess would be that he must have picked it up from a newspaper at the time of the millenary celebration of Alfred's death, a year or two before my birth.

Of late I have come to think it is a pity that we do not keep going our more distinctive Cornish names. Jenifer has come increasingly into use, and a good thing too, for it is a lovely name: the Cornish form of Guinevere. But at the end of the Middle Ages and into the seventeenth century one comes across in the old parish registers the pleasant habit of calling children after the patron saints of the parishes. In the parish of Perranzabuloe, for instance, where the family of Mitchell was the chief one among the farmers, you would come across Perran Mitchell: what could be nicer, or more distinctively Cornish? The softened form Mitchell is our form of Michael, and should be revived as a Christian name. You would find Petrocks, or the later form of Petherick, at Bodmin and elsewhere, where that saint was venerated. The name Petherick survives as a surname, but has died out as a Christian name. In the parishes of St. Columb major and St. Columb minor you would come across Columba, Denis and Clement in their respective parishes. I do not know whether the patron saints of Luxulyan (as also of St. Veep), St. Cyriac and St. Julitta, found favour with parents; but what could be prettier than St. Juliot, near Boscastle — Hardy's St. Juliot?

Then, too, there are all the Arthurian names connected with Cornwall that should be revived: Tristram, Kay, Gawen, Geraint, Mark. We have seen that Tristram was a name in the Carlyon family, and there was in Elizabeth's reign the pathetic figure of John Winslade's son, dispossessed of his estates by his father's treason in the Prayer Book Rebellion, now a Catholic wandering abroad to Douai — of whom Carew says that he 'led a walking life with his harp, to gentlemen's houses, wherethrough, and by his other active qualities, he was entitled "Sir Tristram": neither wanted he (as some say) a "belle Iseult", the more aptly to resemble his pattern'. And true enough, when we find him arriving at Douai, where he is given hospitality for a while, his name is entered in the Diary as 'Tristram Winslade'. A poor, pathetic shade of a man — the last of his family. I must imagine something about him some day, bring him to life again, make up to his wandering ghost for what the man lost in life: give him at least the existence of a name in a story when the men who dispossessed him and kept him out of his father's house have been forgotten.[1]

Gawen was a name in the Carew family; Sir Gawen was brother of that wonderful old ruffian, Sir Peter Carew: he took a lease of Launceston Priory after the Dissolution. Then there are the more exotic names like Hannibal, which was quite common in the family of the Vyvyans of Trelowarren. Charles Henderson told me that in the seventeenth century the Lizard Peninsula was dotted with little Hannibals in honour of the family. There is delicious Justinian Talkarne, Elizabethan governor of St. Mawes Castle, who had to give up his charge for his dealings with pirates; or Sir Ferdinando Gorges, Governor of Plymouth, who nearly came by his end in the Essex Conspiracy. Or what about the baroque flavour of Orlando, or Endymion? There is far too great a plainness about men's names compared with women's, and here in Cornwall, with so many good names lying about unused and with such associations, there is no excuse for it.

[1] For the story of the Winslades, see my *Sir Richard Grenville*, 186-8, and *Tudor Cornwall*, 263-4, 282-3.

I have never been sure whether what I take to be my first memory is in fact a memory or a dream. All I know is that it is a picture in the mind and that it goes back very far, at least to when I was three and possibly before. It is just a photograph in my mind of being brought down early one winter's morning to breakfast: there was the lamp lighted on the kitchen table, myself sitting in the high-up baby's chair with the little tray attached in front, and the most prominent and vigorous object in the whole scene the large enamel blue teapot standing near me on the table. I am still not sure whether I did not dream that scene later; anyway, memory or dream, it is very early — the only association that I remember with myself in the baby's chair.

My mother recalls that I was a very 'forward' child: very early on throwing my bottle out over the cradle and drinking out of a cup, learning to talk early and quickly (I am sure that was true!), and walking away at the age of thirteen months. My brother was backward in these respects, nearly two before he could walk. But he more than made up later in boyhood for his slow start physically, developing into a normal active boy, good at running, throwing stones, climbing, swimming, riding; whereas physically I lost my early start and developed into a timid boyhood, rather feminine, and though quick enough in my movements, all the same awkward, so that I was hopeless at games, and never learned to swim or climb or throw stones or bicycle. Why this curious alternation? It is almost as if developing one's brain goes counter to development on the physical side. I have always thought 'Mens sana in corpore sano', which used to be dinned into us at school, to be nonsense anyway: I was very sure that if you wanted to achieve anything really remarkable you had to put all the eggs into one basket, whichever you chose — or rather, were destined for. And unhappy as that doctrine may be, I think now that it was probably right.

There were other factors entering into this complex out of which my character was formed: I was an imaginative and very easily frightened child; I was brought up in my earlier years largely by my sister; I was at the same time not a passive child, but active, self-willed — I might say strong-willed — and for ever breaking away to go off on long walks on my own, on which I was perfectly capable of looking after myself. Of one of these I have a distinct recollection in all its details.

My mother tells me that I had a way of walking off in the week to where I had been taken with them on Sunday; that once I strayed as far as Mount Charles, where I was found and brought home by a kind soul who ended by drowning herself. But I have no recollection of that walk whatever, whereas of this that I took into the town at the age of three I remember everything.

It was on a Friday, I know, for that was the day on which the scales and weights in the shop were cleaned: whether it was the preoccupation of my mother, or the disturbance of the usual routine, or the smell of the brasso, I don't know, but I disliked Friday: it had an empty desolateness about it. There were other days in the week, too, which I grew to dislike: Monday, because it was washing-day and the kitchen (where we lived) was full of baths and hot water and soapsuds and steam and the odour of clothes-washing, and everything was upset. Saturday I came to detest most of all, for as I grew bigger I had my 'work' to do: there was chopping sticks to light the fire with through the week, weighing up quarter-pecks (8¾ lb.) and half-pecks of flour in the stores and bringing them over into the shop, measuring out lamp-oil at intervals all day for people, sometimes — deepest humiliation of all — going round the village selling oranges, at the end of the day making up books and bills. That was my 'work'. I thought it all loath-some and a detestable waste of time; I wanted to be alone by myself, dreaming my own dreams, reading, writing, dressing up: anything to be away to myself from all these irritating, vexatious calls, 'Do this' or 'Now you go and do that' or 'A quart of lamp-oil, please' — the most hateful of all occupations, for I disliked getting my hands dirty, I detested the smell of lamp-oil, and the moment I had carefully washed my hands from one lot somebody else would want another. And so it went on, I thought, with devilish ingenuity the way the villagers came for oil in the middle of my tea. Why couldn't they all come for their beastly oil at the same time so that I could have one good go at it and finish for the evening? But that would have demanded a rationality, a measure of rationalization, such as human beings are incapable of.

Oddly enough, it never occurred to me to go on strike; I suppose I was too much afraid of my father for that. But similarly, it never occurred to them, simple working-class souls that they were, that *my* work, my reading and writing, was infinitely more important than measuring out a whole oil-field (which I must have almost done, when I consider all the gallons through all the years which I administered to the village). Most people would have been only too glad, I felt, if their boys were willing to do any reading or writing on their own at all. Here was I, with my own life to myself the one thing I cherished, perpetually irritated and vexed by a hundred interruptions. My brother was thought 'willing' by the villagers, and was in consequence popular: quite rightly, he was one of them. I was 'unwilling', and not popular. I did not react passively to that: it only increased my contempt for them. Unable to go on strike, I found my most useful weapon in a sullen ill-temper, 'black looks', etc., which probably saved me from being put upon even more than I was. Now I see that this side to my life as a boy which I most hated was not wholly to be regretted: it must have had the effect of making me prize still more highly the inner life of my mind, 'going away to myself', as a citadel of refuge from all the interruptions and calls of the shop and the house. It was a fortress into which I retreated and shut myself up; nobody could get at that anyway; every moment had a savour of its own, or rather, a thrilling excitement; I infinitely preferred to be alone; I hugged myself with pleasure — and then the shop-bell rang once more, and it was 'A quart of lamp-oil, please.'

Sunday, too, I much disliked: there was something about its atmosphere, stuffy, unnatural, repressed, which made it insufferable. On Sundays we lived in the sitting-room and wore our best clothes; and it was for ever 'Can't you keep quiet?' or 'Stop kickin' your ole feet against they chairs', or 'Mind you look sharp 'ome from church'. There was nothing to do, except to go to Sunday School and church, morning and evening, come home, eat Sunday dinner and tea (the only *pleasures* of the day, for they were on a grander scale, more luscious, and there were always luxuries such as stewed prunes and cream and sponge-cake for tea), and then to bed. No playing on Sundays, no amusements, nothing to do. I hated the day. That made four days in the week which for various reasons I disliked: Friday, Saturday, Sunday, Monday. There was something about the tone, the colour of those days: if the days, like Rimbaud's vowels, may be said to have colour, as they certainly had atmosphere — Friday was a dull neutral buff or grey, Monday was the colour of mud, Saturday the unrelieved black of despair, Sunday a gloomy purple, a day of mourning rather than enjoyment.

But all this is to leap forward from that particular Friday, which is my chief memory of being three. With the yellow glitter of the brass scales clear in my mind, I set off along the road to the town. I was wearing a green overcoat with three little capes *à la* Napoleon, of which I was proud. At the farm one of the older Lewis children asked me where I was going, and I said 'In town'; he didn't seem very friendly and I remember a distinct feeling of rebuff which propelled me on my way. I remember no more until the level-crossing where the railway crosses Tregonissey Road: a rather dangerous spot, one or two people had been knocked down there — it has now been done away with. Here you had to be careful; the gates were closed, a train was passing; you had to wait, and then go through the little gate at the side very carefully. It was market-day in the town, the street full of traffic and people: you had to walk on the pavement, not in the street — you might be run over. So I walked in and out the people on the pavement and arrived at West End, where our great friends the Mays had a butcher's shop and where we visited on Sundays. I was not at all well received, I remember: again this chilling sense of rebuff, of being 'not wanted' — by anybody apparently; I believe I was heaved up into a cart and brought home this time by nice, friendly Will Husband.

One other memory dates back to this very early time, and it is, I believe, my first intimation of aesthetic experience, one of those moments with all

The glory and the freshness of a dream,

which redeem life, and give me a standard, a touchstone by which to estimate all the rest. Wordsworth thought those moments gave one intimations of immortality. It was a still evening in early summer, for the bluebells were out in Doctor's fields up on the hill-side. And it was a Sunday evening, for we were all walking in the fields together, a very rare event: I never remember it happening again. As we walked, we picked bluebells in the cool of the evening. And then from far over the shoulder of the hill-side to the west there came the silvery sound of the bells of St. Mewan ringing to church, so rare a sound, so far away, we very rarely heard them, like church-bells in a dream on a

May morning. The thought of those bells brings tears to my eyes;
their memory speaks to me of my buried childhood, brings back that
moment in the cool evening, the bluebells gathered, the thorn hedges
in leaf, father and mother and the children that we were for once at
one, my father now dead, all of us scattered, the unity broken.

To this feeling of not being wanted there was one great exception,
my sister Hilda, who had a growing girl's devotion to the baby of the
family and whom in consequence I adored. 'Hoola' was on my lips
from morning to night. It was she who brought me up in my early
years — my mother's time and attention being occupied wholly by
house-work, cooking, scrubbing, washing, cleaning, plus looking
after the shop. She had no time over to display much interest in me,
which anyway I don't think she had. It was 'Hoola' who made me say
my prayers, dressed dolls for me, looked after the brown teddy-bear,
and tended me in bed when I had the measles. (No very up-to-date
ideas about hygiene in working-class families in those days; indeed it
was more or less impossible to isolate one child with some infectious
disease, measles or whooping cough, from the others; there wasn't
room: they had just to take their chance. A generation earlier, when
mother's sister Polly had the measles, mother was put in bed with her
so that she might catch it and get it over. In fact, she didn't.) I well
remember having measles — being kept in bed and treated with care
as if one were somebody of importance. I had just started going to the
Infants' School at Carclaze, where I caught it; my sister told me that a
small friend of mine called Clarke had died because he got out of bed
before he was well. I was very much impressed, though dying meant
nothing very clear to me; I felt sad and determined on no account to
throw the bedclothes off the bed or let my arms stray out over, much
as I was tempted by the fever. I was a frightfully good little boy in
those ways — and always have been a good patient in illness, to which
I attribute my survival from the long illness that overshadowed all my
early manhood, from the time I was nineteen till I was thirty-five.

But I was particularly obedient to my sister — the reward of love and
undivided attention. One day I remember my mother stupidly posing
the question before somebody else, 'Oo do 'ee love best?' The answer
was of course, firmly and unquestioningly, 'Hoola'. This was very

ill received, with a frown and a scolding; but I was as obstinate as devoted, and wild horses would not have made me give the expected answer. It wasn't true and I wasn't going to say it: I think there was even thus early an instinctive resentment at the feeling of rejection, the importance of which in my make-up (or case-history) I leave it to the Freudians to disentangle. Being brought up so much by a young sister must have brought out even more strongly the feminine side which so many small boys, *pace* Henry Green, possess and which was very marked in me.[1]

I took great interest in colours, for instance, and clothes and dressing-up. Aunt Lelia (pronounced 'Laylia') was a great, if somewhat remote, admiration of mine. She was Uncle's sister-in-law, Annie Courtenay's mother. Edwin Rowe had been a miner in South Africa, made a bit of money, came home and took a pub at Carthew, died of phthisis at no great age, leaving his widow with some money and house-property in the village. Lelia made a gallant figure, with her black, oiled and curled ringlets, her many gold rings, her gold chains (she wore all of them — a perfect tangle about her neck), her brooches and scarves, her genteelly-pursed lips. But what I most admired were her voluminous skirts which made such a lovely sibillance whenever she moved — which she did in a slow, stately fashion, like a heavily-rigged Spanish galleon, some *Madre de Dios* or *Santo Spirito* bearing down the village, her jewelled hand twitching her skirts up from the mud of road or pavement. (You would never have believed that as a girl she had worked at Polgooth Mine, probably washing 'buddles' — work women did at the mines in those days.) She had a decided streak of grandeur in her: I suppose one would say, to-day, a streak of almost gipsy vulgarity. I think we even thought so then: it was the oiled and ringleted hair we drew the line at. One day, a small boy of three or four, overcome with admiring curiosity, I said: 'Let me see your pretty frockies, Laylia'. 'You are not to call me "Laylia"', the old lady replied, pursing up her lips; 'my name is Laylia Jane.' However, she relented and lifted up her dress to reveal the most splendid coloured skirts, green and purple and black, frilled and watered silk that made that irresistible and impressive rustle when she moved. She was about as voluminous underneath as a

[1] cf. his autobiography *Pack my Bag*, a disappointing book, I think, by an interesting author.

87

really voluptuous purple pickling cabbage. 'This little boy ought to have been a girl', Lelia said.

Later, I am sorry to say, her gentility became a subject of ridicule to the growing boy; and I remember going over to collect an order from her, and coming back to say solemnly: 'I want a pennorth of pipper, and a jilly.' This tickled my mother, who made no effort whatever to 'improve' her speech, or even add an 'h' to her use of language — an accomplishment of which she remained as completely innocent as Walter Savage Landor. We were not on very friendly terms with Lelia and she was never referred to as Aunt Lelia. There had been a quarrel between her and Auntie — who did not ordinarily quarrel with anybody — in the course of which Lelia departed from her usual standards of gentility and revealed the streak of coarseness underneath: 'Hore by name, and whore by nature', she had said — a wildly improbable charge, for Auntie was the soul of respectability. Though uttered in the heat of the moment many, many years before, it was never forgiven. (In the course of my historical researches, I found the women exchanging precisely the same compliment three hundred years before.) In consequence, Lelia and her daughter Annie belonged to the other camp which divided the west end of the village with us, though belonging to the same family; they were friendly with Harry and Polly, and, like them, dealt with the Co-operative Society, not with us.

All young children, I suppose, are extraordinarily observant, but I had the sometimes engaging, but more frequently inconvenient, faculty of expressing my observations in words. There was a commercial traveller who came to the shop (from Furniss's at Truro, who supplied us with gingerbreads, delicious, crisp, golden-brown): this man had an enormous, enlarged nose, more like a limb than a feature, which appeared to my eyes (aged three or four) in the light of a gigantic strawberry. One day, when he came a little too near, I said: 'Go away with your ole strawberry nose.' It was such an exact description that it amused my mother and nettled the poor man, I learned, who must have been all too conscious of the burden he bore. At that point I had to retire. Doctor Stephens, too, who always wore his tall black silk hat on his rounds, was similarly adjured when he pursued me into the sitting-room one day to see 'how I was getting on': 'G'won home with your ole poker-hat.' I think these outbursts were more a form of

defence than anything else, for I was very liable to be frightened by
anybody making a move on me; and, since I was such a nervous child,
everybody in the unimaginative environment of a working-class
family used in consequence to frighten me. It was their idea of a game.
Old Frankie Dewlaps, for example, with his diabolical appearance and
gipsy-black eyes, used to chase me round the corner whenever he
came to see Uncle. It was partly a game on my part, too: all the more
agitating because there was genuine terror in it, as there must be for
young kittens in playing hide-and-seek with them — sometimes
their nerve completely collapses and they escape from the game in
a panic.

There was no element of sport whatever for me in the night-terrors
which tormented me all through childhood, boyhood and adolescence,
and are liable to recur, given certain circumstances, now. As a small
child, I used to be frightened off to bed. Could anything well be more
idiotic? A policy not to be recommended even with stupid and insensitive children, it was very foolish with a nervous and imaginative
child. My brother, who was robust and masculine, didn't take the
slightest notice; but to me 'Wee Willie Winkie' was a figure of mystery
and terror. I would be sitting on my father's knee in front of the fire,
sleepy but very anxious not to be put off to bed, when one or the other
of them would begin:

> Wee Willie Winkie
> Run through the town,
> Upstairs and downstairs
> In his nightgown;
> Tapping at the window,
> Peeping through the lock,
> 'Time all children's in the bed,
> Past eight o'clock.'

But who was Wee Willie Winkie? and what was he doing running
through the town, and in his nightgown? No answer from anybody.
That only made him the more mysterious and frightening. I saw him
huddling along in his nightgown, carrying his candlestick and saying
in that deep, hollow voice which they all put on when they came to
that part:

'Time all children's in the bed,
Past eight o'clock'

(or seven or nine, as the case conveniently might be).
There was another horror too:

Bo! Bo!   Here comes the bogey-man:
Catch'n if you can!

Who was he? The bogey-man was even worse. Wee Willie Winkie, whoever he was, did at least assume the appearance of a child in his nightgown. But the bogey-man was shapeless and vast as the spirit of God that brooded upon the waters. I saw him with a hump on his back, like the old man Dungey, a begrimed ganger on the line, black with tobacco, ill-smelling, his skin so like tanned leather that he could kill wasps with his fingers; he was inseparable from a great hump of a bag which he carried over his shoulder. He had the fixed-lidded eyes of a lizard. He sometimes figured as the bogey-man when I thought who he was. When I asked they only laughed. That was no comfort.

I was taken off to bed, but not to sleep. I lay in bed, my heart beating, hardly daring to breathe, listening, listening for every sound, a creak on the stairs, the scurry of mice in the lumber-room, a rattle at the pane, longing for the time to come when the rest would come to bed. I dared not call out, though I longed to; I should only call down an ill-tempered scolding from my mother on my head. Sometimes I got out of bed in the dark and groped my way to the head of the stairs, whence I could see the warm and friendly glow of light in the shop through the glass window with its muslin curtain. Irresistibly drawn like a moth to the light and warmth, the human conversation of the shop, I would descend a few stairs with infinite care, for, old and rickety, they creaked like the devil and would give me away; sometimes I would be discovered shivering in my shirt in the angle of the stairs and scolded off to bed. (Even a scolding was something warm and human, anyway—it brought one back from the world of the dark, the shadows, the watchfulness of everything.) Sometimes, very rarely, my nerve gave way completely, and after a few vain shouts to somebody to come up, I would burst into a fit of sobs. That would sometimes end with my mother's stern voice coming up the stairs: 'Go sleep', unsympathetic, minatory; sometimes it brought my sister up to comfort me. That was bliss — but a precarious bliss under the threat of the moment when she would inevitably go down again, leaving me a prey to the dark.

When in later years I read the beginning of Proust's *À la Recherche du Temps Perdu* — the first two hundred pages of which are one of the most astonishing tours-de-force in literature — how well I recognized all the symptoms of his agonies as a child at night. His were much more complex and subtle and neurotic, all centred in the desire for his mother; mine were simple, based on that fear of the dark which all Celtic peoples appear to have, but they were not less agonizing. Later on, as a growing boy, with a bedroom to myself downstairs, I got into the habit of looking under the bed every night to see that nobody was there, and I would no more have thought of leaving that downstairs window open than of flying out of it. And so these night-fears went on, into my Oxford days, when it fell to me to inhabit a room with a ghastly memory, which I only learnt of by accident and made myself endure night after night, year after year: it was as important in my life as almost any of my friendships. In the end I exorcised it, though its trace remains in a poem or two and on a few pages of prose.[1]

But how stupid to let a small child fall into these ways — still more to drive him into it and then apply repression as a remedy for the consequences. It is only one other example of the matchless unimaginativeness, the absence of nerves or mind or sensibility, among working people. It would have saved me infinite torture if they had thought for a moment what they were doing and whether it was sensible. But of course the people are more or less incapable of thinking — otherwise they would not be the hewers of wood and drawers of water that they are. I dare say some of the younger working people know better than to frighten their children off to bed; and I dare say with a great many children it doesn't matter anyway. But on this point I did learn from my own experience, when a young relation of mine, whose father had been a miner in South Africa and died of phthisis, came to live with us. I was still a schoolboy; but I could see that he had something of my temperament, that he was nervous and sensitive, artistic and imagin-

[1] cf. the poem 'Waylaid' in *Poems of a Decade*:
What face is that peering from the shadow,
Though I turn not, of the darkened window . . .

ative. And I used to explain to him that everybody felt afraid at night, and that there was no real reason for it, as one recognized in the morning when daylight came. Under this treatment he fairly soon began to grow out of his night-fears.

Not that I am in favour of making everything too easy for children. On the contrary, I have not much sympathy with modern modes of leaving children to do pretty much as they like – the ridiculous fear of anything resembling repression. It is an injustice to children to bring them up as if they will not encounter obstacles and difficulties in the world. It hardly prepares them for what life is really like, besides allowing them to be an infernal nuisance to others in the process. Nor do I endorse the views of modern psychologists about avoiding repression at all costs. The logical end of their endeavours would seem to be to remove the kinks and complexes that make us different and interesting; the ideal from the psychologist's point of view a dead, flat level, with no variations either on one side or the other. I would much prefer to retain the repression (and the complexes) if it has the effect of making people more interesting and odd. There are plenty of characterless specimens in the world, with no individuality or interest in them, already. As for genius, I regard it as the one redemption of the world – it is my religion, what I worship; and in so far as repression, unhappiness, cruelty, misery go to produce the inexplicable state of mind which we call genius (witness, for example, Hobbes, Swift, Beethoven, Newman, even Frederick the Great), I would not wish it otherwise.

Apart from this, there were stories I heard which nursed my terror. I was all ears for such horrors which fed my inner life of imaginative fears. I shall never forget the day on which, at the age of four or five, I heard a ghastly story in the shop – of a man who called at a house late one night with a heavy sack and asked if he might leave it there till the morning. I forget what exactly the dénouement was, but a woman coming down in the night found a man getting out of the sack, and I think he murdered her. The details are not what I remember, but the atmosphere of the shop that cold, bright morning of March wind and sun, the door shut to keep out the cold, the customer standing talking with the shelf of tinned salmon and corned beef behind her head, and the shiver down my spine at the thought of the man emerging from the sack — who would have thought of such a thing? — the sack moving, the knife, the murder.

Enough about night-fears — though it was somehow comforting to find that my contemporary at Oxford, Cyril Connolly, whose own autobiography[1] gives a picture of a background in such contrast to mine, confesses to similar sufferings. In spite of the vast difference between his environment — Bath, South Africa, Mitchelstown, Eton, the Army, Irish ascendancy, public school — and mine, I suppose we have that in common, Celtic temperament, a too lively imagination. He confesses to cowardice, and I think I was a coward, at any rate physically.

I was very timid about new experiences, in spite of an insatiable curiosity: the conflict of the two occasionally brought about a failure of nerve and a sudden panic. One day there was a rumour that the elephants from a visiting circus were going to put up at the farm. I was about three, and was taken over by Uncle to see them. He was wearing his blue apron as he always did when working in the shop; I was all excitement and bravery. I didn't know what I was in for. When I saw these huge, strange creatures lumbering up the road, I was struck with astonishment; I suppose I was expecting something that looked like cows or horses. Falteringly I asked:

'What they g'eat fings called, Uncle?'

Those were the elephants. The news wasn't reassuring as they came nearer and nearer, their sides swaying, trunks hanging like drain-pipes. At the moment when they drew level with us I broke and ran for shelter under Uncle's blue apron, from the security of which I peeped out to see the last of them vanishing into the farmyard.

One habit of Uncle's never ceased to excite my curiosity and comment, and in the end I paid it the tribute of imitation. He had a way of drinking his tea very hot; he used to pour it into his saucer, then shut his eyes completely, screwing them up with a grimace of delicious enjoyment until they couldn't be seen at all, then sipping his tea slowly with a loud, sucking noise and every sign of extreme pleasure. He was in heaven. But what was a mystery to me was why he should close his eyes. It didn't make the tea any less hot. Indeed, he seemed to like his tea as hot as could be and then to pour it out. 'What 'oo shut yours

---

[1] *Enemies of Promise.*

eyes for, Uncle?' I used to ask again and again, mystified. 'No wonder the dear child do ask', Auntie would say, amused — she didn't altogether approve of this habit of Uncle's; it wasn't done in polite society. That didn't stop him from enjoying himself in his own home. And the ritual continued, while I watched, fascinated: nobody else that I knew did it. I ended by doing it too, shutting my eyes fast, screwing them up tight and drinking my tea out of the saucer; until, inevitably, a stop was put to it at home. 'Drink your tea properly out of the cup', etc.

Now for pleasures, for there were pleasures — even, occasionally, in going to bed. When I had migrated to the bedroom downstairs, and on a winter evening my sister played the piano while I was falling asleep, the firelight and candlelight in the sitting-room making a rosy pattern upon the ceiling above my open door, there was a blissful sense of security which lulled me to sleep at the same time as I tried to keep awake to hear my favourite pieces played. Between the two I was in a state of flickering dream, half music, half firelight, and wholly secure. What those favourite pieces were I am now wholly unable to determine; sometimes I think when I play a piece of Chopin that I remember that from those early years. But on the whole I think not; my sister's standards were not high, and I doubt if more than one piece of Chopin figured in the repertory of miscellaneous pieces she possessed.

My cousin, Mamie, who had been adopted by Uncle and Auntie, was supposed to have rather a higher standard; that is, she was taught by a more expensive teacher, a man, and went in for examinations. In the drawing-room at Hillside there were one or two framed certificates on the wall — an odd form of decoration much affected by the lower middle class, and even by the working class, though usually there were no certificates for them to win. What interested me more was a large red morocco-bound volume labelled 'Beethoven'; for in that was a piece called the Moonlight Sonata. At the age of five or six I had a passion to hear this piece, a passion which my cousin as stead-fastly refused to gratify. I looked at the incredibly exciting wavy lines of the notation; it was very recognizable out of the whole book. Alas, four sharps — it was impossible for me to get more than the first notes of it. I believed it to be a piece of astonishing difficulty. Once when I was badgering my cousin to play it, Auntie lent her voice: 'Why don't you play it to'n?' she said. It is my belief now that in spite of the framed certificates on the wall she couldn't play it. So my desire went unsatisfied; though frequently in my sixth and seventh years I would take out that book and look longingly at those moonlit waves in the dark notation. I was reduced to trying the first few bars in the right hand over and over to myself, launching out on uncharted seas of mystery and inexplicable emotion. It was as if a whole world of experience beckoned to me in that piece; the name 'Moonlight Sonata' lured me on, hopelessly, for I could never get beyond the first bar or two.

There was in fact such a world awaiting me; but it did not begin to open out until a few years later when I graduated from Sunday school to church choir. As for the piano, it never occurred to anybody to have me taught, the one member of the family who would have been worth teaching. Playing the piano, among the working and lower middle classes, was essentially an accomplishment for girls. Nor would my parents 'afford' it, though they could have done. There was talk of my sister teaching me, and I had one or two 'lessons' from which I learned the notes. On this slender basis I have built what superstructure of musical performance I have – up to, say, the middle Sonatas of Beethoven, the Sonata con variazioni (Op. 26) being about my standard; half the Preludes and Fugues of Bach.

But there is nothing more aggravating than to get so far and not to be able to get any further: to be able to play the variations of Op. 26, for example, and not to be able to play the infinitely more wonderful ones of Op. 109. The thought that I could never now be first-class at playing the piano, even had I time to practise, made me sell my piano at Oxford to Charles Henderson a few years ago. And then I realized what a foolish thing it was to have done and how much playing the piano meant to me in nervous recreation and renewal. For months it was as if I had cut off my hands; then I gradually got used to it and, of course, hopelessly out of practice. But perhaps it is just as well; one must not disperse one's energies too much. And there is always this feeling of hopelessness when I look at the greatest of the Beethoven Sonatas – Op. 106, 109, 110, 111; or at nos. 5, 8 and 19 of the Chopin Preludes. I feel reduced to the place where G. H. Hardy classes school-mathematics, Hogben-mathematics, as he calls it : which ends where real mathematics begins. So with music, I think when I look at the things

I'd give anything (except years of my life) to play: I feel that I leave off where music begins.

Pleasures were on a very simple scale: nothing like Cyril Connolly's Corsican sunsets, or shaking hands with Captain Scott, the fleet at Simonstown, or having a handsome Moorish guide at Tangier to play with and present one with a drum. I think the high-water mark of pleasure in my early years was picnicking on the beach at Porthpean. We were very simply brought up. We hardly ever left home; the family never went away for a holiday — you couldn't leave the shop and the livestock; we never had any pocket-money; I had never been outside Cornwall until I went to Oxford to try for a scholarship when I was seventeen. (What could be more rootedly Cornish than my roots)?

So going for a family picnic as a child to Porthpean on a Bank Holiday was my equivalent of Cyril's going to South Africa, or Corsica, or Morocco, or Ireland. We children sallied off early in the morning following the trail of the Tregonissey stream in its lower course down Donkey Lane and up under the mysterious and lovely shadow of Gewing's Wood (alas, it disappeared from the landscape in the last war), up the hill to the last exciting dip down to Porthpean. Oh, those delicious days of an all too rare, all-day picnic. You had your boots and stockings off all day, crunching about on sand and shingle and rock and grass. We never bathed in those days; it was only later that my brother, a more independent spirit physically, took the plunge — and loved it. I was content with paddling about all day, eating the pasty brought down by mother and father when they arrived in time for dinner. The chief, and indeed unforgettable, sensation of the day was the way your feet felt when at night you were snug and warm in bed; you could feel the exquisite print of the sand and shingle under-water luxuriously hurting you, as if in bed you were still paddling on Porthpean beach. You nursed the illusion until, footsore and tired out with happiness, you dropped off to sleep. Sometimes at Porthpean it came to summer rain towards the end of the day, or even — a great grievance — before the end. Then we had to pack up and make for home. I remember still the exquisite mingled scent of rain upon the escalonia, upon the pines and fuchsias, soaking into the thirsty summer earth there by Porthpean House where the road bends round to come up the hill.

Going for a picnic to Crinnis was a bigger, more ambitious venture: it involved hiring a wagonette and taking kettles to boil the water in. So usually when we went to Crinnis we went with the Mays and made a large party. That was less pleasurable, since there was always trouble at some point with the small girls, who invariably cried about something. Nor was I a favourite in that quarter. There was something less inviting, positively forbidding even, in the vast spaces of that shapeless beach; the small groups of picnickers were lost in its immense perspectives — so different from the jovial familiarity of the crowded beach at Porthpean. Our first job, arrived on that great prairie of sand beneath the ochre-coloured cliffs, was to collect firewood to boil the kettle; then we were free to scatter and quarrel and get into trouble. My memories of Crinnis picnics are by no means of unalloyed bliss. One of them stands out in a lurid glow like the brazen thunderous day on which it took place: August Bank Holiday 1914, the day when the word went round that war was going to be declared. It was a lowering sulphurous day; as the news went round the beach people began quietly and gloomily to pick up their things and go home. So different from the elation in Berlin! That day was a great dividing-line, and I used to think of this book as starting from that *point de départ*, which it was. It had a strange significance for me, which is not wholly explicable. It was a symbolic day. For the first time I became aware of the outer world, the world beyond the village and the town. I was ten years old.

Among the figures who were closest to me in childhood was Nelius. This was old Mrs. Cornelius, who lived next door up the court. I have already indicated her story: deserted by her husband, who left her with a family of children and went off to America, she brought them up respectably by her own unremitting hard work. She went out to work nearly every day of her life, charring, scrubbing and cleaning; she was a very good needlewoman and such scanty time as she had to herself in her own bare little home she spent ceaselessly sewing. She was never idle. Life had been hard to her, and it had made her hard. She was already an old woman when I was a child, but still she went out to work, not perhaps every day of the week, but most days, walking all the way into the town or to Mrs. Kelly's — who was a generous soul and good to Hannah, as she called her — at Lane End and back. She had the appearance of a child's idea of a witch riding on a broomstick: a very prominent hammer-chin, thin sunken cheeks, toothless save for one frightening tooth of prodigious length and solitariness, bright dark bird-like eyes, thin grey hair plastered sparsely down on the skull parted with a deep line in the middle. People in the village believed that she had the power to ill-wish them, and with regard to some of them she was not perhaps without the will.

She loathed Jack Loam, the young man next door, who was an un-mitigated scamp, neglected his wife and children for other women, stayed away from his work for days and made up for it by poaching and stealing. Nelius kept a watch upon all his goings out and comings in: at night she watched behind the curtain of her bedroom window and always knew from the slightest indication — a feather lying in the court, the smell in the next-door chimney — what had been brought home and cooked that night. She hated Jack with an intense and pursuing hatred. I didn't understand when I was young; but now I see that she was pouring out upon him the vials of wrath and resentment so long stored up against the remote and shadowy figure of her husband. She would grin like a dog and positively growl when her next-door neighbour slunk by. She was right about him, too: he was a scoundrel, whose own life was a tragedy and who made the lives of others a misery and burden to bear. Of him more later: an extra-ordinary story to live cheek by jowl with for years. Poor little Jane, the wife, honest, simple and hard-working, thought that Nelius had ill-wished her — typical of the idiot way the people have of finding a scapegoat, of not being able to face the facts of their situation. (Cf. the whole attitude of the German people since the defeat of 1918.)

Nelius was as hard as any man: she did all her own gardening, built up the hedge (Cornish hedges are of stone) like any hedger. You might have thought that with her appearance and my timidity I should have been frightened. Not a bit of it: in Nelius was all my trust; it was the confidence of absolute love on her part, and on mine, alas, the uncon-scious, unthinking child's assumption of utter devotion and all services rendered. She did anything and everything for me: made all my clothes, pulled out my milk-teeth for me, consoled me in trouble, fought my battles for me, stood up for me even inside my own family, and—most prized attribute of all—out of her hard-earned wage in town she always brought me home a rich banana-wafer. Oh, the flavour of that biscuit: rich even to sickliness as I remember it. It must have cost at least a halfpenny in those days, perhaps a penny—and that meant a lot to her. As I write, I can see her figure with the full skirts in the drab grey-black material, carrying her black satchel, coming round the corner at the end of the village and the small boy glancing along—as we say—to get the so much desired banana-wafer. That was all that Nelius's appearance meant to me: the heartlessness of childhood!

Children, and this small child especially, were the soft spots in this poor lonely old woman's heart. But I am glad to say that, in return for Nelius's goodness to us, mother and father were good to her. She had a great relish for seed-buns—yeast buns flavoured with caraway-seeds, much appreciated in Cornwall, though not by me. Whenever there was a baking of seed-buns, infallibly once or twice in the week, there were a few sent up to Nelius. I think her greatest luxury was at our hands. The last thing on Saturday night, when the shop was shut up and Nelius had gone to bed tired with the week's work, father would carry a boiling hot cup of tea and a new seed-bun up to the old woman in bed. This was pleasure indeed for her: a regular, looked-for ritual which concluded the week. It makes me happy to remember that little act of kindness; sometimes, if father was busy, I took it up to her. I have often thought that just for that little act alone, so simple in itself, meaning so much to her, my father and mother deserved to be rewarded in their last years—as they have been.

No wonder, then, that we children could do as we liked—Nelius thought no ill of us. Once father made a wooden sword for George, with which he made a great show of bravery and ended up by stabbing all Nelius's cabbages to the heart in a row. She came in in a great taking, and said—she was very suspicious by nature—that somebody had an animosity against her; she put it down to Jack Loam, of course. George owned up, and then it was all right. Anything that we did was all right.

Her last years were made easier for her by Lloyd George's Old Age Pension. If anybody ever deserved 5s. a week after a lifetime of honest hard work it was Nelius; and if there was anybody to whom it was an inestimable help it was she. The consequence was that she worshipped the name of Lloyd George — and quite rightly, too. The work of that remote politician away in Westminster, a mere name to her who knew nothing of politics and politicians — any more than any of us did — meant that much concrete security to her last years, so much for tea and sugar and bread and candles and coal and house-rent — there was little enough left over for meat. The seed-buns, thank God, came from next door. When I grew older and was going to school I used to have to fetch her pension every Friday from the Post Office at Lane End. With the best will in the world I could hardly ever remember it. Week after week I would return home from after-noon school, Nelius waiting for her pension to make her few purchases — she never went in debt for anything — and there was no pension. It was like a fatality: I *could* not remember it. My mother used to send me all the way back to Lane End again. Sometimes I felt ashamed and wished I could remember; more often I thought it was a nuisance and was annoyed at having to go all the way back once more.

I well remember the night Nelius went away for good. She had got too old to live by herself and was got down by bronchitis all through the winter. Her daughter was taking her away to live with her at Carthew. It was a night in Christmas week, cold and brilliant with stars; we were having a little party, for Will Jeffery and Mabel were home from South Africa, and there was much playing and singing at the piano, the candles lighted. In the middle of the party the cab arrived to take Nelius away: I remember the feeling of desolation at seeing the bundles being piled in, the big white flour-bag — one of ours — which contained all her bedding, the last bundle of all poor old Nelius crying, for she didn't want to leave her home. Her instinct was right, too, for her son-in-law was very unkind to her and did not want her in the house. One day, after some months there, the old woman got away from Carthew, walked up the steep side of the valley and across Down Park back to Tregonissey, wandering across the downs, and thence up Carclaze Hill to her sister's, where she took to her bed and died in peace. She was eighty-two.

CHAPTER V

ELEMENTARY SCHOOL

I STARTED going to school before I was four — at so early an age that I can hardly remember my first day. I thought I could not remember it at all; but as I write I can just recall the trepidation, the characteristic fear, at finding myself with all those other small children in the tiny armchairs in the babies' class, and the promise to my sister not to cry. Apparently I had several times before this followed her all the way up the hill to Carclaze School, and been sent home by the headmaster as being too young. At last mother sent word that if he wouldn't let me go to school she would have to keep Hilda at home to look after me. That was the foundation on which my schooling started.

I loved it from the first moment, the first scare over at finding myself with so many others: so much more interesting than at home, where there was nobody to play with, nothing much to play with, for we had very little in the way of toys, and my mother had her hands full with house and shop. In the babies' class in the Infants' School — it was really a sort of crèche — there was a nice young woman to play with us and tell us what to do: we played Little Bo Peep, I remember, acting it, crawling all over the floor. Very much more amusing than anything at home, where, if you were minded to crawl about on all fours pretending to be a sheep or a dog, it was 'Stop that noise', or 'Get up from the floor', or 'You'll make your clo'es dirty', etc. Then there were pretty coloured beads that ran up and down the wires on a wooden frame, and you were asked to say what the colours were. I remember saying the names of some, then getting one wrong and being rather vexed at not knowing them all.

However, I soon went up into the second class and began to learn arithmetic and reading. I couldn't understand why little boys didn't like coming to school. I remember the trouble there was to get Jack Hancock to come into the classroom — pretty little boy with a mass of golden curls and pink face all puckered up with crying. It made me cry, too, out of pure sympathy. But there were really no troubles for me at this stage of my school existence, except one day when I brought a bunch of white hawthorn which Hilda had picked for me to take to school from where it grew in the kitchen garden over the Doctor's hedge. The teacher, as superstitious as her parents, refused to have the may indoors, said it was unlucky and threw it away over the railings of the playground into the road. That broke my heart. I was inconsolable; I was desolate. What more awful than to have the flowers picked by my·adored Hilda, in addition to not being valued, just thrown away? It was a terrible grief and nothing would stop the sobs that shook me. At last the teacher took me out to look for them in the playground and over the wall: there they were scattered, broken — too late to do anything about it; I became resigned to their fate. Absurd and childish as was the occasion, I remember few griefs that have been as poignant, as sharp as that: it was the rejection of this offering of love that so cut me to the heart.

It was while I was in this class that it was discovered that I could read. Cyril Connolly tells us in his autobiography that he cannot remember when he could not read. I can just remember learning the letters and words in this class, when I was a little over four; and then suddenly asked to read out loud, it was found that I could read whole sentences: I can hardly remember the process. So up I went into the top class under the headmistress herself, who had a charming smile, great dignity, raven-black hair, and a very nice tin of rich toffee in her desk, from which I used to be helped to a large piece and occasionally kissed when I was a very good boy. In fact I was very much a favourite with her; and on leaving the Infants' School for the big school she presented me with a book, *Granny's Coach and Four*, which I read at home and was inordinately proud of the fact. My first book; it had an impressive inscription: 'For dear Leslie, with love, M. L. Williams', the signature almost as elaborate and self-conscious as those early signatures of Elizabeth which I have come across so often in the Public Record Office.

It was to this time that I date the first awakening of self-consciousness about language when I learned that the word 'chimley' was wrong, and it should be 'chimney'. The chimley had always been called the 'chimley' in our house. I could not believe my ears. Security vanished: it was as if some stone were loosened which was part of the foundation of my universe, and things were a great deal more uncertain than they seemed. However, school was the greater authority with me, in this as in everything else; and I dutifully learnt, a little incredulously at first, to say 'chimney' and even after a while to believe that it was so.

After that, further revelations were not such blows; it was merely annoying to be brought up against the fact that one didn't know what the correct word was, because at home no effort was made about speech at all. Mother talked the Cornish dialect her mother had talked before her, minus the 'h's' which even granny was not entirely without; nor was my father, though he used them sparingly, as they might be aspirins rather than aspirates. My mother could never have cured a headache with any aspirates she possessed. It was humiliating to be caught out not knowing what the right word was. As, for example, when I was sent out to another shop for some 'gurts' — the reader will already have gathered what a favourite dish 'gurty-meat' was with Cornish people: the insides of pigs baked with gurts, i.e. groats, and heavily flavoured with spice. My brother, a true Cornish lad, loved it. I loathed it. When I asked at the shop for 'gurts' the supercilious young woman affected not to know what I wanted, and at last as a great concession suggested, 'Oh, it's *groats* you mean.' My reaction was a very active one: shame, humiliation, indignation with the young woman and a rising tide of anger with the stupidity at home which was responsible for the humiliation. Tears of vexation burned in my eyes all the way up the road, and arriving with the precious packet I threw it on the table, adding: 'And if you want to know' (this very cuttingly) 'it's not called *gurts*, but groats' — and flung out.

It might as well have been addressed to the man in the moon for any effect it had upon my mother. She was quite incorrigible, didn't mind a scrap and couldn't have learned if she had minded. But as the result of this sort of experience I very early began a continuous and persistent effort to speak correct English. It was very much on my own; my sister, who would have had sympathy with it and would have helped, had by this time left home; my brother didn't care a scrap for such things — and in consequence finds himself, at over forty, a lorry-driver. But I was determined to speak as well as I could. It involved an effort, a constant watchfulness, to be on the look-out against lapsing into dialect solecisms and to acquire and acclimatize new words and expressions. It was not, of course, exactly popular with playmates and schoolfellows, and it was a bit difficult keeping to one's standard by oneself alone. But that did not deter me. And, as a matter of fact, there was a great deal less difficulty than a middle-class reader might have expected. School-children are very adaptable and very soon get used to a situation. I think in a short space of time it impressed them and they took it for granted. Then, too, my rapid success at school, where I was always the head of the class, though often the youngest member of it, singled me out as somebody different. That fact, I suppose, became accepted: certainly I can barely remember the time when I did not assume it myself. I remember one day some slight chance reward coming my way for my efforts: some visitor to the district — all visitors were assumed to be Londoners and that conferred the greatest prestige upon them and their cockney accent — happened to be listening to us school-children playing in the New Road (cut across my grandmother's fields), and he said to me: 'But you don't come from here, do you?' This pleased me enormously; it would have been too much to hope to be taken for a Londoner, but this was at any rate tribute to the progress of my efforts. I must have been about nine or ten.

I am well aware that all this will be disapproved of in some quarters, and these efforts deprecated as mistaken, the efforts of a little prig. That reaction is itself, in my opinion, a priggish one, what I call a cliché-reaction. There is in fact among intellectuals of the Left an inverted snobbery about the working class and working-class ways and standards (they call them proletarian). There are well-to-do young men who 'go proletarian' out of boredom with the conventionalism of their environment, who make a cult of the working class (it once used to be called 'proletcult' in a better place). It amuses me in a way: they never take me for a proletarian writer, these middle-class intellectuals, mostly Etonians, like John Strachey and George Orwell, those rising hopes of the stern, unbending workers. Yet here is a genuine working-class writer under their noses, who comes from the people, and therefore has no need to make a cult of them. Genuine writers who have come from the working class, like D. H. Lawrence, can afford to take these things for granted: they know the inanity, the weaknesses of the people, as well as their qualities, their strength. What D. H. Lawrence has to say on the subject in his 'Autobiographical Sketch' is of the greatest interest, and I entirely agree with him: he and I *know*. The truth is, it is not possible to go on living the life of the people once you have developed an intellectual life of your own. For they have none; as Lawrence says, their mental world is altogether too narrow and constricting for us to remain content with it any more. We should stifle.

These blessed middle-class intellectuals who are engaged in a super-fluous pilgrimage to Canossa, standing in a white sheet when nobody asked them to — a slightly ridiculous gesture which the working class does not in the least appreciate, is in fact uneasy with, half-contemp-tuous, wondering whether it is not being laughed at — these same intellectuals do not know what the working people are really like. They see them from the outside; they idealize them; have no concep-tion of how stupid they for the most part are. Hitler knows — that is the tragedy — only too well: he comes from them. There are so many writers in the upper classes going proletarian these days that perhaps it may be taken for originality on my part to make a move in the opposite direction: a proletarian who appreciates and has an altogether higher respect for the standards, the culture, the sense and ability of the upper classes.

There may be people silly enough to think it snobbery to prefer civilized standards and a world of culture and tradition to the great heart of the people. I have no use for the great heart of the people. Or rather that is about all of theirs I have any use for: their emotional life, its depth and sincerity and vitality and directness, is their greatest strength, not their intelligence, their wit, their brilliance, subtlety, variety of conversation or understanding. After all, the magnificent achievements of English literature, of the English political tradition, of English history, English science, are the work of the upper and middle classes, not of the people. I have never much liked Piers Plowman as against Chaucer, the nasty Puritans as against Sir Thomas More and Marlowe and Shakespeare, the fantastic Levellers as against the Cavaliers or Hobbes or Milton, Ebenezer Elliott and the Corn Law Rhymers compared with Tennyson and Arnold, the Socialist tradition in English thought compared with the magnificent line of Bacon-

Hobbes-Locke-Hume-Bentham-Mill. In history I have always been
bored by Popular Movements and Revolts: such fools, led by
such nit-wits — Jack Cade, Robert Aske, John Ket, and the rest of
them. What a dreary quagmire is the history of the Labour Movement — Robert Owen, the Chartists, Bronterre O'Brien, Feargus
O'Connor, the Trade Unions, the Junta, Ramsay MacDonald —
compared with the splendour and magnificent achievement of
Elizabeth and the Cecils, the resplendent services to the nation of the
Churchills, the Pitts, Nelson or Drake. I find an entry in a note-book,
jotted down casually, saying that I can never hear the name of Nelson
without tears coming into my eyes — such genius, such courage, so
transcendent a fate. When William Pitt died, worn out with his labours,
at the age of forty-six, the spirit of European resistance to Napoleon,
at the mention of that name in the Commons, taking their leave of him,
a hush passed over the whole House. Is it any wonder that I prefer
such men to the drab Levellers and all the Chartists and Socialist
Leaguers that ever were?

This digression is a far cry from those early days at the elementary
school, but it at least helps to define one's attitude, which is, after all, the
object of an autobiography. And it does arise directly from the
consideration of the struggle to get away from speaking Cornish
dialect and to speak correct English, a struggle which I began thus
early and pursued consistently with no regret, for was it not the key
which unlocked the door to all that lay beyond — Oxford, the world
of letters, the community of all who speak the King's English, from
which I should otherwise have been infallibly barred? But the struggle
made me very sensitive about language; I hated to be corrected;
nothing more humiliating: and it left me with a complex about
Cornish dialect. The inhibition which I had imposed on myself left me,
by the time I got to Oxford, incapable of speaking it; and for years
the situation, with the censor operating subconsciously, remained
like that. I was too self-conscious to be able to speak the dialect even
if I wanted. It is only in the last year or two, with greater confidence
in myself, after recovering from the long years of illness, that I have
been able to go back and talk the dialect of my earliest youth. Last
year I took down a magnificent dialect story from the lips of Dick

Stephens of Trevissick—how he fought the bear in the town fifty years ago, and I read it over the wireless. But not without trepidation: I was more nervous over it than I was over any broadcast I have given, from the very first, when, with a group of young Oxford poets gathered together by Harold Acton, I read a poem in a B.B.C. programme from Savoy Hill.

But really, this self-consciousness about dialect is not exceptional; I only write down what I felt because it is typical of what all lads like myself go through in the process of emancipation—or, if you like, self-adaptation. Young Welsh friends of mine, with a similar background, have exactly the same self-consciousness about talking Welsh before English people. I have never succeeded in getting Goronwy Rees to say a sentence in Welsh to me, who regard myself as a cousin of the Welsh.

More important in the long run, and wholly desirable, was that the struggle made me sensitive about language and style — though here again my own standards and practice are *different* and have, I hope, some character of their own. English literature and English writing are essentially middle-class. The conventions and assumptions and canons of writing are those of a great corporation to which I do not belong. D. H. Lawrence felt that, too. He was quite right. No need to regret it: in his *difference* lay his contribution to English literature. So far as I am concerned, I know that academic, public-school England has standards which I do not adhere to, conventions which I do not respect, clichés which I do not possess. My own use of language is freer, more unconventional, looser, with inaccuracies and solecisms which I am often aware of and deliberately employ, if they give greater naturalness and spontaneity and vigour. For my belief is that one's style should convey as exact and immediate an impression of personality as possible. I can appreciate dry, academic, impersonal styles, as of the eighteenth century, but when I think of any concrete cases of the best writers — Swift, Johnson, Chesterfield, Gibbon—even in that age, they all appear to be extremely personal. And, in fact, my bias is all in favour of the flexible and emotionally suggestive styles of writers like Newman and Froude. I deliberately disagree with Pater's dictum that writers ought to learn to use English like a learned (i.e. a dead) language. And I believe that I have the writers of my own generation with me, even when they come from Pater's tradition, and have not the same social reason as I have for the line I take.

For all that I am conscious of the difference. All English writing is dominated by the middle class, even that of the Left — such periodicals as the *New Statesman, Horizon, New Writing, Left Review* when it was going. I was brought up against that fact by my divergence from their standards, the kind of question that crops up from time to time between me and the journals for which I write. I know that I do not share their standards, that I differ very often profoundly from their whole approach, their polite point of view, the way to treat opponents, etc., no less than on important issues of policy — for example, from the *New Statesman* as to the issue of Germany and the Germans. I know I do not belong; I often feel like what Carlyle must have felt writing for the *Edinburgh Review*. I do not speak their language, nor think their thoughts. (This is not intended as a complaint: *je constate seulement*: actually I have received very friendly, surprisingly friendly, treatment at the hands of all these journals and more besides. It is only intended to bring out the point of the difference I feel, and that I sometimes doubt if they are aware of the passing frictions that arise and their source — since not one of them treats me as a proletarian writer, which I am. They think George Orwell is, or that Ralph Fox was!)

I suppose all this is only a small part of the complex of differences that arises from being a proletarian: to consider them here would lead into very deep waters. I will only say now that there are middle-class assumptions and judgments as to taste and conduct and morals, the importance attached to being a gentleman — which appears to be the real religion of the public schools — which I neither share nor accept. It amuses me with my very relativist outlook on these matters — Hume is my thinker *à moi* — to see how middle-class and public-school people think of their particular standards, with their very limited frame of reference, economically and socially, as absolute and fixed for everybody to adhere to. (Everybody thinks of his own desires as setting the standard for others. Growing up and becoming adult and rational — which few ever achieve — means to become self-aware about these things, to realize that what you thought were fixed and eternal laws are merely the codified exigencies of your particular class or group, that the 'principles' you would impose on others are merely the expression of your own desires or interests.) The emphasis on being a gentleman amuses me greatly: it is so very middle-class. It is due to the harmless desire on the part of the middle class to blur the line of division between them and the upper class, the gentry, the county. You don't hear the phrase 'gentleman' constantly on the lips of aristocrats: they already know that they are the salt of the earth. They don't need the concept 'gentleman' to elide the distinction between them and the middle class; for them the distinction is too clear all the time.

And really what sacrifices the English middle classes have made, in their decadence and decline over the past twenty years, to that idea! They were so unaware that other people did not regard their code of behaviour as of ubiquitous validity. They knew that the Bolsheviks were not gentlemen — that was too obvious: their nose for their class-interest told them that. But they were so very anxious to give Mussolini a fair trial — twenty years' run they gave him; and many of them were prepared to give the benefit of the doubt to Hitler, Ribbentrop and Göring — there was always Göring to fall back upon: was he not a sportsman?[1] And most of them had no doubts at all about that Christian Gentleman, Franco. It was very provoking when these persons did not behave according to the standards which, it was well known, prevailed among gentlemen, and were inculcated at Rugby (Neville Chamberlain was a Rugbeian), and at Harrow (Baldwin was a Harrovian), and at Fettes (which had the privilege of educating Sir John Simon), and perhaps at Eton (Lord Halifax). All that has happened is that between one and the other of them these gentlemen have fumbled their country and the British Empire into the greatest peril they have ever stood in.

Now I am not a gentleman, I am glad to say. I cannot understand anybody preferring to be a gentleman to being even the most insignificant possessor of a very little genius. To be a writer or an artist or a scientist or a political leader with a real flair for politics is an infinitely greater privilege than to belong to the best society — let alone the rather inferior middle-class society which feels itself glorified by the

---

[1] Cf. the memoirs of the egregious Sir Nevile Henderson, *Failure of a Mission*: an appalling revelation of fatuity in high place.

category of the gentlemanly. Yet there are writers I know — true, of an older generation — who have set more store upon being regarded as gentlemen than they have by their genius. If there was ever such a thing as the sin against the Holy Ghost, that is it! To betray, or let down in any way, the rarest and most priceless of human gifts, the touch of genius — that is unforgivable. Naturally such writers have in consequence not achieved what they might have done with their gift. (In so far as the move to 'go proletarian' amongst younger writers, my middle-class contemporaries, is the converse of this, it has some sense in it. But the older attitude is not worth regarding so seriously as to react thus strongly against it: why can't people take the situation for granted and be what they are?) My own view is quite simple: to be natural, be yourself, keep your own integrity at all costs, make no compromises with or concessions to the stupid, the illiterate, the conventional, the stuffy, the hypocritical, the bourgeois; never say what you don't think in order to please people who don't know, or think they know (they never do); never make any concessions in the realm of what absolute values there are, as regards literature or art or music or plain thinking, for the sake of social expediency. Such sacrifices are the death of the spirit, and for the artist fatal. He must only say what he knows to be true: he cannot live (as an artist) on any other terms. That is why, I suppose, so many of the great writers and artists have had such troubles, and such difficulties with the reception of their works. What matters? Posterity makes it up to them.

I am deliberately and deeply arrogant about all that, as against the contemptible apology of intellectuals for being intellectuals (would they rather be fools?), the *défaitisme* and failure of nerve which makes them seek the anonymity of being ordinary persons (which they are not: and should be shot if they were — when they were endowed with such gifts to make the most of), the attempt to adapt themselves and their behaviour to standards which are not worth a moment's consideration. Flaubert was a thousand times right about all that, with his life-long, loving hatred of the 'bourgeois' and all that it meant. When I read in his Life of how he and his friend Alfred le Poittevin used to go arm-in-arm about the streets of Rouen repeating to the astonished faces of the bourgeois their favourite clichés, 'Comme elle est belle la façade de la cathédrale', etc., adding, to their indignation,

'Et comme elles sont belles aussi, les noyades de Nantes' — I recognized a kindred spirit, and with envious admiration that they could have thought of it as schoolboys, when I was still in the chrysalis stage.

All this would naturally lead on to the consideration of religion and ethics, and the differences there due to being a proletarian. But I must postpone that to a later chapter, a later book.

Back to school! There is not much that I remember about my elementary school education anyway. What do I remember? Episodes like the Inspector calling in Standard II and asking what change you would have from £1 if you had spent so much and so much adding up to 14s. 6½d. — or some awkward figure like that. Several got the amounts added up all right, and then failed at the last hurdle to do the subtraction right in their heads. Only one horrible little boy got the answer right — perhaps practice in the shop enabled me to do sums then which I am sure I couldn't do now. I remember that uproarious, unruly standard, forty children or so, because of the charming habit of the young woman-teacher who couldn't keep us in order and used to retire behind the blackboard to have a good cry, and then come out to face the mob again. In the meantime Bedlam broke loose; children are, in such circumstances, fiends. Then there was the one occasion when I was 'kept in' after school. This was for whistling in the class. I was very ashamed and covered with confusion sitting all alone on the long bench in the vast empty room. (That room held about seventy children in two classes: think of teaching anybody anything in such circumstances!) When I was asked what I had done it for, I confessed, what was the truth, that I didn't know how to whistle and that I thought I would try just to see if I could — and then this unexpectedly piercing note was the result. The teacher couldn't refrain from laughing at this innocent explanation, and I was let off, inexpressibly happy and relieved.

I was moved up the school at a very rapid rate, sometimes jumping a standard altogether. This was put down to my being 'Master's favourite'. But it was really very sensible on the part of the old headmaster, a very interesting character, whose 'favourites', anyway, were the senior girls. I was given the cane once or twice, just to show, I think, that I wasn't a favourite; but though I wasn't caned hard, I resented it extremely. One day when 'Master' was away — he was a member of the County Education Committee and used to go off to Truro once a month or so — there was a regular riot against his under-master, a youngish man called Hunkin from Mevagissey. He was very unpopular with the big boys, was fond of caning them, and they had it in for him. It was an enjoyable experience up to a point for a 'good boy' who was too young, anyway, to take any part in the proceedings, but had a seat in the front row of the stalls. It began very early that afternoon by agreement amongst the older boys, who with one accord refused to do anything they were told. The under-master started punching the boys; some of them hit him back. Soon there was perfect pandemonium. I can see his pinched eager little face now, with the sharp nose, and blue eyes behind the rimless spectacles, his hairy hands shaking with anger and passion, himself white to the gills. There was no other man on the staff to come to his rescue; the women in the next-door classrooms once or twice looked helplessly in on the scene, but there was nothing to be done about it. I began to be quite frightened when I heard that Hunkin was to be 'tabbed' on the way home. School was dissolved early that afternoon, and as he ran the gauntlet of the narrow village street homewards he was pelted with 'tabs' (turfs) and even stones, some of which got home and cut him about the face. I was much too frightened to venture out and see all this. Within a year or two he was, poor fellow, killed in the War.

The War made an enormous difference to our manners and modes, and I cannot imagine this happening at Carclaze School after the War. But the fact was that before the War the boys were a distinctly rough crowd. How I got through these elementary school years as well as I did is rather a mystery to me now. I seem to remember a good deal of going out of the way to avoid trouble; sometimes I recommended myself to the protection of some older and stronger ruffian, much as a weaker Saxon might recommend himself to a feudal lord. I must have been a good deal more diplomatic than I subsequently became when I was capable of standing up for myself. And it was a great advantage that natural tastes and sympathies led me to consort with the girls, who were chiefly my friends in these earlier years. My brother, who had no such gifts but his own strong right arm, and being five years older was among the senior boys, was for ever in trouble fighting with them. I hope he enjoyed it: I wouldn't have had such a life for anything. I remember one occasion when several of the big boys gave him a 'hammering', hitting him over the head and shoulders with their big red handkerchiefs which they had filled with stones and tied up for the purpose. No such things happened to me, though I was completely incapable of defending myself. I remember thinking him — with the superior wisdom of nine to fourteen — a fool for getting involved with them.

Anyway, whether it is illusion or no, I have the impression that after the War elementary schools like ours became much less rough and raw, and altogether quieter. For one thing there were so many fewer children; for another, their parents had been a bit educated by the War and liked fighting and quarrelling among themselves rather less; then, more recently, the elder children have been skimmed off to the senior schools. But I think it is no illusion — the War brought about profound changes in English society; working people became better off and their standards changed. The changes have gone through all classes: in the older Universities the pre-war rowdiness has largely come to an end; the public schools have become immensely less harsh and rigorous than they were.

What about our 'education'? We were taught to write a good plain hand; much store was set by that, the one advantage, I often think, we have over public-school boys. We were given a firm foundation of arithmetic. There was a lot of drawing, which I was not bad at in those days but have never been any good at since. We assembled at nine o'clock, the school-bell clanging harsh and more harshly out over the ugly granite village of Lane End. We marched into our places to the sound of some piece dutifully thumped out on the piano by one of the girls learning music with one of the teachers: a closed circle into which I longed to penetrate — but, alas, I didn't know a piece to play. The register was called and we said 'Present, sir' or 'Present, miss' as the case demanded. (It somehow calls to mind the little girl keeping school at the bottom of the sea in Jules Supervielle's *L'Enfant de la Haute Mer*.) Then we had prayers and a scripture lesson: all this a fearful waste of time — the first and most active-minded three-quarters of an hour in the day wasted. Oh, the unutterable tediousness of Matthew vii: 'Judge not, that ye be not judged. For with what judgment ye judge, ye shall be judged; and with what measure ye mete, it shall be measured to you again.' There were similar passages from Romans and what not, which we chattered away like magpies or jackdaws. And that was the religious instruction which the humbugs of the County Education Committee, or rather all the humbugs of all the County Education Committees in the country, combined to impose on us elementary school children. I can hear the dreary sing-song mumbo-jumbo of it now, Judge-not-that-ye-BE-not-judged, in those high unmeaning children's voices. For, of course, it meant nothing to us. Its only result was to give us a horror of the Bible; it put me off completely, and for years afterwards I never opened it on my own.

Then there was a lot of Silent Reading, it was called, during which our harassed teachers with forty or fifty children on their hands would get on with their mark-books or attendance registers, while we read more or less silently. How well I remember those somnolent after-noons: the hard benches without any backs, the difficulty of finding a comfortable posture, and at length finding one, propping your head up with elbows on the desk, hands over your ears so as not to be interrupted in your self-regarding pleasure; occasionally looking up in a dream, to hear the rustling of leaves being turned, boots scraping the floor, the sparrows chittering or saying their rich 'gulge-gulge' in the eaves. Yes, that is the sound which I associate always with Silent Reading at the elementary school — an automatic mnemonic: if I hear it to-day, my mind goes back thirty years to myself as a child with those other children, when life and hope were new, when there never seemed any end to one's vitality or any diminution to the spirits, when everything came fresh and full of savour to the eager appetite, when one did not know what life had in store for one, and the experience of the moment was its own satisfaction. I had a way — most children have — of naming sounds and actions in a language of my own, in the words that expressed them best to me. The 'gulge-gulge' of sparrows is a nostalgic sound for me, and wherever I hear them brings back those sleepy summer afternoons, the school windows open, the subdued murmur of the hive, myself sunk deep in the dream of my reading.

We didn't have much that was interesting to read—only two or three books that have left any imprint on my memory. One was *John Halifax, Gentleman*; and that I remember for quite the wrong reason — for the extreme sexual excitement I derived from it, from the passage where the wife announces to her husband that she is going to have a baby. It only shows how impossible it is to keep sex out. Nobody on earth could have imagined that this would have been the effect of the chastest of Victorian novels on a small boy of ten — and, indeed, this is all that I remember of the book. The other book was Q.'s *The Splendid Spur*, and that was my favourite. I read it over and over again. You had to read your books over and over again, anyway, if you read at all quickly, they were so few; but I mean that I read this over and over with pleasure. I knew it almost by heart, and I loved its exciting scenes: from the very first moment in the bowling-alley at Oxford where the sinister Mr. Hannibal Tingcombe, with the trailing foot, makes his appearance; then the carousing round the table into which Jack Marvel breaks and escapes by upsetting the lamp (how could he have thought of anything so clever? it would never have occurred to me). I loved his lordly gesture when, 'tossing his gown to the porter' at Trinity, he left Oxford; there was the heart-beating excitement of the escape from the tavern on the Great West Road, Jack's 'sorrel nag' — or was it his pursuer's? — and the hut in the wood where Jack took refuge and the old French gentleman died and was buried in the snow. I am afraid I am remembering it not quite accurately, but I remember it with love.

One afternoon I was so deep in this book, my ears stopped up as usual, that somebody to play a trick upon me told me that 'Master' wanted me at his desk; unquestioningly I went out and stood by the desk, to be asked what I wanted. Instead of ticking me off, the old boy sent me back with a word of praise for having the faculty to get so lost in my book. I suppose I was rather spoiled at school — and that was why I liked it so much; I certainly wasn't spoiled at home. It is amusing to think that nearly thirty years later, earlier this very year, Q. told me how and when he had come to write that book, getting married at Shiplake Church in the middle of it. I think he said he wrote it in six weeks — which seems the dickens of an achievement to me who am accustomed to slave for years at my books on history.

Those early readings of *The Splendid Spur* at the elementary school were the foundation of my lifelong admiration for Q. and all his works, though I didn't know anything about him then and there wasn't anybody to tell me that he lived only across the hills, almost within view, at Fowey.

Two other books I know we read: Scott's *Ivanhoe* and *Tom Brown's Schooldays*. The first left a dim impression, except that my sympathies were wholly Saxon then. *Tom Brown's Schooldays* I loved, though one or two episodes in the book, like the roasting of Tom over the fire in the school hall, the sanguinary fight behind the chapel, gave me a fearsome impression of public-school life. I preferred the gentler scenes, like Tom's farewell to the farmyard at his home in Berkshire before going to school. (Am I right in thinking of it as taking place at sweet Uffington under the lee of the Downs, which I often pass by in the train going from Oxford down to Cornwall?)

Other reading was even more restricted: I mean books from which we read out loud. I remember once the teacher — it was my friend Miss Clemo, now headmistress at Charlestown, under the hill from here — got out *Julius Caesar* as an experiment and handed out the parts. We were given a few minutes to prepare ourselves, and then I started off very dramatically

'Hence, home you idle creatures, get you home!'

with all the 'h's' in place and very aspirated. It had an electric effect on the class and even on myself. I was very excited: it went to my head. Nobody laughed; they all sat up. But we couldn't keep it up; certainly they couldn't, and I doubt if I could: the scene tailed off at the end, and I do not remember that those green-bound *Julius Caesars* ever made their appearance again.

One day in class 'Master' was surprised to find that I knew a thing or two about Mary Tudor, whom nobody else had heard of, for the Tudors had never yet come our way. The fact was that Auntie had a book in which I liked reading about history. On my way home from school I used to call in at Auntie's. She would sit in her chair under the little bookcase fixed to the wall, red-faced, rotund little figure, tight-corseted. In these days she often used to 'feel queer'; she would have what she called an 'attack' in which she would go off: it was like a faint; she would go blue at the lips, her eyes remain in a fixed stare, and afterwards she wouldn't remember anything about it. It was very eerie: she seemed so strange when she was coming round, not at all like her loving, cheerful self; she would speak as if she did not know you. The attacks came fairly frequently and I was present several times when they happened. We took no serious notice of them. Auntie always wanted to know all the news, especially about home — had father been beating George lately? what had so-and-so said? etc.; and I used to get into such trouble for telling all the news, and having too 'long a tongue', as mother put it, that eventually I decided silence was the only safe policy. So I would remain mum under Auntie's barrage of questions, bored as she was with the long empty days at Hillside and Uncle still out going his china-rounds, though he was always promising to retire. 'I dunt know what sort of children yours are, Aunt Annie,' she once said, 'when they come up my place, they shove their nose in a book and you can't get a word out of 'em.'

It was not only safer that way, but more interesting; there were no books to read at home, not a single one. Whereas I liked Auntie's green history book. I opened it at my favourite page, the illustration of Bloody Mary — it must have been some horrible Protestant text-book, which so worked up my indignation against Bloody Mary for her burnings that I ended by scrabbling the page all over and, if Auntie hadn't protested, would have torn the portrait of Mary out of the book. It is curious to me to think that here I am thirty years later, still scratching away at Tudor history; other affections, other passions have come, and some gone, for music, church, poetry, politics; but my earliest devotion of all — to Tudor history — still remains with me. I often think of it as perhaps an instance of the way in which our earliest impressions unconsciously form and direct our tastes and choices. What has changed is not the affection, but the judgment: I have gone a long way from the Protestant text-book's line about Bloody Mary.

It happens that my old school-teacher, Miss Clemo, has preserved a writing-book of mine from this time, from which I can reconstruct something of the progress of my education up to the age of eleven. It is a faded, grey exercise-book, such as we used, with the arms of the Duchy of Cornwall on the front, the ducal coronet above, the

Cornish motto 'One and All' beneath. On the back, a map of Cornwall, which was thus so much more familiar to us than the map of England, along with some information, such as 'Area, 1356 square miles; Population in 1901, 322,957', chief towns, industries, physical features, distinguished Cornishmen, including a misleading piece of information, for it begins with William Pitt, who, though the Pitts owned Boconnoc for a time, was not a Cornishman at all.

The chief thing that comes as a surprise to me, after the quarter of a century since I saw that book last, is to find how knowledgeable we were about current affairs. I learn, for instance, that Lord Pentland was the Secretary for Scotland in the Cabinet, that the Chief Censor was Sir Stanley Buckmaster, that Sir John French continually complained in his despatches of not having enough munitions (how little the War Office changes!), that Petrograd was the new name given to the capital of Russia, and that there was a large street there called the Novski Prospect.[1] All this in the course of putting words into sentences in order to show their correct use. Occasionally I was defeated, as with 'The person accused with the murder of Lady Stanthropean [wonderful invention, in which the presence of Porthpean is obvious] proved to be an alibi.' The law-courts were evidently too much for me.

Not so the War, which occupies a very prominent part in these lucid pages. A month ago, we are told, 'a squadron under Sir David Beatty sunk the *Bleücher*'. A recruiting march of the D.C.L.I. about the district on May 8th, 1915, is next described: one might almost write a local history of the early stage of the War from this exercise-book. At Lane End the headmaster joined the officers, some of whom made speeches: 'one recruit volunteered, whose name was Mr. Chubbs'. Poor lad, for his pains, he came back minus a leg from the War. At the end of the day, in the town, 'seventy men came forward and offered their services for their King, and were accepted. On the whole the day passed very pleasantly'.

I was very patriotic. There are 'compositions', i.e. short essays, on St. George's Day and Empire Day, a letter to a British prisoner of war, beginning, 'We are all sorry to hear that British prisoners are in a state of semi-starvation'. Then comes a letter to Count Zeppelin, a very

[1] I have, of course, left the mistakes in spelling, etc., as they stand.

rhetorical work, written 'three days after the last raid. You think that we English subjects are frightened at such atrocities that, through you, have been committed.... But Beware! I say, there is a greater trial yet, and you will suffer.' There is a still more oracular remonstrance addressed to 'His Imperial Majesty the Emperor of Germany': 'I have addressed you by your full coronation title; but I am sure you are not worthy of such an honour.' The Kaiser's attention is drawn to such considerations as the sinking of the *Lusitania*, the German bullying of Europe since 1866, the treatment of Belgium. He is reminded of the fate of 'the last tyrant Napoleon: who died of a cansor (through sorrow,) without any one to love him, in the lonely isle of St. Helena'. The letter concludes with an outburst of eloquence which might have done well on Coalition platforms in the Khaki Election of 1918: 'Well however, you who impute all your victories to God, I suppose you go to church. Have your chaplain ever preached you a sermon on "Repent, or ye shall all likewise perish". You and your sect have not repented, therefore you will perish in the torments of Hell! Well, Good-bye, you monument of holiness.'

Scripture provided some lighter moments. Joshua, we learn, 'sent out two men from Shittim'. (Was there really such a place, I wonder? Or did I mean, perhaps, Shechem?) These two men apparently came to Jericho to spy out the land, but 'when it was dark went into the house of a harlot, Rahab by name'. Very understandable; but can I really have known what a harlot meant? If the Education authorities only knew what risks they take by prescribing the Bible for the minds of the young!

There is a great deal about ships. I knew all the dimensions of the *Lusitania*, and rather more about the affairs of the Cunard Company than I have known since I became a shareholder in that great concern. I knew that the *Titanic* was travelling at an average speed of twenty-one knots when she ran into the iceberg. There is an essay on the American War of Independence, of which the hero is George Washington, the point of view more American than the Americans, as is usual in all English schools on that subject. The Americans were right. Indeed, it is not until the quite recent rise of a band of American historical scholars that we have realized that there was even another side to the question.

But the most surprising thing in this little book is the paraphrase of a poem, which clearly gave rein to the child's imagination. It is, I think, a rendering of a poem of Longfellow's:

A man lay beside some ungathered rice, in his hand he held a sickle. His tangled hair was buried in the sand. As he lay in the shadowy land of sleep, he dreamt of the land of his birth. Wide through the land of his dreams, the great river Niger flowed. He strode once more a king underneath the trees of his plains. He also heard the bells of the caravans descending the hill. His wife, standing among her children was present in his dream. They kissed, embraced and spoke kind words to him. From his eyelid burst a tear, and it fell on to the sand. Then along the Niger's bank he rode, his bridle reins were of gold; and he could feel at each bound his sword smiting his horse. Bright flamingoes flew before him and he followed them until he came to the Caffre huts, with the ocean in his view. At night he heard the wild animals roar and scream; and he heard the hippopotamii crush the reeds of a hidden stream. All shouted with liberty, as he passed through the forest; and the hoots in the desert cried with a wild and free note. He started in his sleep and smiled at the triumph of everything. The burning heat of noon nor the slave-driver's whip had any effect on him for he had passed from the Land of Sleep, to the Land of the Dead.

When. I reflect how much has perished of my memory of those early years at the elementary school, I am all the more grateful that my old teacher should have preserved that one exercise-book; for from it I see that we were altogether better taught than I had remembered, that we were talked to about current affairs, the imagination appealed to in a way to which a clever child could respond. No wonder I liked going to school so much, and never missed if I could possibly help it. It was so much more interesting than staying at home. The little faded, grey-backed book, with my name and Carclaze Elementary School written in the headmaster's bold, free hand, makes me realize all the more acutely the debt I owe to those elementary-school teachers of thirty years ago.

Two events in the world at large made an extraordinary impression on my mind at this time: I think they were the first occasions on which the newspapers impinged on my consciousness. We didn't take in a daily paper in those days; we waited for the full impact of the news to reach us on Sunday mornings, when we took in, not the *News of the World*, but the other one — I think it was *Lloyd's News*. I well remember the sensation in the household when we read about the *Titanic*'s going down: you might have thought that we had lost half our family on the ship. The fact that a Mount Charles man had gone down on her brought the disaster somehow very near to us. I think we all wept. I was appalled. In fact, so strong was the impression, that the loss of the *Titanic* made a permanent mark on my mind: it confirmed the fear of the sea which I got from my grandmother ('the hungry sea') and from my father. In father and mother's bedroom there were two photographs of ships wrecked on the Cornish coast: one a four-masted schooner wedged in a V-shaped cleft in the cliffs; another of a liner, with two or three funnels, stuck fast on the rocks near inshore. And when we went to visit our Falmouth cousins, the Richardsons, the talk was very often about another liner, the *City of Paris*, that had struck the Manacles in a fog, the lights of the ship going out, the vessel sinking swiftly, the hundreds of people drowned, the bodies washed in at St. Keverne.

So that the loss of the *Titanic* had something to go upon in my mind. I took in every detail avidly: the luxury of the great ship, the forebodings, the ill-omens before she set sail, the passengers singing 'Nearer, my God, to Thee' as she went down, the intense cold, the iceberg, the boats getting away, the vast ship blazing with lights from stem to stern — and then, darkness and silence. The result was that anything about the *Titanic* ever afterwards excited my attention. Ten years later, at Oxford, one bitter March afternoon, I came across an account of the disaster, a little book on the shelves in the open air by the bookshop which used to occupy the Octagon in the Broad. All through the afternoon I stood there at that draughty corner, absorbed, oblivious of time, the gusts of March wind, while that amazing scene re-enacted itself in my mind as when I was a child of ten. A further result was to increase my horror of the sea, or rather of going on the sea — so unnatural, you might say, in someone who had lived all his life within sight of the sea — until it achieved almost the character of a love-hate complex. Whenever I have had to go by sea abroad, I have always been conscious of the sensation Turgeniev diagnosed so well: so long as all is going without a hitch on board the steamer all is well and the passengers are happy; but the moment a hitch occurs, their latent anxiety comes at once to the surface and reveals the fear in the background.

The Crippen murder case had (I hope) no such lasting effect upon my mind, though at the time it made for a deplorable excitement. I was well up in all the lurid details of that squalid affair, as presented by the Sunday newspaper: the doctor's wife, La Belle Elmore, generous and vulgar, who was apparently no better than she should be, the doctor's fancy, Miss Ethel Le Neve — it might have been the stage-name of a Gaiety star — the discovery of the remains under the floor of the cellar, the flight across the Atlantic, Miss Le Neve dressed as a boy, the doctor's impassivity on being put the question: 'Did you murder your wife?', the accusing blush upon his neck. I have never been able to forget these details: I think I might almost have won a D.Phil. with a thesis on the subject at the London School of Economics.

The first time I ever bought a newspaper for myself was in the last days of July 1914, in all the excitement of the War approaching. I think it was the *Daily Mirror*, or the *Daily Sketch*, that I bought, and felt very worked up at the photographs of tunnels and bridges guarded by soldiers. I read the news with all the impressive long words — diplomatic démarche, ambassador, ultimatum; there were all the foreign names, M. This and M. That: I called them, not Mr. — Monsieur I hadn't heard of — but plain 'M'.

One other public event, of a local character, must not be omitted: the china-clay strike of 1913. The average wage of a china-clay worker was about £1 a week: I think that is what my father was paid. It is wonderful how those working-class women brought up their families, fed and clothed and housed them, paid their rent and kept their fires going on such a miserable pittance. Meanwhile, in and around St. Austell there was a handful of china-clay families, all inter-related and with their numerous sons-in-law forked into jobs in their offices in the town, or as 'buyers' or travellers for their firms, or, when they were no good for anything else, as

'cap'ns' of clay-works. They were a dismal, uncultivated lot, these
china-clay families, with all the vulgarity and congested self-
complacency of their worship of money. For they were prospering
and making money in those years. On the airy western slopes of
the town their showy new houses were going up: enlarged and
glorified cottages, like their minds; ugly, shapeless, with innumerable
gables and an infinity of knick-knacks, without taste, without
civilization. But they had money, and they let everybody know that
they had: that was what they really worshipped, Sunday by Sunday,
in the chapels in which they continued, most of them, to cut a figure.
(One or two of them went up a peg, and went to church.) Their
sons were learning to play golf, their daughters tennis; one or two of
them learnt to ride; they inhabited

> The land of lobelias and tennis flannels . . .
> Their only monument the asphalt road
> And a thousand lost golf-balls.

I did not appreciate their inanity at the time; they did not come across
my path much as a boy; and if they had, I should have paid them the
compliment of envying them their money — as we all did: such was
the standard of that china-clay community from top to bottom.

But it is an amusing, and a revealing, reflection now to think that
of these moneyed families of my native town — one of them sold the
works where my father was employed for not less than £300,000 —
not a single one of their sons, that I ever heard of, went to the University.
For all their money, they continued to live in their enlarged suburban
houses on an income of five or ten or fifteen thousand, as they had
lived before on so many hundred. Not one of them ever moved into
a country house. They continued to huddle in and about the town,
close to business, the club and golf-course. They had no taste. What
went on inside their minds, their conception, if the term may be used,
of how to live their lives — constricted, congested, constipated — would
make a wonderful study: a subject some day for a novel.

But they managed to beat the strike all right. They would.

The men were not well organized. The old General Workers'
Union took them in hand and did its best to bring all the men into the
Union. So far as they could, they prepared the ground for the strike,

aided by the eloquence of a Baptist minister, an idealist Radical of an older type, by name Booth Coventry: so different from the nauseating hangers-on to power, the conformists to Chamberlainism, of the post-war period. Booth Coventry toured the whole district with the trade-union leaders, did his best to get the men to stand together — most difficult of all in the county whose motto is 'One and All'. The men came out on strike. The strongholds of the strikers were the little villages on the western escarpment behind St. Austell: Foxhole, Trethosa, St. Stephens, Treviscoe, Nanpean, St. Dennis — now strongholds of Labour votes. The leadership of the men came from there: in particular, a magnificent old warrior, Samuel Jacobs, who had been a soldier in youth and killed his man on the North-West Frontier. He was a natural leader of men, firm as a rock, like a rock in physique, staunch and unbreakable; uneducated, but with a great respect for education, a touching humility towards the educated, as modest and shy with them as a child. When I came to be Labour candidate, he was my strong support, a venerable old patriarch now, looked up to and respected by the whole district: everybody came to him with their troubles. I admired him infinitely. He had just that combination of great strength and sweetness which is the finest foundation for a man's character. I have never admired anyone in life more than Sam Jacobs of Trethosa.

We knew little enough of what went on during the strike. We were very little affected by it in our village on the edge of the plain. We heard exciting rumours of what was going on in the 'Higher Quarter' — and put it down to the natural roughness of the Higher Quarter people. There was very little real trouble, only an occasional disturbance as the strike deepened: the noise usually made by the women, as funds became short and the children went hungry. But the china-clay owners seized what opportunity there was to bring in a lot of Glamorgan police, a rough crew, who were used to strike-breaking in South Wales: they were billeted in the Bible Christian Sunday School, I remember. They had a very fearsome reputation among the gentle-hearted Cornish people. And not many weeks after their arrival the strike was broken and the men went back to work at the same wages.

My father came out with the other men, and went back when they went back. (A few of the cap'ns' favourites, who were graced by the men with a less elegant term, never came out at all.) But owing to the shop, the strike affected us very little: merely indirectly, in so far as one or two of the strikers' families ran up bills, which they conscientiously, gradually paid, when the strike was over. We never went short ourselves, we never did at any time. I am afraid I never realized then how much we owed to the shop.

By quick promotions I had arrived at the top of the school by the time I was eleven; most of the boys and girls in what was called the ex-seventh were thirteen and fourteen, at which age they left school. 'Master' had evidently had it in mind that I should take a minor scholarship and go to the secondary school. There was no very good feeling between us and the 'secondary school kids': we felt that they were superior and we were jealous. In those days secondary schools were a new thing in Cornwall, and not all of them were successful — the one at St. Austell had not been so far; it had had a rather chequered career. Then, too, it was a definite sacrifice on the part of an elementary schoolmaster to send away his best pupils. However, it was decided by him that I was to go in for a scholarship. With my usual respect for whatever was said at school I went home and announced that I was going to try. I remember now standing inside the rickety old double door of the shop and telling my mother. She wasn't very interested: I think she would have preferred that I left school. But I was too young for that anyway, so what did it matter what I did? Elementary school or secondary school, it was all the same to her.

So I went in for the examination — like Lawrence, whose course, little did I know it, I was following. I felt a good deal of stage-fright. I had a vague idea that I ought to be doing homework beforehand, a thing not done at the elementary school. We were free in the evenings to play in the village road. And what evenings those were: I remember them now, particularly for some reason, those of autumn, when the friendly mists of October came down upon the village and the evenings were closing in earlier, and we played on in the twilight, at rounders, against the side of Mrs. May's house, or at skippety-bed with the girls in Back Lane, until bathed in sweat and tired out I heard the inevitable voice calling me in at the bottom of the court. There was the acrid, unmistakable smell of autumn in the garden fires; voices were mellower; lights were lighted in the cottage windows, the lights of those delicious days of boyhood now for ever gone. Those evenings of care-free play with the boys I went to school with day by day were soon to be over. I was going to the secondary school, alone of the village-boys. That made a barrier; there had not been one before.

I just remember sitting for the examination, and feeling that I had not done justice to myself; I bungled a question or two in the arithmetic paper which I could have done better. We heard no news of the results. I was sure I had not got through — after all, I had done no homework: the school couldn't run to giving me any coaching for the examination. Then one afternoon Master arrived home from Truro, his face wreathed with pleasure, his large voluptuous nose giving that familiar twitch when he was pleased. I had not only got a scholarship but was placed first in our district, and about fifth for the whole of Cornwall. This was very unexpected and I hardly knew where I was, except a very real pang when the time came to leave my old school and Master and teachers who had been so very kind to me.

Auntie had promised me half-a-crown if I won a scholarship: no interest in the matter at home. When the news came, she was no longer there to display hers. One day towards the end of my time at Carclaze, somebody told me on my way home that I'd better hurry on, my Auntie was dead. With my first experience of grief of that sort clutching hold of me, hoping against hope, praying it might not be so, I rushed in at the familiar gate to find the place in a turmoil. The house was full of neighbours. My mother had been sent for; she and Annie Courtenay went up and with two other women carried her upstairs in a sheet and laid her forth. Butcher Hancock said he had never seen four finer-looking women than these four. I was sent home out of the way, desolate with grief, the sharp pangs of a child's grief, which heals quickly, but was a genuine tribute of my love for her. Uncle had been stopped somewhere out on his round and told that she was very ill; but he knew the truth at once and was inconsolable. He loved her very dearly; and life never meant anything to him again without her. He just sat there, lingering on a year or two, longing to die, to join her. His love for her was far the best thing about him; for she had the best and truest of natures, a golden heart. Gone were all the happy days associated with 'up Auntie's': no more the Christmas good cheer she delighted to provide, the gaslight upon the wine-red wallpaper and the dates and walnuts; no more Auntie 'quizzing' me when I was on my way home from school, to know what was doing at home; no more songs from Uncle to her delighted applause and pride in him. Sometimes afterwards Uncle would begin to quaver one of his old songs, one of the melancholy ones, and then stop, his voice falter — he had seen a vision of her with whom he had lived the best years of his life and whom, it was literally true to say, he prized more than life itself.

There was the funeral, of which I remember little, except that we all wore black gloves. I had been taken up to say good-bye to Auntie as she lay there in her coffin by her best half-tester bed with the dark-red hangings: the spare front bedroom. I was told to kiss her forehead; there was a little foam at the corners of her lips. She was cold as marble. I was very unhappy and frightened. It was the first time that death had come near me or touched anyone I loved. Dear, kind heart, that held nothing but kindness for everybody, I have at length, after all these years, when most of those in the house that day have gone, rendered you justice!

With Auntie's death and the closing of the ever-open hospitable house on my way to and from Carclaze School, and with my winning a scholarship, which took me a rather shorter distance in the opposite direction to school, a noticeable change had come about in my life. A new world was opening out before me.

CHAPTER VI

CHURCH

So far I have said hardly anything about going to church; and yet in some ways, certainly aesthetically, it was the chief influence in my early life. As with the medieval Church's mission to the barbarians of pagan Europe, so with me, the Church's influence was mainly a civilizing one. This was the point, St. Austell parish church, at which my small, rather isolated and ignored existence, having to develop for itself, hinged on to the civilization of the past, to history, breathing something of the sense of history, this atom of remote Cornish life yet in some touch with the Europe of which it was part, but of which it was totally unaware.

My brother and sister had begun by going to the Bible Christian chapel and Sunday School, as father had done. But, after some children's squabble or other, mother took them away because it was too rough and there was 'more reverence to church'. By the time I arrived we were a church-going family, and I was duly christened by the curate, Fred Carr, who subsequently became one of the best-known of Cornish clergy, Vicar of St. Mary's, Penzance. Aunt Rowe was my godmother, supported by Lelia, and Mrs. Vague, who carried me.

We were rather exceptional in going to church. All the people in the village went to chapel, of one sort or another, most of them to Bethesda, at Carclaze. In the town and over the whole parish — as over Cornwall as a whole — the vast majority went to chapel. I have since reflected, particularly in relation to politics, that it is a considerable handicap not to have been born a Nonconformist. (There are advantages, of course, which more than make up for the handicap; for instance, one has so much better a chance of being civilized.) All the same, it was exceptional: one belonged to a minority again, a minority which considered that it was superior. The local gentry were, of course, all Church: the idea of a Nonconformist landowning gentry is a very odd one — a contradiction in terms. But nearly all the business and moneyed people of the town went to the various chapels, of which indeed there was a plethora; the most businesslike and the

128

most moneyed went to the Wesleyan chapel, that temple of the worship of money and success.

Where the Church assembled the bulk of its congregation from I cannot now make out: there was one Church butcher, at least one Church grocer, a keeper of a high-class stables, with their respective families and employees — one sees the economic tie-up of that: it was good business — there was a sprinkling of policemen and young men, a good many devout old ladies of the pious rentier type, and a few working-class families who for one reason or another were not attending chapel, as they would normally have done. Altogether it added up to a fair congregation, to which the presence of the town gentry, the Coodes, in the absence of the Graves-Sawles — who were very remote — gave a cachet; they set the standard. A curious, reserved, shy, honourable family, they occupied as of right the two front pews (I don't know if they still do: there can be few of them left). Nobody would dream of occupying their seats, if the rest of the church was packed and there were a few places still vacant in those front pews. And those of us who knew what was what, and how things were, would have been shocked if some stranger astray had got into the sacred pound. I think there would have been such a concentration of disapproving looks on him that he would have known there was something wrong. I believe I once saw such a mistake happen; it did not happen again.

Church Sunday School, like chapel in this respect, was a good institution for getting children out of the way on Sundays, while the Sunday dinner was being cooked, etc. (The etc. no doubt happened in the afternoon.) The result was that for us Sundays were an orgy of church and Sunday School going. We began by going to Sunday School at 10 o'clock; we went on to church at 11. In the afternoon we returned to Sunday School at 2.30, sometimes going on to church for Catechism. In the evening we went to church again at 6.15. To this we added, when we grew older, occasional (I think that is the word) Communions at 8 a.m. Each of these involved a mile or so walk into the town and back again. We were kept out of mischief pretty satisfactorily on Sundays, and ended up the day tired with our religious avocations. No wonder Sunday does not stand out as a particularly agreeable day in my memory.

I have a distinct recollection of what I might almost consider my first attendance at church service, at the age of three. Mother and Hilda had gone to church one Sunday evening and afterwards father had taken me for a walk into the town and stood me up against the railings in Church Street to listen to the singing. Long after the singing had stopped and the service lapsed into a silent patch, the small voice continued to sing high and clear outside; mother and Hilda heard it, without knowing who it was. I remember being brushed by father's best pocket silk handkerchief as I was got down: I didn't like that handkerchief; the texture tickled one, like hairs on the face. On another occasion when I was taken to Harvest Festival at Bethesda by my cousin and her young man (who became, rather earlier than was intended, though not too soon, her husband) I disgraced myself by singing out, quite loud, a quite different tune, above the congregation.

I had a clear, pretty voice as a child, which became a really remarkable singing voice as I grew into boyhood; with that, and the musical gift that came from the Rowses, singing was my one obvious talent in all these years, the one that brought me a great deal of local *réclame*, that turned my head — in so far as it was turned — by a lot of early publicity, my chief emotional outlet and mode of expression. Not writing or reading or playing or working, but singing: something exceptional, apart in my life. Of that later; it meant so much to me.

I was taken to Sunday School very young in the wake of Hilda, from whom I was inseparable. I remember being taken into the big girls' class, where I was in my element, petted by Hilda's friends, wearing my blue velvet suit with the lace collar, and taking out my handkerchief to kneel on on the bare boards. I was very particular and girlish, brought up by my sister in her ways, which I wouldn't cross for the world, such was my love for her. I remember only one outburst into tears, one failure of nerve; after that I was acclimatized and went into the infant class with the others. The vicar was a very Olympian and impressive figure, with a bushy black beard and a terrifying way of looking out over his glasses. He was a stern disciplinarian and we were all afraid of him. He kept marvellous order when he was present. And then came a thunder-clap, which assumed the proportions of a catastrophe in those quiet days of the reign of

Edward VII, when such a happening in so small a sphere shook the very foundations of society.

I just remember that figure in Sunday School and at church, gliding out from the priests' vestry behind the organ, the rustle of cassock and surplice, the scent of the so carefully kept linen, the flowers upon the altar, the opulent lilies, the gleam of polished brass and silver. The vicar was a good-looking man with the appearance of the late Lord Salisbury—handsome dark beard, bald candid forehead, a distinguished pallor and fine features. He had a very melancholy, parsonic voice: that was fashionable and much admired, I think, in those days. He was married to a wife much older than himself, 'dressed op like an ole gipsy', said mother, of her first appearance in the village. What wonder that such a man was the target of many female admirers? There were the devout and sour-looking Miss Goods, pince-nez and all, who were always to be seen sharing his carriage with him on the way to service at Pentewan. There was Miss Manger, a curious little creature, who had been cast off by her family and come down here to live on a small allowance and a small job in a small shop. We knew her very well. She frequently came to tea. She had some affection of the throat which made it difficult for her to swallow: that impressed us very much, it was so lady-like. It was, I think, purely psychological and very recognizable—a Freudian symptom. She was not one of the inner circle of devout ladies; she was very devout, but she worshipped from afar.

It was not one of these elderly spinsters who was the poor vicar's undoing. There was the natural attraction of the bushy black beard for a bright head of golden hair; one Sunday evening the vicar preached a more than usually moralizing sermon on the subject of the young men and women spooning in the Truro Road—he was a stern moralist—and behold next day he had decamped, furniture and all—gone off from the station. It was a sensation of the first order. Let the historian, though it be his duty to record everything, draw a veil over the rumours, the stories, the suggestions, the excitements of that time. Only a Renan, or an Anatole France, could do justice to it. But the autobiographer is in duty bound to recall significant impressions upon his mind. The Nonconformists were jubilant at this fall; the good and the respectable were crestfallen. My Nonconformist teacher at the

Infants' School could not restrain herself from asking me, aged six: 'What do you think of your parson now?' — a question which she must have had the pleasure of putting a score of times. I didn't know what to think; I didn't quite understand what he had been up to, but had an idea that it was something unsuitable. Jack Loam, the scamp who lived up the court, took the opportunity to tease me unmercifully for my churchiness. Out in the court, shaving before his mirror fixed up to the doorway, his shirt open to reveal an expanse of hairy chest, he would put his maddening question about what the vicar had done, and follow it up with, 'Have you got hairs like that?' I turned my back on the disgusting spectacle, glanced down the court furiously vexed, and took refuge indoors.

Once, years later, a Sunday School teacher of those days told me a dictum of an ardent church-worker at the time: 'After Brownbeard went,' she said, 'we thoroughly *scoured* the communion-cup.' An interesting example of something like sympathetic magic remaining among these simple people. What one wants is not so much anthropology of savage peoples as anthropological investigation of the so-called civilized. This *Autobiography* is a small contribution to that study, and I hope of use to anthropologists. I remember a most fascinating discussion with Bertrand Russell one evening about the hypocritical reactions people allow themselves on these subjects. (As if, *à propos* of the poor vicar, people had never heard of human nature!) Russell put it down to the insistence of society upon *decorum*, the necessity of decorum, etc. — almost entered upon a defence of it; very funny from him! I do not disagree with him; but I do not regard hypocrisy as any the less deplorable for being a herd-manifestation rather than an individual one. *Ecrasez l'infame!*

After this agreeable episode we had a locum tenens with a hole in the roof of his mouth. Then came Dr. Thomas Simcox Lea, a dear old curiosity, who remained vicar during all the time I continued going to church, until I went to Oxford. We didn't know then — we thought he was wonderfully learned; a few people may have had a shrewd idea how the land lay. He was an amiable old eccentric, of a most lovable disposition, who wouldn't say bo to a goose (he had a great many geese in his parish). I only once saw him angry, and that after the most intolerable provocation. He was a perfect old dear; but his relation to other human beings was too oblique and elusive for us to be fond of him in any personal way, except as an old character. We were rather proud of him. After all was he not a D.D., and an Oxford man? I sometimes wondered in my innocence why he was not made a bishop. He was never even made an honorary canon or rural dean.

His real interest had been originally in natural science, and he possessed a curious and uncanny knowledge of botany and the ways of natural history, butterflies, bats, frogs, wasps, moths, lepidoptera of all kinds. He bore a resemblance to some species of lepidoptera, in the odd way that people get to look like their subjects—horsey men like horses, etc. He had a very fine, innumerably creased and wrinkled parchment skin, very sunbrowned (he had travelled a good deal in his younger days), a mop of grizzled hair curly and going white, large, cricketer's hands; he was very short-sighted, or long-sighted—I can't remember which, at any rate odd-sighted—and he had a remarkable side-long way of walking, like a crab. His sermons were intolerably tedious.

All the more so because his real intellectual interest was in the Coptic-Gnostic Cabbala, on which he wrote a book, published at his own expense. Where he picked up this rubbish from I cannot think, but he smuggled it into his sermons on the least excuse, or none at all; and once, on a festival day, perhaps Trinity Sunday itself, he treated us to a long rigmarole of this stuff from beginning to end; it may have been from proofs of his forthcoming book and perhaps the old innocent had not been able to resist the incipient pride of authorship. He may have been ticked off at the Parochial Church Council for this: the ruling power at church in those days was Sidney Hancock, a gruff and bearded estate agent, who was people's warden and of whom the poor Doctor stood in considerable terror. Old Sidney was a rugose personality who knew everything there was to be known about old St. Austell; but he never would impart his information to anybody and it died with him. I am bound to say that, rough-edged as he was with everybody, he was always very kind to me as a choirboy and schoolboy.

I forgot to explain what this Gnostic rigmarole was that so possessed the good Doctor's heart and mind, and made him so absent-minded, with that rapt and far-away look that came into his eyes. I wonder how he got through the services without a mishap; sometimes there was a pause while we waited for him to collect himself from one of his reveries. He would look vague, lost, then shake himself, make a furtive dive towards the collection-plate which was awaiting him, church-wardens, sidesmen and all (the elevation of the collection-plate with the greatest solemnity was our form of ritualism), sometimes lose his balance in his hurry and surprise on waking up to the facts of life. But this happened more often on the slippery, polished marble steps on his way over to the pulpit, where I have seen him do a perfect skid, arms flung up in his long-sleeved surplice, huge D.D. hood hanging sideways like a coal-sack. Oh, those slippery chancel-steps: how well I remember them as a perfect trap for small choirboys with their best, creaking Sunday boots. I wonder if they are still as dangerous as they were?

I doubt if I can explain the Gnostic Cabbala that so interested him: it all rested upon taking the numerals which the Greek letters of Holy Writ represented, adding them up and recombining them until you got the number 666, the Number of the Beast, which clearly referred to the Kaiser. There were similar enlightenments to be obtained everywhere in Holy Scripture; I think it had something to do, too, with the measurements of the Pyramids. It was certainly related in some way to the Fourth Dimension. A harmless hobby, according to the excellent definition of a hobby: 'no sense at all, and no finality: just what a hobby ought to be'. It was very much on a par with British Israel or Christadelphianism. The dear Doctor was not very ecclesiastical, and not in the least priestly. He was not so much High Church, or Low Church, or Broad Church as — Old-Fashioned Church. That I rather resented in my later Anglo-Catholic phase; now I see that he was a figure who had stepped out of the eighteenth or early nineteenth century — pre-Oxford Movement. His mind was essentially academic. What he loved was not dressing up in chasubles and copes and things, indeed he never even wore a stole — a great grievance with me — but trailing round in his full Oxford robes as a Doctor of Divinity, all black and scarlet. So it was that he looked forward to his annual invigilation of the School Certificate examination at the County School with great pleasure. One saw him side-stepping along the country road between the vicarage and the school with that characteristic crab-wise progression, but in full regalia as if it were the High or the Broad at Oxford.

The reader will gather the deep impression made by Church upon my infant mind when I say that my firm intention from five onwards was to become Archbishop of Canterbury, until I found that grown-ups would ask me what I was going to become in order to laugh at the expected answer. But that did not make me relinquish the intention; it only taught me to keep quiet about it. For a time I deserted that ambition for the more compassable objective of church organist: my heart was seduced by the great variety of noises you could make with a church organ. So that the court was rendered almost uninhabitable by my attempts to reproduce these noises, sitting ensconced in the tree with various convenient branches as pedals and stops to pull in and out, and roaring like Tregeagle.[1] After that I went back to my earlier ambition, and I don't think I wavered until I went to Oxford and saw for myself how impossible was the intellectual foundation which supported that precarious (and in these days unsatisfactory) eminence.

My imagination was stimulated by, and in turn fed upon, the ritual of the Church. There were occasional visits of the Bishop, all purple or scarlet, with white lawn sleeves and pectoral cross, and complete with chaplain to carry his pastoral staff. I remember once seeing Stubbs, the successor of dear Bishop Gott, whom I have portrayed in my poem *Invocation for a Cornish House*: Stubbs had a wonderful appearance with his noble profile and silver-white hair and beard, every inch a bishop, as you might say, looking at the portrait of him turned out with his opulent astrakhan collar. Burrows was less exciting: a heavy scholar and somewhat constipated athlete who had taken too many Firsts at the University to be very human.[2] What I chiefly remember about him was the unexpectedly heavy weight of his hands upon my head at Confirmation — 'Defend, O

[1] cf. the china-clay worker who had bought an American harmonium for his daughter and told father: 'Aw, she can play'n 'ansome. She do maake'n roar like a g'eat Tregaglon.'

[2] There is a rather comic portrait of him at Bernard Walke's induction to St. Hilary, in Walke's *Twenty Years at St. Hilary*. The induction took place on a fast-day, so therefore, the Bishop could be given no meat at lunch. On the other hand, an induction was something of a festal occasion. So Walke compromised by offering the Bishop a collation of oysters and champagne. The Bishop was a teetotaller, and couldn't bear oysters!

Lord, this thy child', etc. — I wriggled a little, it felt so very committal and might, I thought, give one a headache. He was succeeded by Warman, kind but unimpressive and regrettably Low Church: a good preacher to C.E.M.S. gatherings.

Then came Frere, who was my ideal of a bishop in every way: a scholar, an artist, a saint, a prince of the Church but very unaffected and easy to talk to; a monk but also a man of the world, who knew Europe from one end to the other, who knew Russian; a musician, an ascetic who appreciated the good things of life; a man who looked even more the part than Stubbs had done (that was a trifle too opulent for a Christian Socialist). Very important that people should look their part. Frere was unpopular with the people who didn't know him, especially with the Nonconformists, who could not have appreciated such a man. And as for the Protestant *canaille* who made his last years at Truro unhappy — well, it is wonderful what professed Christians can do for each other. But this is rushing on years ahead: Frere was too late for me. By the time he came I was already away at Oxford. And wonderfully persuasive as his personality was — I used to dream about him and think that if anybody could persuade one it was he — not even Frere could have retained me once I had begun to think out my position clearly for myself, and with whatever emotional regrets, 'hoping it might be so'.

By now you may have guessed that I had become a choirboy, like those distinguished contemporaries, Noel Coward,[1] William Walton, Laurence Olivier. It is a naughty occupation, and choirboys are liable to turn out to be 'no good' because of their too early familiarity with the holy of holies. It was a bright idea of mine one choir-practice night, when the organist was late, that we should all make for different quarters of the dark church and when he arrived converge crawling upon him from the various aisles, from the south door, Lady Chapel door, vestry and west door. I gave myself the last post, because it was farthest and so arrived on the scene last, having seen and heard all the fun. On another occasion I was one of the ringleaders, and certainly the most obstinate, in a strike we declared.

[1] On consulting Mr. Noel Coward's autobiography, *Present Indicative*, I find I am mistaken: he was rejected after trial for admission to the Chapel Royal, much to his and his mother's indignation. Perhaps we should say, then, a failed choirboy.

We considered that we were unfairly treated in being watched and reported on by the head-boy, whose voice had broken and who was paid at a higher rate than we were. We middle-boys did all the effective singing and we weren't going to have it. We arranged not to sing the Sunday evening service, which happened to be the appalling Stanford in B flat, that begins with two screeching notes, top F and top G. There are a good many high notes in that service, which was one of our star-turns. But that evening there was nobody to sing them: the top-boys whose voices had broken were helpless, the very junior were inaudible and morally browbeaten. It had a disintegrating effect on the service: the men didn't know what was happening, the curate (now Canon Shaw of Penzance) didn't know what was happening; they thought we had lost our voices and sang all the louder to make up for us. That made the effect all the more obvious. It was deliciously enjoyable — even the reckoning was when it came. We felt we had been in the right. Nothing gives one a better appetite; and though some of our pay was stopped, I felt that I had rather scored in the discussion with the organist at the next choir-practice, and in the end we won the substance of our claim: the useless top-boys went; we took their places.

Mine was on the Cantoris side, beginning with the lowest, at the altar end, and gradually progressing up the seat until I was promoted to the top pew, very grand on my own, immediately under the curate's reading-desk. This was a crucial strategic position to occupy in church, a very conspicuous and favoured one; and, to tell the truth, after my voice broke and I had in the end to evacuate what I had come to consider as my special and privileged place in church in the choir, and after so many years, I had no heart for (and no intention of) taking an ordinary back seat with the rest of the congregation; so I ceased to go. My brother, who was in the choir for a short while with me and then left, sat always on the Decani side. There was as much rivalry between Cantoris and Decani as between two houses at a school. Which was superior to which? The fact that the vicar's pew was on the Decani side might have been taken to end the argument in their favour had it not been that, when a special chair was installed in the sanctuary for the bishop, it was placed on ours. Very childish; very human: lesser matters have caused civil wars in the past.

We had many good times in the choir and at Sunday School. So much of my life in early boyhood was bound up with church that most of the good times were associated with it. It was not until later that school gained upon it. In addition to the weekly ritual of choir-practice on two evenings of the week, Tuesday and Friday, and two or three services on Sunday, there were the excitements of choir-outings and choir-festivals, besides Sunday School outings and plays at Christmas. Life would have been infinitely poorer without all this to fill it up and keep us busy. For we were hardly ever taken anywhere by our people: one summer holiday at Falmouth with my cousins when I was five for long stood out in my memory as a Paradise to which there was to be apparently no second entry. The shop made it impossible for mother to go away anywhere, and in those days father had no holidays: none of the clay-workers had, except Bank Holidays. Then, too, we had no regular pocket-money, or very little pocket-money at all, even occasionally. It was all very well for Uncle to impress upon me: 'Take care of the pence, and the pounds will take care of themselves'; I had very few pence to take care of, let alone pounds.

I am very much struck at the altogether better times in these respects children have to-day than we had. They have much more to spend; they have many more amusements, pictures and wireless and bicycles; they appear to get around and be taken about the country far more than we ever were. Are they any better off for it? I doubt it. In some ways worse off: their attention and enjoyment more dispersed, they can have much less time for reading and dreaming than I had: nothing like such an intense concentration upon the inner life of one's own imagination. Far too great an importance can be attached to the improvement of external 'standards'. of life: the Labour Party, all Labour Parties, have made this mistake. Better that they attached more importance to the real standards that signify; but of them they have no comprehension. Such standards are essentially aristocratic, aesthetic, qualitative not quantitative, private:

> Of the unequal I assert the sense,
> The valued quality, the difference.

In early childhood there was the excitement of those Sunday School outings to Pentewan. Not a far cry: three miles down the valley from St. Austell to the little china-clay harbour with its large beach and 'Winnick' — grass-covered towans, a splendid play-place. But the excitement was increased a hundredfold by the fact that we went down the valley, not by the road, but by the diminutive railway that carried the china clay to the harbour and coal back to the town. The trucks were cleaned out for this annual event, and filled with Sunday School forms: we were a small, shrieking, gesticulating, singing trainload, children, parents — as child-like as the children — Sunday School teachers very prim and lady-like (I must add I was attached to them as to my school-teachers), for were they not under the eye of the dear vicar, complete with curate? (I just remember the presence of that formidable black beard on the earliest of these occasions.)

But what violent pleasure it was: we couldn't have been more excited and tingling with expectancy if we were making a journey into Darkest Africa. And actually when we left the obviousness of the roadway behind us and the track took us beside the river skirting King's Wood, the river might have been the Limpopo and the wood equatorial forest, it was all so exotic and thrilling. The overhanging vegetation plucked your cap off before you knew where you were; the dragon-flies darted gorgeously by on the wing; the honeysuckles reached their fingers into the truck and tickled your neck; there was a rank vegetation of every sort of flower, yellow and purple and red, alongside the track; there were moorhens flitting in and out the flags of the swamps; and as we arrived at our destination, the little ponds that fed the dock-basin were the splendidest of lakes for me. When we were decanted there were the dangers of the beach with the white river to be warned against: so-and-so had been drowned here so many years before. We paddled; hardly anybody bathed in those days: I wouldn't have bathed for anything. We ran about the Winnick, played games and quarrelled. And then we had tea: each of us an enormous, round, golden saffron bun, corrugated with currants and flavoured with lemon-peel. Never were there such saffron buns as those! Dear Sunday School teachers of my childhood, of those innocent years before the War, thirty years ago — before the world, a red and sinister moon, had looked over the horizon at us, when we knew of nothing beyond the boundaries of our parish and life itself had no greater perspective than a Sunday School outing at Pentewan

— here is one of your little boys, who then passed unnoticed among the rest, to celebrate your kindness, your goodness of heart, and see to it that those days are not utterly forgotten!

When at the end of a day's racing about on the beach, on the Winnick, we were gathered once more into the trucks, on our return journey through the woods, darkening and mysterious with evening, there was a quieter mood prevailing. We sang. But I for my part remember nothing but a delicious sensation of stupor and tiredness in all my limbs; and I never remember arriving at the other end at all, nor how we got home: I must have slept on my legs. The mood of happy fatigue sometimes communicated itself to the little engine, which came to a dead stop in the middle of Africa. I felt a feeling of alarm: there we were in the middle of the woods, darkness closing in on us — suppose if we couldn't go on? It was a delicious sense of trepidation, dispelled by the amusement caused by my companion, Alec, who declared of the engine: 'She's ferted'. Everybody knew what this good dialect word meant, though none of the grown-ups would have used it for the world on this polite occasion.

I celebrate these outings to Pentewan at length, for they have long since ceased. When the War came the little track was taken up — to be laid again in who knows what battlefields of France or Flanders or Palestine? — the trucks and engine dispersed. It ended the prosperity of the little harbour, and the ships came there less and less. But, for us, it meant perhaps more: it was the end of an epoch, the end of childhood.

At Christmas-time there were plays in which we performed, for the benefit of our elders. (As I write, I think of the plays performed by Elizabethan schoolboys: Christopher Marlowe at King's School, Canterbury, and, no doubt, William Shakespeare at the Grammar School at Stratford — from which there was such an astonishing flowering.) Our performances were very simple and elementary: nothing like the wonderful achievements of St. Hilary under Bernard Walke. They were not so productive to me of pleasure as of stage-fright: I liked the bustle and the excitement, and I liked having a prominent part; but, all the same, whether it was in acting, or singing solos, or speaking at school, or, later on, lecturing and making political speeches, I was very nervous. Everybody said that they didn't notice it, and took it for granted that I would get through. They never knew what agonies of nervousness I suffered: every time I had to sing a solo part at church in the evening, my Sunday tea was ruined. I always wished that something catastrophic would happen to put it off; that I might fall ill, or (wildly) that they might forget the service or find that it was the wrong day. Anything, anything would do. Meanwhile the inexorable hour of 6.15 would approach; the church-bells were ringing; I must hurry. One passed through the service in a confused blur, until the agonizing moment when one's voice sounded through the crowded church alone. I never once 'broke down'; and no doubt everybody thought it was easy. Mother used to attend church on these evenings with the completest confidence that it would be all right. I was so nervous that I didn't like my own people to come to church when I was singing; it made me more so. Little did they realize that every time I sang it was a fearful struggle; and, when it was over, the sense of relief and triumph was tremendous.

Years later I remember Q. telling me, what consoled me greatly, that all the best speakers were nervous; that if you weren't worked up beforehand, the probability was that you were a bad speaker. The truth of the converse of that was borne in upon me when I reflected on the ease and comparative absence of any sign of nerves with which the more loquacious of local councillors bored us at school-prize-givings. It was obvious that they hadn't a nerve in their whole bodies. Later I learned what a state of nervous expectancy a great speaker like Lloyd George or Winston Churchill gets into before delivering a big speech. No doubt Hitler does, too. The fact is that these men are all artists. When I was secretary and chairman of the University Labour Club at Oxford as an undergraduate I still couldn't make a speech for nerves. What aggravated me was that I knew that, if only I could get over my excessive nervousness, I had the temperament of an orator and should be a first-class speaker. It was consoling therefore to hear Bertrand Russell say one evening before addressing the Labour Club how nervous he felt, that he always wished beforehand that the earth would open and swallow him up, or that he might fall down and break a leg. That gave me not only fellow-feeling, but a little more confidence.

It was not, however, until I became a political candidate and had to address any and every sort of meeting — a hostile crowd on the quay, a dreary gathering of four people under an umbrella in a downpour of rain (of whom three were already converted), a dispersed body of distracted listeners at a four-corners where two or three bus-routes met, a strung-out gathering in the Moors at Falmouth competing with a stentorian loud-speaker in a gramophone shop, etc.— that I became more or less hardened and got my nerves under control.

My attendance at Sunday School ended with a triumph. The classes used to compete for an examination in knowledge of the Prayer Book, under some foundation of the redoubtable Bishop Phillpotts of Exeter — a nauseating character, I subsequently discovered; a nasty political pamphleteer who recommended himself thus for ecclesiastical promotion to the Tory reactionaries of before the Reform Bill, who recommended himself still more by marrying Lord Eldon's niece, a grabber of every scrap of church preferment he could lay hands on to serve his family — he had seven sons in Orders and almost as many sons-in-law; who kept clear of his cathedral city the whole time of the cholera, an oppressor of the poor, who built himself a fine marine villa at Torquay (now the Palace Hotel), from which he administered his diocese and went up to speak in the House of Lords on behalf of every bad cause: in short, a complete Tory. It is amusing to think now how utterly ignorant one was then of this man, of everything but his unpleasant-sounding name. When in the senior class we were prepared for the examination by the senior curate; and after the examination I learned, to my surprise, that I was first in Cornwall. I received a very splendid Prayer Book in leather, printed on India paper at the University Press, the cover resplendent with the seal of Henry Phillpotts Bishop of Exeter, the mitre, keys of St. Peter and all.

That was the end of my church-schooling. But it remains to say that I did find the Prayer Book more congenial than the Bible, another thing which marked one off from the Nonconformists. Whether it was the liturgical character of the language which appealed to me:

> Hear what comfortable words our Saviour Christ saith unto all that truly turn to him.
>
> Come unto me all that travail and are heavy laden, and I will refresh you.

It is very meet, right, and our bounden duty, that we should at all times, and in all places, give thanks unto thee, O Lord, Holy Father, Almighty Everlasting God.

Therefore with Angels and Archangels, and with all the company of heaven, we laud and magnify thy glorious Name; ever more praising thee, and saying,
Holy, holy, holy, Lord God of hosts, heaven and earth are full of thy glory: Glory be to thee, O Lord most High.

And I believe one Catholic and Apostolic Church. I acknowledge one Baptism for the remission of sins. And I look for the Resurrection of the dead, And the life of the world to come.

(How can one ever forget such language, once it has been so implanted in the ear? *O hoher Baum im Ohr.* I believe that its rhythms, the shape and repetitiveness of Cranmer's sentences, exert a hidden pull upon mine to-day.) Whether it was that, or the Prayer Book's connection with the background of Tudor history, which already had an attraction for me, I do not know, but naturally, after all those years singing them, it is the Prayer-Book version of the Psalms that still rings in my ears and comes back to me in scraps:

Like as the hart desireth the water-brooks: so longeth my soul after thee, O God.
My soul is athirst for God, yea, even for the living God: when shall I come to appear before the presence of God?

Have mercy upon me, O God, after thy great goodness: according to the multitude of thy mercies do away mine offences.
Wash me throughly from my wickedness: and cleanse me from my sin.

By the waters of Babylon we sat down and wept: when we remembered thee, O Sion.
As for our harps, we hangèd them up: upon the trees that are therein.
For they that led us away captive required of us then a song, and melody, in our heaviness: Sing us one of the songs of Sion.

The choir had outings too, on a grander scale than our little Sunday School jaunts to Pentewan. They were called choir-trips, and we went at first in wagonettes, and later, to our great excitement, in motor-coaches to such places as Fowey and Looe, Perranporth and Newquay, and, last of my choir-trips, to St. Ives. I find a description of this last in an early volume of my Diary: myself sitting in front with the two churchwardens, noting all the architectural points of the churches we passed — my schoolboy Diary is as full of piscinae and holy-water stoups as any Wykehamist's:

> But not for him those autumn days,
> He shuts them out with heavy baize;
> He gives his Ovaltine a stir,
> And nibbles at a 'petit beurre',
> And satisfying fleshy wants,
> He settles down to Norman fonts.

And then I find myself launching out upon the defence of my head-master and the vicar against the attack of the redoubtable old bear, the people's warden. It ends up with a prim little comment, very disapproving: 'Dr. Lea, the other subject of criticism, we will not discuss.' The vicar was above criticism to this seventeen-year-old supporter of divine right.

The joke to me now is that these elderlies were prepared to accept me on their footing and listen seriously to what I had to say. Stupider people have done less since! I think I must have been very solemn and serious, or early got myself into the position of a licensed libertine, who could say what he liked. But it was a game which had its intellectual excitement, for old Sidney, blinking sententiously behind his gold-rimmed spectacles, was a difficult customer: however, though he led the vicar and curates a dance, he never once said anything harsh to me. I think he liked the tribute of my respect for his antiquarian knowledge of the parish and county; indeed, I credited him with knowing everything there was to be known about both, and always loved to get him to talk about these things. That must have seduced the heart that was evidently present behind that formidable exterior, the burly person always dressed in double-breasted dark suit. Greatly daring, I even asked him once what sort of person the previous vicar had been — that figure from the vanished past who so haunted my imagination. The old man merely replied defensively: 'He was a very good parish priest.' Then silence, absolute, complete. On an earlier choir-trip, when I was a good deal younger, I remember being fascinated by the way he ate cheese at lunch (we called it dinner): he just speared the little pieces of cheese on the tip of his knife and popped them like that into his mouth. We never had cheese at home, or hardly ever. So *that* was the proper way to eat cheese! I was very impressed.

But I was most of all struck by my one glimpse into upper-class ways of living, which came in consequence of my singing. I was taken by the organist to sing a solo, I cannot remember what — 'Hear my prayer', or some such thing — at the Harvest Festival at St. Stephen's. The rector of St. Stephen's was an affluent person, who lived in considerable style — carriages and horses and servants: an extinct type. Very kindly, if less considerately, he asked the organist and me to dinner; for, for me, it was both an extreme pleasure and an ordeal. I had never seen this kind of interior in my life before. Half-asleep with tiredness and the sense of relief that always came after an agitating triumph, I was driven along in the carriage from church to the rectory: I remember the dark drive, the lights in the house; in the dining-room the low light given by the rose-coloured shades of the lamps, the gleam of glass and china and silver, the soft steps of servants on the thick carpet, the melancholy drawl of the rector, the silvery voice of his sister. A scene out of Trollope. Never was there such a delicious meal. I remember the flavour of those new potatoes, the mint-sauce, to this day. But oh, the agony of so many knives and forks, the attraction of those little silver sweet-dishes with their chocolates and not knowing how to help oneself. Were you helped? Did you have to wait till they were handed round? Or did you, ever so politely, put out a fork, like some small wild animal of the jungle, temporarily domesticated, putting out a claw? It was very vexing not to know. I remember no more: tired out, I must have slept all the way home.

Choral Festivals were another pleasant variation in our routine. Our choir was the leading one in our rural deanery, the deanery of Powder, and our organist was the leading figure in these orgies of church-music, when the church would be full with all the little choirs from all over the deanery, each with its organist conducting away, taking the beat from our organist upon a pedestal erected in some central position. Proud as we were of him at all times, we were never more proud than at these Choral Festivals, which were his field-days, when he was the most important person in the proceedings. Every second year of three we went away to some other church. Once we went to Fowey: we were cramped together like pilchards in the small choir of that splendid church, so unworthily furnished. (Why don't they do something about it? As at Bodmin, which has been resurrected from a similar state of dreary indignity in recent years, and the whole interior turned into a thing of beauty. But that sort of thing needs an Anglo-Catholic with good taste, one of Frere's men; whereas the Fowey living is in the hands of the deplorable Simeon Trustees.) Of that occasion there is a dreadful image printed in my memory: the blind organist, seized with a fit of asthma before the service, standing in the churchyard under the limes that lead down to the Ship Inn — the old Elizabethan house of the Rashleighs — the bent, bearded man shaken with spasms over the little tray upon which something was burning, the acrid smell, the fearful coughs, the trail of brown smoke fuming across the churchyard.

Carol-singing at Christmas was the greatest pleasure of all, and the most profitable. We were paid some three or four shillings a quarter in the choir, in accordance with our attendance: a very useful adjunct to our exiguous pocket-money. I was not paid any more for being the solo-boy: honour and glory were the only reward. So we looked forward to Christmas-time as our chief opportunity of making money on a more generous scale. Besides this it was very exciting in itself. The boys went round in two different bands, seniors and juniors; and woe betide the juniors if they were found trespassing on the better preserves of the seniors. Stories were told of the treatment meted out by the big boys; there was a tradition in these matters, and great was our trepidation in going in at the gate and up the dark drive of one or other of the grander houses of St. Austell at the rumour that the big boys were about. In that first Christmas we made about 3s. 6d. each. The second year I was taken along, for the sake of my voice, with the big boys.

The Coodes were our chief victims, our most promising objectives, and their houses, which ringed the town like the castles of robber-barons a medieval Rhineland city, were saved up for Christmas Eve, the culmination of our campaign which had begun perhaps a week before. There was Mrs. John, at Polcarne — you did not need to add the surname: everybody with any self-respect knew whom you meant; did we not see them every Sunday of our lives at church, occupying their family seat? There was Mrs. Arthur at Trevarthian, that imperious old lady, more impressive to us than Queen Victoria, with her lofty way of holding herself, her mincing, tripping way of walking, her airs and graces, her condescension, her generous heart, her love of singing, her head nodding time to the music in church, her *hauteur*, which I now suspect was more than slightly exhibitionist. But she was always away at Christmas: she spent it at Exeter she once told me (she, too, took notice of the growing choirboy and occasionally chatted to me as I went up the hill from church): she always stayed at the Rougemont Hotel and went to all the services at the Cathedral. There was Mrs. Willie at Polkyth and Mr. Melville at Wellington Terrace, and old Miss Caroline at Palace Road. We used to be asked into the lobby or hall and there we'd sing our regular numbers. I remember once an impressive vision of Miss Caroline, who was to be seen any day walking down Station Hill, very old-fashioned and dowdy, waddling like a duck, on Christmas Eve slowly descending the stairs in a very low-necked evening dress with an immense, rustling black train.

Our furthest journey was to Carthew, usually arranged beforehand, on the afternoon of Boxing Day: here we were shown into the low, old-fashioned dining-room, sang our best and received 10s. or £1. Then there was a round of prosperous middle-class houses in and about the Truro Road, at Tremena and so on. It was a special pleasure to go to Mrs. Morley Richards's, for she, a good musician herself, asked for the music and would play the romantic accompaniment to Stubbs's carol, 'The Cornish Bells', on the piano inside while we sang in the hall. That pleased me extremely, for I could never play that accompaniment; it was too difficult.

> O merry ring the Christmas bells
>   across the Western land,
> From Launceston's town to Michael's Mount,
>   from Bude to Sennen Sand

The joyous echo sweeps along
　far spaces by the sea,
And church bells answer church bells with
　their 'Gloria Domine!'
　　O Cornish bells, ring far, ring free,
　　Ring — 'Gloria tibi Domine!'

Our favourite, which we sang most frequently, was:

Fair the night in Bethlem land,
Sweet the song of angel band;
　Fall snow so lightly!
Jesu, born of Mary maid,
In an oxen-stall was laid,
　O star, shine brightly!

Three men rode from out the wild,
Came to greet the Christmas Child,
　Fall snow so lightly!
Gaspar, Melchior, Baltazar,
Magian pilgrims from afar,
　O star, shine brightly!

What a beautiful old superstition it is! As I write out the words, and
the tunes come back into my mind after twenty-five years — a quarter
of a century filled with what changes, what disillusionments and disasters — there come back the memories of the boys that we were, some
of them already dead, all of them dispersed and I alone remaining to
keep faithful witness to those clear starlit nights, sometimes a Christmas
moon bathing all the hills about in such an unreal and lovely light
that one could more than half imagine the shepherds on our hillsides,
the choirs of angels, and Gaspar, Melchior, Baltazar on the road to
Bethlehem, as it might be across the bay. Has all that changed? I only
know that the bells which rang out on Christmas morning early, which
rang out the old year and rang in the new, which rang us to church all
through the year, their brazen tongues clamouring loudly in the narrow
streets of the town, echoing softly over the shoulder of the hill at
Tregonissey, have been long stilled now — for the barbarian is abroad

once more in Europe, as he has been before, wrecking so many innocent homes and lives and all that ancient peace.

We ended up the Christmas tired and pleased, with hoarse throats, but
plenty of oranges, dates, chocolates and sweets. One of us was given
the charge of the money and sharing it out, usually me in later years.
We made sometimes 12s. 6d., sometimes 15s., and once something
short of a pound. I determined to buy mother a present; went into a
ladies' shop, and with some confusion, asked the price of a black-and-
white silk scarf. I had expected it to be 10s. at the most. It was 15s. 6d.
Inwardly horrified, but too shy and proud to retreat, I bought it:
practically all my carol-singing money vanished at one go! However,
the scarf still exists; it was evidently good value.

From those winter nights of choir-practice one scene is imprinted
on my mind which may throw some light on the choirboy and his
fellows — life in the choir. One evening there had been, rare event for
us, a fall of snow: the walls of the church rose up black and ominous
from the strange, pure pall of white. At the end of choir-practice for
us boys, when the men were still left with the organist going over their
parts, I sensed that something was afoot. I was a little late gathering
up and putting away the service-books — the instinct of the born
librarian; by the time I was ready to go home there was a concentration
of all the others waiting, *pour faute de mieux*, to have a good game at
snowballing me on my own. They were all good shots; I was a deplorable one, while with my rotund figure I presented an irresistible
target. I was frightened, but even more furiously indignant: so like
boys to join together against the one who was weaker and defenceless.
That was their idea of a joke.

But I was not wholly defenceless. I had brains: I was not going to
be caught by these fools if I could help it. I hung about waiting in the
vestry till the men's practice should be over and I could slip out with
them. The senior boy was sent in like a weasel to extract the skulking
rabbit. The rabbit was dragged, struggling all the way, to the vestry-
door, where he entrenched himself, foot against the door, refusing to
budge. The bigger boy could hardly both open the door and get me
through it. Meanwhile through the chink I could see the brutes,
maddened by the snow, waiting for their reluctant, but certain, prey.

I struck a Macchiavellian bargain with that weak-minded senior boy: if he would go outside the door, I would come out of my own accord. It is well recognized that promises made under duress are of no moral force. No sooner had he gone outside than I slipped the bolt fast and locked him out.

But how to get away home myself? I could not wait on for ever for the men to come out, and there they were still in the choir droning away at their parts: from the darkness of the vestry I could see their lighted security, as an outcast might look in through the lighted window of his former home, with regret and longing for that scene of domestic comfort. But I could not disturb the men's choir-practice: that would be too shameless; yet I had to get home. Outside, I could hear those treacherous choirboys, tired of waiting for me, beginning to spend their accumulated ammunition on each other. I suddenly thought of the only other door by which I could get out: the door of the clergy-vestry, which was never used by anybody, hardly ever opened. Would they have thought of posting a sentry outside it? Since it was never used, nobody had thought that it might be. Greatly daring, I felt my way into the dark unfamiliarity of the clergy-vestry and gently turned the harsh, grinding, unused key.

Outside, nobody! I could hear the others away on the other side snow-balling each other happily, in friendly fashion, while they waited for their real game. Their quarry was just about to elude them. Shutting the door softly I sped across the snow-covered grass of the church-yard the better to deaden my footsteps, instead of the path, among the black shadows of the chestnut trees, which in May bore their candelabras of red blossom, the thorn-tree which I thought of as Joseph of Arimathea's thorn — out into the freedom of High Cross Street, my heart beating furiously with triumph, exultation, fear released, contempt. Never have I been so possessed with a wild hatred of my fellow-creatures. I could, like Richard II at Conway, have had them flayed alive for their presumption, their treachery, their crowd-impulse, their foolery. Unlike Richard, I was free. I felt I had been betrayed by the other Tregonissey boys who came down to church choir-practice week by week with me. I think I ran almost all the way up the steep hill home, out of breath, panting — to make sure they wouldn't catch up with me. Arrived home, I set about making my own little store of ammunition with which to surprise them when at length, weary with their fruitless waiting for me, having turned for their fun upon each other, they came home through the village.

That night, a policeman making his round of the church found the door of the clergy-vestry, very surprisingly, unlocked. He went up over the hill to rouse the organist, who had to get up from bed and come down to church again in the snow to lock it. But I fear, when I heard of this, I was quite unrepentant: it merely added a little piquancy at having outwitted a lot of fools. Nor did I ever have any more trouble of that sort during all the years that I was in the choir.

Of singing as experience, and what it meant to me, there is little enough that I can say; and I daresay it is the same with other people who have been singers. All I can say is that it was my one talent, a very remarkable gift, to judge from the impression it made on people who heard me and from the memories of it that remain in the district. My subsequent *réclame*, what with politics, books, broadcasting, lectures, scholarships, the University — all dates back really to that. What I know is that, when my voice went, it was utter misery to me. I experienced all the anguish of a *prima donna* whose powers are failing and who is eclipsed by a rival. I never said anything at the time: it was a very lonely time for me and there was no one to confide in. I should have been too proud to anyway. And it was a slow process: my voice didn't break all at once; it rather subsided gradually into a lower register — like the central tower of Chichester Cathedral, a story which has always amused me. The celebrated Dean Hook was at work in his study one day, and happening to look up at the window, his astonished gaze saw the Cathedral tower slowly give way and subside upon its haunches. It was a disintegrating moment. The good Victorian Dean knew what to do, however: he flung himself upon his knees in prayer.

In my case, too, I resorted rather more to prayer: not to arrest my voice — I knew that was hopeless anyway, short of the drastic steps which, I recalled, were resorted to with the papal choir of Renaissance times, but which would have been out of place in Georgian (V) England. Not so: it happened that this coincided, as is often the case, with my Anglo-Catholic phase. So religion became more important. More *i*mportant still — it was a blessing it was so — my work at school was gathering momentum; I was on the way to trying for scholarships at the University. Without that I should have been lost. Even as it was I was let down lightly; for, a year or two after my voice began to break, I continued to sing in the choir, being promoted for a while to sing alto with the men. Though this was less satisfactory, and may ultimately have been rather damaging to the proper development of my man's voice, it was better than nothing.

While as a boy my voice was at the height of its power, there is little to say — singing was so natural to me. I sang like a bird, and didn't think much about it. True, I did what I could with the gift. We were well trained by the organist, who taught us to produce our voices naturally and well. Mine was not especially remarkable in range — though it went up to B flat easily enough — but in quality, a rich mezzo-soprano, and in expression, which was that of a boy of exceptional intelligence and emotional capacity. It was from some cheap book, which impressed me greatly—I think *The Rosary*—that I learnt something important, that in singing you should throw yourself into the part, forget yourself, so far as you can, in what you are singing. This, though obvious enough now, was a great discovery for a boy of twelve.

What did I sing? I can remember little enough, though the name comes back to me of the anthem in which I sang my first solo: 'O for a closer walk with God', a very sentimental piece of work which plucked at the heartstrings and became a favourite with me. We prided ourselves on adhering to a Cathedral standard, and so it was, a rather small Victorian Cathedral in the provinces, which sang Stainer and Stanford, J. B. Dykes and Berthold Tours. We occasionally tackled something better and bigger, Haydn's *Creation* or a chorus from Brahms's *Requiem*: 'All Flesh is as the Grass'. We always sang an oratorio on Good Friday, in which I took all the soprano solos and recitative. My favourite pieces were Mendelssohn's 'I waited for the Lord' from *Elijah*, and the lovely pastoral 'He shall feed his flock' from Handel's *Messiah*. The last I had been taught to sing for a recital after the church service. This was very popular, and there came a request that I should sing it one Sunday evening after service at the Baptist chapel. I sang it, and to my astonishment there broke out a round of applause. I had to sing it again. There followed a request from another chapel, where I sang. Then it was stopped. The organist said that I was a member of the church choir and that I shouldn't sing outside. No demur on my part. But if they had had any sense of responsibility they would have sent me off to a Cathedral choir-school and given me a good education. A younger namesake of mine, with a much less good voice and more intelligent parents, went into the choir of Winchester Cathedral. I rather think I must have been too good a proposition to lose. Between one and the other of them, at home and in the choir, they never even had me taught the piano. What I learnt I picked up for myself; naturally I learnt to read music pretty well. My one regret was that I never sang 'I know that my Redeemer liveth'; it was suggested that I might one Easter, but it was put off and I never did. If I had done, I should have made it something to remember.

At these organ recitals after church on Sunday evenings I would steal alone in my cassock into a pew in the darkened Lady Chapel and give myself up to an exquisite wandering dream, induced by the music. I did not follow it intellectually, and in those days I did not like Bach Fugues; I just sat in the darkling and thought my own thoughts, while the music ebbed and flowed among the pillars of the lighted church, and came and went in my heart and along my nerves. The walls of the little chapel were filled with the memorials of the Sawles of Penrice; here a fine big decorated monument of the time of Queen Anne, the gilt upon the arms gleaming out of the darkness above the aumbry; here a black, draped urn of the Georges; there a marble relief of a lady in Greek draperies mourning over a bier, very Regency; the plainer slabs of the Victorians. The dream was a period-dream, of the quint-essence of the eighteenth century: one could not lay one's finger upon its core, for it was only a succession of images, in which the 'white gate on the road to Trenarren' always appeared, and the young heir return-ing from service at sea from some Portobello or Louisburg or Lagos. I saw him in his three-cornered hat, his tie-wig, the formal pose, the gestures of the time. Or there was a moon through the flickering trees along the path of childhood that led by Gewing's Wood to Penrice. Or it was summer-time and I saw the lovely lateral lights of the wood within, the shadowed light upon the silver boles of vanished beeches, the romance and mystery of the house in the wood. Or there was grief and mourning in the great house – a young man killed before his time, and I remembered that it was war-time, the young heir to all these monuments indeed dead. The music came to an end, and with it my ecstasy.

I do not know why Mr. Symons in his *Quest for Corvo* speaks of 'that nostalgia of the past which, of all temptations of the mind, is the most destructive of contentment'. There is a sense indeed in which it is hopeless, like so much of the ideal life of the mind, or of the activity of the passions, of love as much as of grief, for two can never be one, as love of its very nature demands. But this nostalgia is not more destructive of contentment than any other; and in so far as it encourages unrest of the mind, it is a stimulant to creation, a greater source of joy than anything else in life. Cyril Connolly begins his autobiography with the clever, too clever, sentence: 'I have always disliked myself at any given moment; the sum of these moments is my life.' Smart, but pathetic. When I think of my life as a whole, I do not in the end think of myself, but of the sum of those moments of ecstasy which is my real inner life. They constitute my revealed religion – a revelation of the world as beauty.

There are similar moments all along the way, which I can resort to at will and which have nourished me in anguish of body and mind, in misery and extreme disillusionment about human beings, and when I have lain at death's door. I have in fact a technique of resorting to them: hearing the rooks cawing round Mrs. Arthur's trees, that most nostalgic of sounds, on bright Sunday mornings of summer in childhood, or calling up the rich glow of the setting sun making a coloured pathway up the aisle from the western window in the tower till at last it rested a blood-red gleam upon the altar, on those Wednesday night Inter-cession services which we held all through the War, hearing the list of the dead lads from our parish grow longer, while we prayed in the intensity of silence (I know that I prayed) that it might not reach our loved ones and that the War might end; or coming home from choir-practice and up the hill-side to where, turning the corner by the school, you suddenly felt the pure keen air of the uplands coming down from the moors and ran the remaining way, frightened of the shadows that lurked in the hedges, with a keener appetite for supper round that lighted table in the kitchen, the family circle unbroken then, undispersed, the nest warm, complete, the fledglings unflown, and with no thought for what would come next.

So that side of my childhood passed away.

With adolescence there came an increased interest in, or rather excitement about, religion; for religion of this kind is very much a function of adolescence — or of delayed adolescence, from which a good many grown-ups never emerge. I was confirmed early, and took it all very solemnly. But preparation for Confirmation meant nothing intellectually; the reason remained unawakened — quite naturally, since there was nothing rational to awaken it. One learnt doctrine and catechism, like geometry, by rote. How well one remembers the rigmarole, its unmeaning mnemonic rhythm of so many children in unison, like the multiplication table.

Q. Who gave you this name?
A. My-godmothers-and-godfathers-in-my-Baptism-wherein-I-was-made (pause to take breath) a-member-of-Christ-the-child-of-God-and-an-inheritor-of-the-kingdom-of-heaven.

Nothing was registered upon the mind, merely upon the memory.

Q. What is thy duty towards thy neighbour?
A. . . . To honour and obey the king, and all that are put in authority under him: To submit myself to all my governors, teachers, spiritual pastors and masters: To order myself lowly and reverently to all my betters. . . . Not to covet nor desire other men's goods; but to learn and labour truly to get mine own living, and to do my duty in that state of life, unto which it shall please God to call me.

Really, it is too obvious: the ideology of the Tudor governing class, beautifully calculated in its own interest to keep the people in their place. It is true the idiots appear to have been only too anxious to be kept in their place. But I was not one of them. Being kept in my place was the last thing that I desired. I always assumed for myself a very special place. I never for a moment understood why humility should be regarded as a virtue: I thought it contemptible. Now I understand why it was regarded as so very virtuous: no humility, no authority, no governing class. I think that even then the word 'betters' aroused an incipient reaction; 'to order myself lowly and reverently to all my betters': obedient as I willingly was to my teachers (if I liked them), I did not recognize that anybody was my 'betters'. I regarded myself as *pheusi* — to use a later word — on a level with the best.

So religion meant nothing much to me intellectually. Sermons on such texts as 'God is love' conveyed nothing, for I could attach no meaning to either term in the equation. And in the end this came to annoy me. I remember hearing a sermon on that particular text at the church of the Cowley Fathers in Oxford when I was an undergraduate, which so vexed me that I had to rush out of church in the middle of it, the blood streaming from my nose. But perhaps it was merely the summer heat, or the illness which was beginning to get a hold on me after so much strain in getting to the University. Anyway, I don't suppose now that our pastors, vicar and curates, and the rest of them, understood any better than I did. They held what they held by rote, as we children learned by rote. The difference was that there was one child who *wanted* to understand, and nothing was ever made intelligible to him. There was no appeal to his reason as such; and in consequence it remained quite undeveloped until he went to Oxford, and that was the great thing that Oxford did for him. But really it is all very understandable now, looking back on it from a position reached after a long process of thought and development: there was nothing to understand; it was a world of illusion that they, like most human beings, inhabited. Or, rather, what there was to understand was a matter so sophisticated that it is only now that I understand it: the significance of religion, not as truth, but as a social phenomenon, to be studied and understood anthropologically, a study which enables one to appreciate, such is one's scepticism, the utility and even, in some cases, the desirability of illusion.[1]

Ethically the Church meant a great deal more: the constant, and rather deplorable, effort to 'be good', the insistence upon purity, which only aggravated my anxiety-complex, for I took it very seriously. (Actually the effect of preparation for Confirmation was to increase my sexual interest and excitement.) Perhaps the struggle between a very ardent emotional nature and the repressive effort made by a

[1] Any reader who wants to pursue this position further should read Freud's *The Future of an Illusion*, with which I am in general agreement.

strong will (I thought it was weak — evidence of the strength of the effort) may have had useful consequences later, but it certainly made me very unhappy at the time. (How different all this sounds from the sophistication, the worldliness, the effortlessness of Connolly's Eton: ten years in advance of me in my isolated struggle!) I find a charming naïf entry in my Diary at this time — in French; I could not trust my-self to say it in English, apparently — namely, that there was one sin above all which I must learn to conquer. I imagine that most adolescent boys would have the same confession to make; and really, how absurd the effort! It only added a bitter edge to my extreme Puritanism and denial of life, which it took me years to recover from; though at the time that same passionate temperament was responsible for lapses, for there were not wanting one or two shadowy figures in the dark lanes of war-time ready to take our education, if that is the word, in hand.

After Confirmation I expected going to Communion to open the gates of a great mystery to me; and certainly nobody can have awaited, or prayed for, the revelation with more intensity of expectation. I knelt in the darkness at the back of the early-morning church, breakfast-less, for I would not have gone to Communion unfasting, intent upon the distant altar, the surpliced figures moving, the candles lighted, fearful of the moment of drawing near:

> We do not presume to come to this thy Table. . . . We are not
> worthy so much as to gather up the crumbs under thy Table . . .

unhappy with the sense of unworthiness, of not being good enough, of this standard impossible to attain. There was never any joy in it. And gradually the sense of extreme expectancy began with time to fade away. Perhaps there wasn't any mystery, any revelation? Then one day the curate, who was a hard-voiced man whom I didn't like, ticked me off for not coming more frequently to Communion. I was annoyed; I didn't tell him that the reason was that I didn't feel good enough. But that was really the reason why I desisted. I never went again. And gradually the scales began to drop from my eyes. It was not that I thought then that the ethical effort was mistaken, but just that it was intolerable. I had a fund of solid Cornish common sense through all this; and perhaps the effort was in large part due to the fact that I had never ceased from early childhood to entertain the hope of going into the Church. But the effort was both intolerable and mistaken.

What wonder, then, that the Church's most lasting influence was in the sphere where I was happiest, in the aesthetic and the emotional, on the side of ritual, the sense of tradition and history? Intellectually null, ethically unattractive and, I am now inclined to think, even deplorable, its influence here was all to the good. I owe it an immense debt in this field, which I would now not have been without for worlds. The Church of England is the church that I don't go to, so to say; but there it remains in the background, inseparable from my childhood and growth into manhood; its ritual phrases come readily to my lips. I think if I never went again I should still after years know where to stand up and where to kneel down, and where to bow and what to say in the responses. And no doubt when I am old and dying, the comforting phrases will come back upon my lips all the more surely for my having forgotten so much of what has gone between, with the force of their having been among the earliest upon my lips in childhood. There is no doubt that the right thing, in England, is to have been an Anglican.

With these sympathies of mind, it is obvious that in adolescence I should have been attracted by Anglo-Catholicism. I never had any liking for Protestantism or Low or Broad Churchmanship; nor have I now: I loathe Protestantism. As for Modernism, how can one have any devotion to what is a mere smell, and that a not very attractive one? or respect for the processes of peeling the onion — while holding on to all the emoluments and privileges? Bertrand Russell has a distinction between Low Church unbelievers and High Church unbelievers. He himself is a Low Church unbeliever; I am a High Church unbeliever. My latent High Church sympathies — as a boy they were all in favour of King Charles the Martyr and the Royalists: I detested Parliament and still do not like Parliamentarians; my sympathies were Tory as against the Whigs, Roman as against the Nonconformists — these latent sympathies were elicited and brought out in adolescence by one or two older men who took me up and to whose friendship I owed a great deal. They lent me books and periodicals which I had never heard of. I felt terribly ignorant, and I was very lonely. There was nobody among the people whom I knew who cared for the things I cared for, or was in the least interested.

Both of these men were Anglo-Catholics; and far as I have moved out of their intellectual range since then, I am grateful to them for the kindness they showed me when I was a boy. One was a Londoner, with all the prestige of a Londoner, an Income-Tax Inspector, a member of the choir. The other was a St. Austell man, who had intended to go into the Church, had been at Cambridge and through the War. The latter lent me Chesterton, whom I had not so much as heard of: I have not forgotten the impression his earlier brilliancy made upon me; I had never come across anything so clever. Then there were early volumes of the *London Mercury*, through which I first made contact with contemporary literature. I read them late at night on winter evenings in the kitchen after my homework was done, and everybody gone to bed: I read into the morning, the cockroaches coming out all round me, and stumbled dizzy with reading to bed, sometimes so tired I forgot to put the lamp out and woke up with horror in the night to find it still burning.

The interests of my other friend were more religious and musical. He lent me little manuals of devotion which I used at Communion, telling you where to cross yourself and when to genuflect. He would have been glad if I had gone to Confession. I had too much common sense for that. He used to lend me, so that I read regularly, it is odd to think, the parish magazine of All Saints', Margaret Street, a church which I never even saw until the other day. But I knew all about the goings-on of Prebendary Mackay and Roscoe Shedden, Bishop of Nassau, and Frank (not — Ugh! — Buchman. *Conspuez-le!*) but Frank, Bishop of Zanzibar. I knew all the little High Church jokes and rhymes like:

> There once was a Zanzibarbarian,
> Who dreamed that the whole world was Aryan:
> He would find, I suspect,
> Even Peter's own sect
> Insufficiently authoritarian!

It amuses me to think that in my remote Cornish parish I was a regular follower of the doings at this London church, where all unknown to me a somewhat younger boy, Douglas Jay — a great friend of mine now — was a devout member of the congregation in those days when the exquisite-looking choirboy, Laurence Olivier, was giving proof of his talent by an astonishing performance as Katherine in *The Taming of the Shrew*. Then, too, I read the *Church Times* regularly: it was edited by a clergyman who had a pretty turn for the spiteful and wrote deliciously malicious notes about Protestants who were *bêtes noirs* of his and mine, like Dean Inge. I found that very amusing. On the other hand the paper was politically reactionary, which I was already beginning to disapprove of. The other day I looked at it again, after twenty years. It had become distinctly progressive and sympathetic to the Left in the interval; but, alas, all the old spite and sauce had gone. The letters, however, I recognized: they were the same after twenty years, the same phrases, the same clichés, the same addresses — so it seemed to me.

All this was part of the excitement of the immediate post-war years, when Jack Bucknall — by some mistake of the authorities, or sheer inadvertency on the part of the vicar getting vaguer than ever, and who, more than ever like a fish out of water, cannot have known what he was letting himself in for — came to us as curate. He was a great sensation with his more than six feet of good looks, his pipe and shabby cassock which he wore everywhere, those dark lambent eyes, those *risqué* sermons which gave us such a kick. The church was crowded whenever he preached. And, strangely enough, he was, what nobody else was, an attraction to the young men as well as the women. He could have done anything, or almost anything, with me. But he did not choose to exert his power. I think now that he must have been much of an exhibitionist, who enjoyed his effect on the mass. It was certainly prodigious, electric. He was a Christian Bolshevik, an Anglo-Catholic Socialist, a Mirfield monk who had married and gone out into the world, a fine footballer, a protégé of Conrad Noel (whom I afterwards met at Lady Warwick's), a member of the Thaxted circle. What more promising, more exciting? Excited as I was by him, my native Cornish caution held me back from endorsing his eccentricities. I would have gone so far, but no further. He was not interested in me anyway, if he was interested in anybody; I was not his type, and he must have sensed the instinctive reserve in my attitude.

But I admired him, and I was furiously indignant at the treatment meted out to him by the old guard of the congregation, the little clique led by Sidney Hancock, who treated him abominably. They loathed his Christian Communism, they feared and resented his influence with the

young. If he had been able to stay he would have riven the congregation in two, or attracted a new and much bigger one on his lines,
leaving the old guard isolated. But they moved from sullen, passive
resistance to active measures. During the last months of his time, the
people's warden after a long persecution never spoke to him, and then
they cut off supplies. I well remember his last sermon on the text from
the Book of Revelation: 'And I saw a new heaven and a new earth: for
the first heaven and the first earth were passed away. . . . And God
shall wipe away all tears from their eyes; and there shall be no more
death, neither sorrow nor crying, neither shall there be any more pain:
for the former things are passed away.' (Or was it from Isaiah? — 'For
behold, I create new heavens and a new earth: and the former shall not
be remembered, nor come into mind. But be ye glad and rejoice for ever
in that which I create: for behold, I create Jerusalem a rejoicing, and
her people a joy. And I will rejoice in Jerusalem, and joy in my
people: and the voice of weeping shall be heard no more in her, the
voice of crying.')

I must have left the choir, for I heard that sermon from among the
congregation. I heard it with sickness at heart and a kind of dismay,
the tears held back in my eyes. I was conscious enough of the issue by
this time, though not of the full significance of the struggle of which
it was a symbol in our own remote parish. *It was a victory of the old
men against the young*: not the last nor the most important of those which
I shall have to relate if I continue this Autobiography. My reaction,
instinctive rather than deliberate at that age, was perfectly right. I
ceased to be interested in going to church. The unconscious implica-
tion was: very well, have it your own way, but you do not carry me
with you. That may not mean very much at the present moment; but
we shall see who will win in the end. In that particular instance it meant
that there was not much of a younger generation to take the place
of the old in the way they were determined to have things; and so the
institution has slid downhill out of inanition and for want precisely of
the vitality of those younger men whom they thought they could ignore
or even safely antagonize. Probably they would have lost them in any
case; but in my particular instance this was the occasion of my going.
All my energies were now directed towards getting to Oxford, and
there were other things to interest me.

And that was the way to treat the old men in their determination to hold on to power. Since they possessed all the means of power, if they were determined to hold on, let them do so and find that they were grasping a skeleton. Subsequently, in the infinitely more important field of politics, that same determination of the old to hold on to power at all costs I found to be the dominating factor in the twenty years between the last war and this: the reason for the decline in vitality, enthusiasm, belief, achievement in this disgraceful period — the worst in our history since that which lost us America.

One lasting influence this short but significant episode left. It gave me a glimpse, no more, into a new — in reality a very old — world of far higher musical values. From the moment when I first heard Gregorian plain-chant, the ancient music of the Church, it spoke immediately to my heart without any preparation or hesitation. I knew that that was the music for me. I felt at once all the insipidity and commonness of the Stainer and Dykes and Tours we had been brought up on in the choir. The organist, whose vistas were not very wide, held to the old Victorians; he disliked plain-song and used to make a mock of it. That annoyed me: I thought it cheap, besides being bad taste to prefer the sugary sentimentalities of the Victorians. I did not have much opportunity to explore this new world that was suggested for a moment — I only once, I think, heard the Merbecke music that was written for the Prayer Book back in the days of Elizabeth; I longed to hear Byrd and Tallis and the rest of them. The hope closed down when Jack Bucknall went, and back we were at the eternal Stainer & Company. (They still are.) I ceased to be interested.

There can be few people who are touched so deeply and immediately by the music of the sixteenth century as I am. (Vaughan Williams is one; and that is why I like his music so much.) But the intensity of the emotion is such that I still cannot explain its hold fully, certainly not in cool, rational terms of analysis. I have only to hear the opening harmonies of a plain-song service, of a motet by Byrd or a Palestrina mass, to find myself gripped by an overpowering emotion that reduces me, as nothing else can, to tears. There are friends of mine upon whom the idiom — or is it the undertone? — of the Viennese school, that characteristic poise upon the verge of laughter and tears, the gaiety with the tragic undertone, which you get at its apogee in later Mozart, has a similar effect. But it could not be more acute, more penetrating into the secret crevices of the heart, than Tudor music is with me. It has such an extraordinary pathos for me, as if I listened to their very heart-beats, the heart-beats of these men dead for over three hundred years, in the madrigals of Dowland or Weelkes, an air of Tallis. It is much the same quality as that which moves me in

> When that I was and a little tiny boy,
> With hey, ho! the wind and the rain,

or in

> O mistress mine, where are you roaming?

But it is at a more intense pitch, an even deeper level, in their church-music; for I am sure that its power with me is bound up with the vanished world of religious belief, and the emotion is, once more, nostalgia. These harmonies open a window upon that inner world which might have been, but can never be now. I do not want to analyze it too far, though it may be that my introduction to it came at the very moment of the parting of the ways. But the pathos which it holds is a pathos of its own, as I am very sure it is for Vaughan Williams, whose mind naturally inhabits that world, as mine might have done. Now it is a world for ever lost, of which I get a glimpse, which still shakes me, though it does not shatter, through the casements of the music of the Church.

It was a fortunate thing that these influences, aesthetic and historical, the appeal of ritual and music to the emotional nature of a growing boy, were not stronger than they were and not reinforced by any intellectual position. They might have bound me. It is quite clear from Newman's novel, *Loss and Gain* — in many ways more revealing than the *Apologia* where he was consciously making a case for himself, — and also from what we know of his early life (devotion to Charles I, etc.), that it was the ritual and the emotion that came first and settled his attitude for him, and the intellectual position that came afterwards. It was really *ex post facto*, a mere rationalization of what he wanted to think anyway; in that like so much of human thinking, and what makes one now — in adult years — set so much less store by what anybody thinks, or rather thinks he thinks. (The whole position of Pareto, which I share: namely, that adult scepticism of all pretences, intellectual posturings, so many façades for what they want, whether in politics, religion, thought or ordinary human intercourse, which now underlies the whole of my thought on every subject. It is indeed cardinal to a really adult view of life.)

What was true of Newman (Newman, significantly enough, made a defence of it in his last great book, *The Grammar of Assent*) was also true of Gore, who arrived at his emotional sympathies in these matters first — and intellectualized them afterwards. *They* determined his position through life. The same (I am sure) was true of Frere, whom as Bishop I came to know quite well and feel a deep affection for. He was an artist and a churchman first and foremost: that formed his intellectual position, which for the rest was not a strong one. I do not suppose he liked facing it: he was not an intellectual. I remember once getting involved in a discussion about Newman with Evelyn Underhill at the Bishop's supper-table at Lis Escop, a subject which Frere quite evidently shied away from.

I have taken the opposite line to these men. The same sympathies — for my emotional sympathies were at one with theirs — would have taken me with them, if I had been prepared to allow my emotions to determine my intellectual position. Time and circumstances were no doubt very important factors, too: this was not the nineteenth century; I belonged to the post-war generation. And the great thing Oxford did for me was to enable me to develop an intellectual position for myself, one which, though it was historically founded, was in keeping with the circumstances and conditions and exigencies of our time, not of the nineteenth century. So that this intellectual position developed in disjunction from my emotional sympathies and the strong bias of my early life. It was a source of unhappiness and a certain amount of psychological malaise. But I knew which had to be sacrificed.

The sacrifice was made; yet the nostalgia remains, as it remained all his days with Thomas Hardy. Nothing can touch me like the phrases and liturgical scraps that bring back that vanished world of my childhood, a world of security and faith, now dissolved like a 'dream remembered on waking'. It is all very natural: for so many years the alternation of the seasons was marked for me by the seasons of the Church: the changes in the altar-frontals meant more to me than the changes from flower to berry, from honeysuckle to hips and haws. There was the purple of Advent and Lent, the white of the great festivals of the Church — Easter Day and Christmas and Trinity Sunday — the red of Whitsuntide, green for the ordinary occasions of the year. There were the events of the Church Calendar, the sequence of Epiphany, Septuagesima, Sexagesima, Quinquagesima and Lent. There was the distribution of palms on Palm Sunday, the desolation and gloom of Holy Week, Good Friday with the altar stripped of its ornaments, ourselves in black cassocks singing the Passion. There were the processions, the sweet-smelling flowers in the flower-decorated church on Easter Day, Whit Sunday, Trinity Sunday, the fruit and vegetables of harvest festival. Then there was the long hiatus, an ecclesiastical desert, of those interminable Sundays after Trinity, up to the Twenty-Seventh, in which nothing seemed to happen, and August came down on us and the congregation thinned out and people went away for their holidays and even the organist went for a fortnight on his. With autumn and the colours coming out in the hedges, they came back again and things at church began to liven up. And on Sunday evenings I would go down the road with my cousin, Kate·Courtenay, her husband away at the War, or the friendly, good-natured girl at the farm, for I was growing older and more staid and serious, no longer a boy; together we went down the familiar lane of which we knew every turn, every tree, every bush, to the sound of the church-bells ringing us to church. Though they are silent now, I hear them still.

CHAPTER VII

SECONDARY SCHOOL

The last chapter has carried me far beyond the point when, at the age of eleven, the new world of the secondary school opened before me. In spite of Auntie's death I was given my half-crown for winning the scholarship, and set off downhill every morning in the new-found glory of a school-cap with a great many yellow-ribbon rings around it and a badge in front, and with a satchel to carry my homework books in. Homework added a new responsibility to life, which I took very seriously: gone were the old carefree evenings in which I could play at rounders with the boys, or skippety-bed with the girls in the village, to my heart's content with no thought of the morrow. The morrow brought with it the necessity of showing up your homework of the night before — a very good way of keeping children off the roads in the evenings. Impressed with the duty of doing my homework then, I am all in favour of it now.

My first impressions of the new school were of new smells: the almost aggressive cleanliness of the buildings that rose up and smote the nostrils with the ubiquitous odour of carbolic soap. Then there was the smell of new paper, stationery, pencils, rubbers, exercise-books, on a much more generous scale than at the elementary school: a smell which I have always been partial to, like Trotsky, who tells us in his autobiography how he always liked the smell and feel of paper and ink and print. (He certainly must have consumed a great deal of each all told!) Then there was that more exotic scent from the brewery next door, of malt or hops or of I do not know what aromatic spices they used in brewing, which the west wind blew across our playing-fields, enveloping the school in its warm, soft, sweet, drowsy, liquorous smell, that insinuated itself into the passages and corridors and class-rooms, came in puffs in at the windows, lurked heavily about the lower quarters of the school — and, in short, so wound itself into my mind that often when I think of those schooldays the memory of that nostalgic smell is entwined with them. And conversely, so great is the associative power of smell, that whenever I have been in late years near the village when the brewery has been brewing and the wind was in the west, that has brought back like nothing else the very atmosphere and feeling of those mornings at school, the emotional vacuity, the hiatus between lessons, 'break' during which we went out into the playing-ground on our way to the lavatories, the obscure sense of nostalgia which even then that scent brought with it: as if one realized in the moment, through its power, there would come a time when one would regret its passing, for it bore with it the innocence, the emptiness, the waiting, the sense of expectation of one's boyhood.

Unlike the elementary school, the school premises were too large for our numbers. This new secondary school, one of the girdle of schools built about the county as a result of the Education Act of 1902, had so far had rather a chequered, and even contentious, existence. It was by no means a success, nor had the people of the district as yet taken to the idea of secondary education. We were that term 120 in number, in buildings which were built to hold 200. So one had a great sense of space: empty classrooms unused, wide corridors, a staircase which we thought magnificent, an upper story with windows giving on to the football field and looking out across to the bay. (How different the circumstances to-day: the school so much bigger, divided into two, the boys and girls separated, and a large school evacuated there from Plymouth's agony.) It was very grand: one was impressed and happy from the first moment.

There were so many differences that struck the eye at once. You had a desk of your own, with books of your own provided by the County Education Committee for the benefit of minor scholars. You had separate books for different subjects and a sweet little book in which to enter up your homework. You had a hymn-book of your own, a special little school hymn-book, from which you sang at prayers in the morning. The masters and mistresses, no longer plain 'teachers', wore gowns: I think that was what impressed me most. And they changed with each lesson; you didn't have the same person teaching you (or not) all the day; masters and mistresses came and went with their subjects. It was thrilling.

In addition the 'form', another difference, had a form-master or mistress under whose special care you were. Our form-mistress was

Miss Blank, odd name, who came from Camelford, golden-haired and blue-eyed, a strict Wesleyan. But that did not prevent me from developing a *schwärmerei* for her, which lasted all my schooldays and, of course, made me work better for her than for anybody else. I had a very special feeling for her: she was my patron saint. It hurt exceedingly to be ticked off by her; and correspondingly one would rather earn her approval than anybody else's. And naturally, too, one liked her subject best, which was English. I think the clever, ambitious, comically fat boy was a favourite with her, until he grew into the awkward, callow, voice-breaking stage; and very soon after that she left, and he transferred his affections, with the subject, to her successor, an immensely tall, melancholy Irishman, who was very kind and sympathetic, and had the comic name of Fogarty. She left to marry a missionary in India: I remember the schoolboy resentment at that; it seemed like a betrayal—and a missionary, above all! With it there came a curious presentiment, the first of several such experiences which came later and which I put down to my Cornishry, the intuitive feeling that nothing good would come of this marriage. I remember feeling that very intensely when she left. She went to India; within a year she was dead. All that I have of her is my name written in her plain forward-sloping hand in a book that she gave me, my Shakespeare; and the manuscript of a sonnet she wrote, pasted in a volume of my schoolboy Diary, when I heard of her death.

It was she who gave us our first French lesson that first day in our new life. There we were gathered together, a class of which the core was formed by the dozen minor scholars who entered together that year. They were a humble lot compared with the Cecil Beatons and George Orwells, the Roger Mynors and Eddie Marjoribanks, who appear in Connolly's autobiography. But this was the new and much wider circle of acquaintance, boys and girls from the town and all the district around—Mevagissey, St. Ewe, Sticker, Roche, Bugle, etc., with whom I was to keep company for seven years, going up the school year by year with them, until at the end our ways diverged and I was left alone to make my way to Oxford. We were a friendly lot, though I found my friends, to begin with, more among the girls, who were my competitors for the first place in the form, than among the boys.

All this was to the good, so much so that as the result of my pleasant experience of schooldays I have always been strongly in favour of co-education. It worked very well; there were never any 'problems'. (There were boy-and-girl friendships, a few quite close attachments — and a very good thing, too!) The effect on school-work was wholly admirable, certainly so far as I was concerned. The girls indubitably worked harder than the boys, especially at their homework; they were more conscientious, as one finds again at the University. The result was that any boy who wanted to keep the top place in the form, or anywhere near it, had to do some work in order to keep ahead of the girls, who did work. If there had been no girls, I should have been head of the form easily without doing much work at home in the evenings; as it was I had to. So the form-lists always came out, with myself at the head, then four or five of the best girls, then the next boy, whoever that was. Later on, from the time when we were about sixteen, the interests of the boys and girls began to show a more marked divergence. The boys were always better at science, at mathematics, physics and chemistry; and the girls, in general, better at languages, English, French, Latin, and at history. (We can neglect Scripture — Religious Knowledge — as not serious: wholly a waste of time here as at the elementary school.)

That first French lesson was perhaps the chief difference that struck me in changing over from the elementary to the secondary school — a small symbol of the new world of intellectual interest that change was to lead to. It was an excitement and a pleasure from the first moment: I shall never forget that lesson, the first French words I learnt, the strangeness of the pronunciation. The first word — appropriately enough for a fanatical lover of cats from childhood — was 'le chat': pronounced like 'Shah' (as the Parisians impressed upon a visiting Shah of Persia in the eighties, by setting up a fearful miaowing and caterwauling in the streets: he thought it a form of greeting). It was very surprising and ridiculous that you didn't pronounce the 't' at the end of the word: that took some getting used to; I had to suppress a fit of the giggles at its oddity. And the same with 'rat' — which was pronounced 'rah'. It was a little unbelievable: could it be that we were being had on? But no, impossible; whatever teachers said must *ipso facto* be right. So I accepted it on trust, and at the end of the lesson we had achieved our first French sentence:

169

Le chat mange le rat.

It was a new world opening before me indeed. I was thrilled, as never by any lesson before or since. It was as if I stood upon that peak in Darien and caught a glimpse of the Pacific. Coming home to dinner I trod on air: *Le chat mange le rat*, I said over and over to myself. My excitement was a right intuition, for though I had no conception of what it would lead to, that simple ridiculous sentence out of a French grammar was the narrow door which led to a whole world of thought and experience, only second to that occupied by my own language: to Daudet, Anatole France, Verlaine, Rimbaud, Gide, Valéry, Mauriac — something in that order — to Stendhal and Balzac, in the end to Proust and Flaubert.

I have already spoken of my French sympathies as opposed to the German affiliations of my slightly junior contemporaries at Oxford, Auden and Spender. I, too, did my German *Reise* — though illness cut it short, perhaps fortunately; I might have been sucked into that vortex like them. But I think not — something held me back: an instinctive reserve towards them, compared with the way I naturally fell for Paris the moment I set eyes on it — and the constant feeling that this was so inferior. In Germany that winter of 1926-7, in Munich, I spent my time reading French books. I could not make myself learn German: I had an instinctive contempt, it is not too much to say, for it and them. A contempt for the former, I know now, was wrong, and I regret my insecure hold on the language; my dislike of them, however, was only too justified.

The first French book, I think, that I read at school was Daudet's *Lettres de Mon Moulin*, and for that I fell at once, completely and for ever. From the very first sentence: 'Ce sont les lapins qui ont été étonnés', and the description of the old mill with the owl for tenant upstairs. I can't define what it was that so attracted me in Daudet: it was like falling in love; I think there was some bond of sympathy, of which I was unconscious, between the temperament of the schoolboy and his. I was drawn to that gaiety and vivacity, the sentiment, the sparkle of the Mediterranean landscape; I was in sympathy with his form of humour, the exaggeration of it, the wink behind the tall yarn, the vein of fantasy. He was my writer, perhaps even more than Q. — my two earliest and most constant admirations. From that time, for years and years, I always meant to write a Cornish *Lettres de Mon Moulin*; oddly enough I have never yet achieved it, though I have often thought about it, made plans of what it should contain, half written it. It wasn't a bore for me to prepare bits for the next day's lesson; I read on and on far beyond the allotted task, and stories outside those which we were officially reading.

So I came to know the book as I know few others, to see it in the mind's eye—the blue distances of the Alpilles, hear the sheep-bells ringing the flocks down from their summer pasture in the mountains when autumn came, smell the scent of thyme, the thick white dust upon the straight roads of Provence. I was fascinated by the Sous-Préfet aux Champs, having to prepare his speech, 'Messieurs et chers admin-istrés', but finding the beauty of the fields too much for him, seduced by the violets and the birds: who falls to making verses instead, his speech completely forgotten. How often have I thought of him since, when I have had some boring political speech to prepare for some audience or other, and have been led away to poetry or history instead.

Then there was the charming 'Mule du Pape', with its portrait of the good Pope Boniface followed by his cardinals going out on his mule over the Pont St. Bénézèt to bask at his villa in the evening sunshine. Innumerable other touches I have stored up since my schooldays: the very sense of that hot dusty walk across country to the convent of the Orphélines in 'Les Vieux', the contrast of the coolness of the long corridor inside; the genial Révérend Père Gaucher, who made the wonderful elixir, jeopardizing his soul for the sake of the prosperity of his house; the pathetic story of the two inns: 'C'était en revenant de Nîmes, une après midi de juillet. Il faisait une chaleur accablante': the words sent me off into a dream of a place I had never seen, a time that could never be again. There was the starlight, very clear upon the mountains, in 'Les Etoiles', the visit to Frédéric Mistral at his house at Maillane: I thought of that in terms of my own walking to Fowey to see Q.— though Mistral and Daudet were contemporaries and there were precisely forty years between Q. and me. There was the mistral blowing up the valley of the Rhone, *à grands pas de loups*, or the mistral *en colère* beating all night against the mill, shaking its sails and agitating the pines on the hill-side. Time to go back to Paris: to Paris, with its mud and orange peel in the streets, its November fog, the lights coming out along the *quais* that follow the Seine.

I saw it all, years before I went there: so that going to France was like going home, or to some beloved spot where I had been in a dream. Actually it was not until four years ago that I went to Provence; it was absurdly like what I had learned to expect: the Palace of the Popes at Avignon just like the illustration in my old crumpled copy of the *Lettres*, even grander and more spectacular, the little garden upon the summit of the Rocher at the end looking down upon the Rhone, the medieval atmosphere of the city with its innumerable Gothic churches; the countryside beyond, the long white dusty roads which one could imagine Daudet traversing to visit his friend Mistral, the blue hills in the distance, the great *mas* with their substantial farm buildings around them, the view of the Mill itself at Fontvieille up on the slopes, from the road coming from Montmajour.

But a long pursuit of Daudet had lain between that first reading by the ardent schoolboy and the long-postponed visit to Provence, twenty years later, of the sick man, stricken by years of illness, febrile, dyspeptic, disillusioned by human folly. It was then too late, or too soon, to enjoy anything; but it was, at any rate, some consolation to be there, to have got there at last. In the interval I had read a great deal of Daudet: the *Contes du Lundi*, *Numa Roumestan*, the remarkable social novel which first won him success and the prize of the Academy — *Fromont Jeune et Risler Aîné*, *Sapho*, the most perfect of his works. Now, resting in bed in my hotel that looked out upon the narrow Rue Saint Agricole, the windows shuttered against the mistral, or lying in the sun in the Jardin du Rocher, the gorge of the Rhone on one side, on the other the great mass of the Palace, with the little cathedral of Notre Dame, from the pulpit of which Pope John XXIII uttered his heresies on the subject of the Beatific Vision — here, then, I read at last Daudet's own autobiography, *Le Petit Chose*, that simple, affecting record of his own youthful humiliations, the poverty of his family, his struggle to make his way in the world.

What wonder that with this feeling for Daudet's book I should have won my first small literary prize with an essay on it. A periodical called *English*, set on foot in those promising years after the War, offered a prize for an essay on a favourite book. *Les Lettres de Mon Moulin* was mine. I sent in my essay, and it got the prize — £2, which, to my intense resentment, I was made at home to spend upon boots. It was the first of a series of prizes which I won. There was a Navy League essay which I went in for and was placed second in the country; I think the subject was that 'Naval power was less aggressive than military power' — a view which I upheld and which I now find myself, for altogether more sufficient and subtle reasons, still in agreement with. Then there was another prize — some Empire League essay, for which I won a prize of books; and a story competition in the *Queen*, for which I wrote my story about Cuthbert Mayne, and got a small prize — £2. It pleases me to think that after so long a devotion to Daudet, beginning with a schoolboy essay, I wrote *The Times* leader on his centenary in 1940; and if only one is accorded the time and the circumstances — and life in this island not made unlivable by the barbarian — I yet have hope of writing a Cornish parallel to the *Lettres de Mon Moulin*, which, however much less good, may not be utterly unworthy of it.

My sympathies for or against my teachers and their subjects were very decided all through my schooldays. Miss Blank, and her subject, were my favourites. There was equally no doubt about my dislikes. I found nothing whatever in mathematics to interest me: physics and chemistry I loathed with a cordial detestation as equally a waste of time (it was) and positively offensive; handicraft (carpentry) I thought beneath the attention of an intelligent boy — I really regarded it as something between an insult and an injury. Not for me the delights of fretwork and wielding the plane, which so pleased the vapid minds of those who could take in nothing else. After a term of this dreary time-killing, I put a stop to it by an active form of malingering: I ran a gimlet into my finger, partly accidentally and partly experimentally. It had the desired effect; I did no more carpentering. Rather the school choir than that. Physics and chemistry were a more long-drawn-out agony and went on, I suppose, for some years until I got near the top of the school and could specialize on my own in what I wanted to learn. What I learned from those dank periods over years in the chemistry laboratory, except to hate the place, it is now impossible to say. Merely a distaste for the smell and the bottles and test-tubes and gas-burners and the waste of time, I think. For when it happens to me nowadays to be shown over the science laboratories of their schools by proud headmasters and I have to affect an interest out of politeness, I am still only conscious of a vague distaste coming from my schooldays brought back by the atmosphere. What was the point of making those odious smells, those horrible acrid fumes, those fatuous formulae?

In short, I shared from the first the aversion which nearly all the most intelligent men I have met since have had for science, and most of them for mathematics. It amused me the other day when my great school-friend — though I made his friendship after we had both left school — himself a scientist of distinction who has made his way entirely through science, commented to me very markedly on the second-rateness of mind of scientists in general. Well, it was not for me to say, I thought — but I had assumed as much from my schooldays. It is true that I was very badly and unsympathetically taught in both mathematics and science. Not bad at arithmetic and algebra, I had no aptitude for or interest in geometry. I had no logical faculty: or rather, it was never aroused at school; all that came later with maturity and the endless discussions of undergraduate life at Oxford. It comes under the heading of 'What I Owe to Oxford'. Once, when asked why two isosceles triangles with two equal angles should be equal in all and I had replied that they looked like it, I was laughed at and chaffed: 'If I had said that you looked like a bishop', etc. — everybody knew the joke about my intending to be a bishop. Chaff was no good with me — I merely ceased to attend. When it was necessary later on to do a minimum of mathematics to pass my examinations I was reduced to learning these miserable propositions of Euclid by heart; they had no other rationale for me. I still remember the effort of learning the longest of them, the one about the square on the hypotenuse of a right-angled triangle. And I passed my examinations in mathematics all right, in algebra quite well; that was all that mattered. Still, if I had been told something about the fascinating history of mathematics and the men of genius who built up this body of knowledge it would have been quite different: my interest would have been aroused, as I can see now from such books as Charles Singer's *Short History of Science*, or J. G. Crowther's *The Social Basis of Science*, or Lancelot Hogben's *Mathematics for the Million*.

Now it is too late. I am not merely uninterested, I am positively anti-scientist. I regard it as essentially a specialist activity for people to take to *after* they have been educated. Educate them first. Let them take to science afterwards. And of course I regard the tremendous cult made of science in modern society as very exaggerated: scientists have been very skilful in putting themselves across, and they have a vociferous and docile claque to support them in their claims. They assert that modern society rests upon scientific foundations. Perhaps so: but in the sense that a modern town rests upon a proper sewage and drainage system. One expects it to be well done: it should be well done; then one can take it for granted and go on with the infinitely more difficult and more satisfying work of society. The idea sometimes put about that it is for scientists to take over and run society, since it is so badly run by statesmen and politicians, is the most puerile nonsense. The only sense in this position is in so far as it shows that scientists are beginning to realize something of their responsibilities to society: a realization which is very recent among scientists in general, who have been all too content to remain a-political and reactionary enough in their attitude to social and political trends. With the contemporary movement among scientists, most of them friends of mine, to educate their ignorant colleagues — a movement associated with such names as Julian Huxley, J. B. S. Haldane, Hogben, Blackett, Bernal, Crowther — I am in entire sympathy.

And that is all. With history, it is a completely different matter. There is a much more profound sense in which this is a historically-minded age than it is scientifically-minded — though few people realize it. Our deepest and most urgent problems are not those to which physical science can give us any answer: some of our problems are only worsened by the strides which physical science has made, so much increasing the capacity for destruction. Our problems are essentially political and social: how best to order society, to understand and direct the forces at work. To that end, no amount of physics and chemistry will help one; but a knowledge of history may and should.

For the rest of the staff at school, as the War went on they came more and more to resemble Bradley's 'ghostly ballet of bloodless categories'. The men went one by one, and their places were taken by Welsh and Irish. One of the former made a pleasing impression upon me: wavy black hair, intense grey eyes and sensitive features, a sweet tenor voice ('Wales, whose nightingales have no tongues'), I liked him in spite of the adhesive effect of his dentures, and began to learn Latin with him. He went away one week to take his M.A. and came back very self-conscious as he stood there by the screen at prayers in his voluminous new gown. Shortly after he went back to teach at his Welsh University College. He had a very odd self-conscious triangular writing. His place was taken by an unprepossessing Irishman, both ginger and pock-marked, with a beak of a nose, reptilian blue eyes and a spluttering way of speaking that made me withdraw my book for protection whenever he approached. Out of a hopeless and touching loyalty to his predecessor I found it difficult to learn Latin from him, and being ticked off by him one day, I refused to continue. That was my first significant experience of the delicious, and dangerous, game of cutting off my nose to spite my face — a strong characteristic which I got from my grandmother and which I have frequently indulged since. It is an intellectual pleasure always well within reach, and the pleasure has usually outweighed the price one had to pay.

In this case, I knew at the time it was silly; for in order to take the examinations to get to the University I had to have Latin. Nobody stopped me having my way: it was a peculiar pleasure to tick him off back, since I was the best in his class at the subject. But it was a nuisance later; for we never had as good a teacher of it, and I missed several terms, which meant putting in extra work later on when it came to the indispensable exams. The foundations of my knowledge of Latin were always rickety, not merely in consequence of this wilfulness. For, shortly after, he went too, and we were left for a bit with not a man on the staff, except the acting headmaster. I was free to take up the subject again, but with a succession of women who were really not much use. On the whole I think my Latin was a war-casualty, rather than a sacrifice to the peculiar game.

The headmaster was away at the War, and we hardly ever saw him, at most not more than once or twice, until peace came. So that he meant nothing to my generation; but from those that did remember him there came a suggestion of a stern, forbidding, rather alarming personality, a strict disciplinarian, which greatly impressed me. For me there was this presence of a headmaster I had never so much as seen, waiting behind the hiatus of the present. I knew what he looked like: there was the dark, square face, with stern, set jaw and fixed eyes staring out beneath the college mortar-board from photographs of staff and prefects of before the War. That mortar-board was for me a symbol—a symbol of authority, style, distinction, Oxford. No one else wore one. There were one or two evidences of his suspended presence: an Oxford M.A. gown hanging on a peg in the corner of his room through all the years of the War, getting more and more rusty and sun-faded. (It was one of my greatest pleasures to try it on surreptitiously and march around in it when everybody had safely left the school premises, or on Saturday afternoons, when a few of us came up to play pranks together in the deserted buildings.) I must say it was a tribute to the strength of his personality that his deputy never put the gown away in all those years. There in the cupboard was the mortar-board itself. There were a few fragments of his handwriting that remained: the neat, small, Oxonian script of a classical scholar, of a man who knew Greek, not too easily legible, a little sententious, self-conscious, but, above all, possessing *style*. I was fascinated by this handwriting; used to look for it, when nobody was about, in the headmaster's report-books that reposed on the shelf in his room, and in time my own handwriting was considerably influenced by my admiration. From very early on I even transferred some of my feeling for this impressive, unknown, mysterious figure to the head boy, a person of an almost endearing ugliness, because he had known the headmaster, and to me therefore enjoyed a reflected glory. There was the odd circumstance, too, that their names were very similar.

I do not think that the imaginations of my schoolmates were compelled by these considerations; and they were rather a secret source of excitement to me. The school went along very happily and contentedly under his kindly substitute. Hardly anybody was ever beaten; there was no need to resort to the cane. We were more like a happy family. I was very happy at school: I loved it. I always turned my steps homeward with regret; I was usually the last to leave, and though it was no more than five minutes' walk, I invariably arrived home late, moving slowly up the road, dreaming contentedly by myself, as often as not reading a book all the way. It is such a contrast to the experience of so many subsequent friends of mine at their public schools. When I read the reminiscences collected by Graham Greene in The Old School, still more accounts of Victorian prep-schools like that of Lord Berners's *First Childhood*, it seems to me that they inhabited dens of misery, whereas my schooldays were just happiness all the way along. It is a great tribute to day-schools.

I did not even have any trouble with the other boys, such as I should certainly have had at a public-school, from my ungainly figure and my utter helplessness at games. I can quite conceive that at some boarding-schools my life would have been rendered miserable; whereas at my own small day-school I was free to do what I liked in the matter; free even to express my own superiority to, and contempt for, games. I wasn't any good at any of them; I wasn't interested and it would have been waste of time to try. There were so many other interests at school that my time was all too fully occupied. When I was quite young, my beloved Miss Blank, noticing my eager interest in books and ambitious desire to help her — she was in charge of the School Library — made me librarian, a post which I took very seriously, ran efficiently and enjoyed to my heart's content. It enabled me to take out what books I liked, gave me the first choice of what books there were, and later on, when the War ended and we got more money for purchases, gave me the opportunity of making my own suggestions as to books we should buy. So that during practically the whole period of my schooldays I was school librarian: I remember still the fear and trembling with which I drew up my first report for the school magazine.

And in time all sorts of other offices came my way: I was made secretary of the Literary and Debating Society, arranging the very juvenile and unsuccessful debates we staged. (I had a perfect terror of speaking, which lasted all through my undergraduate days at Oxford, in spite of my being chairman and secretary of the University Labour Club. How I contrived to hold these offices I cannot think. However, I made myself speak — anguish in my heart, confusion in my head — as I made myself sing at church. It was not until I became a political candidate that I got over my nervousness and became a good and practised speaker — the only thing that was of any use to come out of that disillusioning servitude.) Then, too, I became joint editor of the school magazine with one of the girls. That was really interesting and useful practice: I remember so well my ignorance of how you corrected proof. And I was always contributing to it, reports and then poems and essays, finally editorials — but never, so far as I can recollect, stories. There was another boy of my age, very moody and highly-strung, with angry blue eyes and a sullen way of speaking, who was for ever writing interminably long stories. I was greatly impressed by his facility.

In due course I became a prefect and, in spite of my uselessness at games, was made head boy, which I remained for at least two years, since I stayed on an unduly long time in order to go on to the University. Then there were school concerts in which I sang, followed, when the War was over, by school plays in which I acted. It was a very full life, which held my interest from start to finish. Never, never was I bored, and hardly ever — so far as I remember — idle. When I turn over the pages of the school magazines of those years, all of which, out of loyalty to the past, I have faithfully kept, I see myself an eager, ambitious, excitable schoolboy, concerned in everything that took place at school, except games, a sort of Lord High Everything Else.

From the first I had no difficulty in defending myself, as I might have apprehended at a public school. Though I had a *mauvais quart d'heure* or two my first few days: I thought my very worst suspicions of superior school life, gathered from school yarns, were about to be confirmed. There was a very large, ungainly lout with a Dickensian name who had been left behind in the form in which we dozen minor scholars had been placed. He was much older than we were and very backward, with loose lips, hang-dog, threatening expression and a shuffling gait. He was determined to copy my homework; I was determined that he should not. I had never put up with such a thing and I was not going to. He just took my books by *force majeure* and placidly copied out what he wanted, while I waited, furious. Greatly daring and fearfully alarmed for the consequences, I reported what had happened. I expected the worst, but in fact I had no further trouble from him. Then for two or three days in succession I was borne down upon by an exceedingly ginger boy, whose passion it was to think of himself as a train. He was a bit of a persecutor at 'break' for a day or two, until, pressed beyond endurance, in a fit of anger I hit him fair and square in the solar plexus. He protested that it was below the belt. I didn't care if it was. It was his Waterloo. After that I enjoyed a hundred years of unbroken security. For the rest of my school life, fat as I was, I had complete peace.

Peace and happiness: what more could one want?

Well, there was one thing one could have had more of, one thing that was wanting — friendship: though we were a friendly lot, we minor scholars of that year 1915; we never quarrelled; there were no feuds among us.

There was a feud among the women of the staff, between my admired Miss Blank and two other mistresses who held together: a feud in which I was a convinced and as far as I could be an open, partisan. My contribution took the form of an obstinate unwillingness to do anything for the mistress I disapproved of: since she was in charge of the choir, I refused to sing; then I tried to get out of it and, when this was refused, I groaned instead. This was varied with a caricature of my *bête noir*'s sententious way of speaking with an unnatural emphasizing of terminal consonants. It had a very catching effect with the rest of the form — children are imitative animals — to add 'st' or 'sp' to the end of words, or double the effect of 'd's' and 't's' by accentuating them loudly. Soon all the form was talking like that. I ceased to sing in the choir. We minor scholars in the form held together — not in the least an oppressed class; we were rather the *élite*, noticeably more intelligent than the better-off, paying pupils who occupied the lower half of the form-list, where we occupied the top half.

Here, as at the elementary school, I was on closer terms with the girls than with the boys. We were friendly, but it didn't mean much. And as I grew older, I began to be a little more conscious of the loneliness which was to be my lot in life, which had always been mine, though as a boy I had been perhaps too busy to notice it much. It was in the nature of things: it could not be helped; it was in my own nature and the way that I had chosen for myself. I was different: I always assumed as much, and this was the price I had to pay. At moments I felt it bitterly. I watched a group of boys go off together on equal terms, no secrets among themselves, or a couple of boy-and-girl sweethearts shyly walking home together through what we in the village called kissing-gates — sometimes I watched them with a pang at the heart, realizing not so much unconsciously as with an intuitive feeling of the future that it was my nature and fate to be for ever outside.

How often have I felt that corroborated since, known that sensation of a door closed in one's face, the sense of emptiness when all that one asks is understanding, sympathy, a little affection — one would not dare to ask for any more. The pity of it was that I had an extremely affectionate nature as a child, which after the departure of my sister from home had no encouragement. It was, rather, denied, turned away, unwanted. I have often thought since that it was that more than any thing else which made me so excessively ambitious, an energy turned in upon itself. But it was too much to expect understanding or sympathy from children of my own age: it was enough that they were not unfriendly. I always longed for an elder brother; I had an elder brother, but he was quite useless, had no interest in the things that I was interested in, had no conception of the remarkable (and surely very interesting) younger brother he had, his youthful head full of play and increasingly of the girls. He didn't like me, of that I was sure; and I reciprocated desperately with interest. Understanding, of a sort, didn't come till many years later; after he had had his fill of experience of life and I had long graduated in the school of disillusionment with human beings.

No doubt it was as it had to be, and this loneliness in childhood and youth was the best preparation for the way of life that was to be mine. For I remember with passionate agreement Flaubert's saying that the life of a writer is essentially lonely; he has to live among the interests and creations of his own mind, and therefore he has above all things, as a condition of his work, to accustom himself to loneliness. To this I was already so inured by the circumstances of my home life that I was astonished when I came to Oxford to find that some of the very ablest undergraduates I knew could not bear being in their rooms by themselves: they had to have company. I suppose this was the result of the close intimacy of their public-school life. There were moments of exaltation, particularly and always the after-tea hour, when I positively loved being by myself, and to have a room of my own was a permanent source of pleasure. Naturally there were times when one wanted the company of friends—it was at Oxford that I really came to know what friendship was. But if I may add a prescription of my own to Cyril Connolly's suggestions as to the best conditions for literary work, I should say — loneliness mitigated by friendship.

Friendship was the one thing wanting, but a foretaste of what it could be came to me when I was rather more than half-way up the school.

Perhaps I should say here that of the hot-house emotional atmosphere which brought to early maturity the sensitive plants of intelligence and precocious wit portrayed in Connolly's picture of Eton there was at my school, alas, nothing. It was in the nature of a day-school education that on all this side of life we should have been — to me now inconceivably — naif, ingenuous, innocent, unaware. I often think now that public-school boys by the end of their time are ten years ahead of us day-school boys in sophistication, knowledge of the world, of human beings. There are, of course, some disadvantages as against this great advantage they have over us. For one thing, I think we are more interested in subjects in and for themselves than we are in personalities.

Public-school people are apt to be so exclusively interested in personalities and the intricacies of personal relations. It is liable to become very sterilizing, a blind alley. I remember on first enjoying the society of senior common-rooms being quite shocked at the intimacy with which people discussed other people's affairs and personalities down to the very crevices of their characters and concerns. It seemed to me that there was nothing that they would not say. I was very shocked. I ended by learning the game. But I cannot conceal from myself my original bias that the game is not really worth while, except perhaps in so far as it provides material for writing. On the other hand, it is extraordinary the degree of ingenuousness, of unawareness, among the people in such matters, the environment in which I was brought up. So unstimulating intellectually. But everything was. When all is said and done, it is a great advantage that public-school boys have over against us in this respect. Before they are thrown out upon the world and have to wrestle with the relations of human beings to each other in all seriousness, they have already had a pretty good apprenticeship in the torrid conditions of boarding-school life; a good many of them have already had a considerable (and useful) experience in the ways of the human heart, before they come to deal, more seriously, with women.

My own brief foretaste of friendship at school had no such element of passion; it was wrought simply out of mutual sympathy and kindliness, and, on my friend's side, an extraordinarily sweet nature. There came to the school, when I was about fifteen, two London lads, whose father had been shifted to the income-tax office at St. Austell: John and Reg Clark. They were both of them very nice boys, and had the additional prestige of being Londoners. They talked in what we imagined to be standard English, but what was in fact a considerable degree of cockney. They had been choirboys at Christ Church, Lancaster Gate — additional prestige — and now joined our church choir. The brothers were great pals — to me a very ideal and unhoped-for state of affairs. Reg, the younger, was very good at games. John was much more my type — quiet, gentle, a little girlish. We became friends — a friendship in which I took the lead; he was a year older than me, but less forceful. In my vicarious feud with the choir-mistress, for instance, he followed my lead, and we groaned and giggled together. It was very enjoyable. The disapproved mistress with the sibilant consonants had him up and charged him with being nothing but my shadow. There was some truth in this, as I, rather flattered when it was reported to me, recognized. I liked him the more; he was very loyal — a sweet nature. I remember now the shy way he brought a present to one of the girls, when he learned it was her birthday, pressing it into her hand, blushing. He was generous with his pocket-money. I, of course, had none.

At Christmas the brothers asked me to their house to tea. Then there arose the awful problem of asking them back. I was never allowed to ask friends of mine to the house, so perhaps it was just as well that I hadn't any. But after a good deal of pestering my mother, I was allowed to have them back. Still there was the feeling of shame-facedness at asking them to our old-fashioned, tumble-down house. They lived in a new, or comparatively new, bow-windowed house in Highfield Avenue. We lived in the house that Uncle Rowe had knocked together out of two cottages, where Granny Collins had taught school — low-ceilinged, floors sloping, dry rot in it, an army of cockroaches, a fair contingent of mice, ants, woodlice (sow-pigs we called them), no water indoors, no lavatory, no bathroom. The front door opened with great difficulty, so it was never used. We always went through the shop, or in through the kitchen door. We lived in the kitchen, except on Sundays, when we migrated to the sitting-room — a remove I did not much welcome, for I liked to have the sitting-room to myself to do my work in, never happier than when by myself;

until the inevitable cry to go out in the rain and up the court in the dark to measure lamp-oil came. However, there it was. My mother was a wonderful cook, and we had a very good spread for tea. I remember John and Reg now sitting apparently very contentedly together on the low horsehair sofa in the lamplight, while I hovered on the edge to attend to what was wanted — an occasional summons into the shop, returning with nuts and fruit. We played cards. I played the piano a bit. They seemed to have enjoyed their evening immensely. I was surprised and relieved — surprised that they could enjoy themselves at our house.

John wasn't at all clever; he was just a sensitive, nice lad, quite intelligent. He didn't do particularly well in the Senior Oxford, but he got through, and his people, instead of keeping him on at school, sent him to a job in London. He must have been about seventeen. I was sure that this was too young for anybody to go to London on their own, forgetting that London was his home, while I thought of it with fear and trembling as a vast alien world, almost the end of the world for me. I have the impression that we must have drifted a little apart; his voice broke before mine and he may have had a job in the town, so that I saw less of him. We had been inseparable. Then he went to London and within a few weeks was dead of pneumonia. They found an unfinished letter to me among his things, which they sent on to me after his death. I had a little snap of him which was taken in front of the school, sunlight and shadow upon his face, the shy, slightly deprecatory smile which I knew so well. He must have given me that when he left. Through all the years, with their subsequent experiences of friendship and death, of long illness and unhappiness and loneliness, I have always kept that little photograph between the pages of the beautiful Prayer Book that I won as a prize, at the service for the Burial of the Dead.

His death was a great grief to me; it was my first experience, and he was my only friend. It was all so sudden and unbelievable; it had the effect of bringing him more closely to me than ever he had been before. With the curious loyalism in my character, which makes me attach myself deeply to causes and emotions that are hopeless — for the person, the end, has vanished — where many more practical people would cut their losses, I grieved bitterly for him. I am sure no one at school knew, but in the evenings when the premises were deserted I used to go down to school from home and moon about the playgrounds where we had been inseparable companions, neither of us interested in games, and enjoying our own jokes and each other's company; there I could cry to myself to my heart's content, without anybody knowing. The blow of his death came at the time when I was already entering upon the moodiness of puberty, that liability to black moods of misery and gloom which continued for years, right on into the thirties. In the depth of those passions of grief I wished that I might die too, and once went so far as to lie down in the wet grass hoping to catch pneumonia.

That was the end of my only friendship at school that was based on a mutual attraction and affectionate sympathy. There was very little to it: John was seventeen when he died, I was sixteen. But I have always cherished his memory as something very fragrant and sweet. Sometimes in later years it has happened to me to dream of him: when I have seen him by my side, he is always his own gentle, quiet self with the shy smile, half grin; but I always know in the dream that he is really dead, and I wake up to find myself crying as when I was a lad of sixteen.

It would seem also that the public schools have the advantage over the secondary schools in the training of character. After all that is their chief claim, from the time of Dr. Arnold on: they have insisted all along on the virtues of character, rather than of intelligence. (Dr. Arnold's more distinguished son, a man of genius, put the emphasis on the other foot.) Naturally, boarding-schools in which boys spend the greater part of the year living together, learning to accommodate themselves to each other, for ever in company with their fellow creatures, are a much tougher test of endurance, and they are at an advantage in impressing a uniform mark upon those who have come through the process — even upon those who have come through not at all happily. There is a much greater homogeneity of outlook, a uniformity of type, an acceptance of common assumptions among public-school men. That is quite natural; they belong to the governing class: the public schools are the sausage-machines for producing them. That is why public-school men get on together better than we do: they accept, often without questioning, unconsciously, the same standards and assumptions: they understand each other—and so they govern.

The secondary schools are at once less effective, more varied and have greater potentialities. They will never be able to compete with the public schools as character-producing machines; I do not think it desirable that they should. I do not want to see the secondary schools aping, rather badly, the public schools: increasing homogeneity, greater uniformity, compulsory games, team-spirit, the insistence upon character rather than intelligence—particularly at a moment when the standards of a public school governing class in decadence have ceased to be advantageous, on balance, to the nation and become a handicap. Their nineteenth-century achievement was a great one. But we are having to pay a heavy price to-day for their consistent denigration of intelligence, their cult of the amateur, their pathetic belief that gentlemanliness was enough, that fair play (in a dangerously competitive world!) would see you through; that good form, in short, was better than good brains. The contemporary world is strewn with the wreckage of these public-school standards. Whatever one thinks of the Nazis — and I regard them as criminals, the enemies of humanity — they have at any rate been intelligent, and knocked spots off those public-school gentlemen, Baldwin and Chamberlain, Halifax and Nevile Henderson, not to mention the dreary succession of incompetent generals with the best social credentials.

Rather than those men of character, Baldwin and Chamberlain, who together wellnigh ruined their country, I would prefer those men of intelligence—the Lloyd George of 1914-1918, the Winston Churchill of to-day. Both of them men of intelligence, of genius; neither of them paralysed, like public-school mediocrities, by the exigencies of good form, or apt to pay much attention to appearances. Men of intelligence and ability themselves, they respected and exemplified real standards of worth, not the false and the bogus: they even wrote books. It is very interesting that at this crisis in our history, after twenty years of unmitigated public-school men of the middle class who have brought us to this, we have to turn to save ourselves to a coalition of the old aristocracy and the working class—neither of them noticeably public-school in their assumptions or behaviour.

The potentialities of the secondary schools are to be found in their greater variety, the scope they leave for the development of individual intelligence; between school and home the day-school boy has greater liberty, and is more free to think for himself than under the constant surveillance of public-school opinion. He need not so much take on the protective colouring of his environment. He is free to develop his own individuality. He has more chance of standing on his own legs intellectually, of charting his own course and developing his own bent. At any rate, that is what I found. This whole book is the record of such a self-development in such conditions.

I must leave it to the reader to determine how far this course justified itself in my case. I am aware that there were losses (not all such as he would expect) as well as gains, disadvantages as well as advantages. I have often had reason since to wish that I had been at a better school than my small Cornish secondary school was, where one was ill taught on the whole and ill enough provided for; I have often wished that I had been better educated. (Later in life, I have been surprised to find cases of friends of mine at the best schools in the land, particularly Eton, who were no better educated than I.) But as against that, I now see what an enormous advantage it was to me to have been able to follow my own course, explore my own bent, develop my own gifts, such as they were. It was, on looking back, an inestimable advantage to have had the freedom to grow in the way one liked. It would have been deplorable to have been made in a mould. It happened that I liked the things of the mind; and, left a great deal to myself, I read much of the best English literature, and something of French, before ever I came up to the University.

It will be evident from this book that, as to the respective importance of character and intelligence, I do not share the prejudice of Dr. Arnold, but agree with his more distinguished (and half-Cornish) son.[1]

The War was going on and on: there seemed no end to it; we took it for granted as the normal background of our existence. In the first years it made little enough impression upon us. One or two circumstances struck the attention of the growing boy. I remember the eldest son at the farm returning to the village in his khaki riding-breeches

[1] v. my article on 'Matthew Arnold as Cornishman', *New Statesman*, August 9th, 1941.

and yellow-leather leggings, and going away again. (Autumn was in the hedges there by the farm where I saw him last, riding away towards the town.) Then there were the days in which a cruiser, which had, so it was said, been built for Turkey, was in our bay with an attendant destroyer. We were prey to all sorts of rumours — about the Russian Army marching through England — the usual stock-in-trade of the popular mind. One night it was said that a German submarine had appeared at Charlestown and that some of the old women had packed up their things and come up to Mount Charles. But for all we knew we might have been living in a profound peace: so different from the present war with its blitzes on Plymouth, visible over half the county, the constant stray bombs on small Cornish towns and villages, the gun-fire at sea, the perpetual watch on the coast.

The impression of a profound peace was added to by the absence of the men away on service, the increasing desertedness of town and village of traffic and men alike. There was a blessed quiet upon the roads. For me the most important consequence of the War was that it took my father away from home. That I regarded as a great blessing. For as I grew into the awkward age my relations with my father grew worse. There was no bond of mutual interest or understanding; and he, poor man, as I see now, must have sometimes wondered what sort of ugly duckling this was that he had nurtured in the bosom of his family. Not only so incompetent physically — which he was not: he was well-knit, muscular and strong — but with not the slightest interest in his avocations: gardening — he was an excellent gardener; putting up chicken-runs — he was for ever busy making something with his hands; horses and ponies and traps and jingles — which he loved and for which I had an evident distaste, it might be described more exactly as disdain; his tool-house, full of rusty nails and bits and bridles and gimlets and saws and things I couldn't even remember the names of, and never knew the difference between one and the other when he sent me to fetch something for him. Sometimes he used to send me purposely by way of making me learn, but it usually ended in his having to fetch the thing himself. It was really no use; I despised his miserable tools: I never could tell the difference between an adze and a dag, or whatever it was, and by his insisting I only came, quite wrongly but no less fiercely, to despise him.

He was a man of a most irritable impatience: if I get anything from him, it is that. He expected you to understand how to do a thing without explaining it at all — a characteristic which I notice in myself years later in dealing with the young or with the electorate, and which makes me loathe teaching the stupid or having to expound anything political to people incapable of understanding what you say. But I wasn't a fool — only I had no natural aptitude for things in his sphere: the cricket-ball didn't fall as by magic into my hands as it did into other people's (fortunately he didn't approve much of wasting time on games anyway); with me the tools didn't rise up and offer themselves when I went to look for them, wondering which the devil they were; the harness, when I was sent to put the donkey in the shay or jingle, didn't naturally fall into place. Getting it right was a worry and demanded intellectual effort — unlike these naturals, who, like Pavlov's decorticated cat, would still, if thrown from a high place, have fallen upon their feet. (I should infallibly land on my head.)

When I was a child we had a succession of ponies, and father liked them spirited. My mother couldn't cope with them. As she grew middle-aged, rheumatism clamped itself down upon her limbs, arthritis in hips and thighs, which made it impossible for her to walk much. She wanted a donkey, which she could manage to drive. One day my father arrived home with the smartest little donkey and jingle, which held two comfortably and at a pinch three. One more addition to the work for me at home: I now had to look after the donkey, help to harness him and learn to drive, without, of course, the slightest interest on my part. My brother was interested, took to harnessing him and driving and riding on his back, as he took to climbing trees, dogs, and a gun, quite naturally, as a duck takes to water. Not so me: I never rode him, after I discovered how difficult it was to keep on a donkey trotting, that horrible unsteady motion which invariably ended in my falling off. Faster to walk; besides, you could always read a book while you led him by the bridle. In this guise, Neddy browsing on the grass as we came slowly up the road from the field to the village and I with my nose in a book, were familiar figures in the Tregonissey scene.

But my father was not at all helpful when it came to harnessing him to the jingle, all those complicated straps which went either over or under each other, I didn't know which; and he hadn't the sense to show me first, he expected me to know. Similarly with driving. I didn't want to drive at all. I was very nervous. Neddy was fed on oats, was as mettlesome as a pony, was young and newly broken in, and displayed a desire to race anything on the road that showed a tendency to get ahead of him. He had a horror of trains, and so anywhere near the railway line was a dangerous place to be caught in; he invariably tried to run away under Holmbush railway arch, or to race the train, which came to the same thing. He was very strong and my father, who had been used to having a pony and was rather humiliated to have descended to a donkey, drove him like a pony. But I loathed him trying to run away. I drove gingerly along, keeping very much to my side of the road, on tenterhooks at the prospect of passing anything, fearful of the emergence of a railway train on the horizon.

Once when we were coming back downhill along a strange bit of road, my father criticizing every bit of the way — how I held the reins, now they were too slack, now they were too tight (he was impossible to please), I saw to my horror a fearful *impasse* before me: two large china-clay wagons, one coming up, the other going down, which would about meet at the narrow nip in the road at the moment we reached that point. Was I to slow down and wait for them to pass each other? or make for the narrowing gap? Driven to desperation by my father's carping, with a feeling of diabolical exultation, I made straight for the gap. We got through with about an inch or two on either side. I wouldn't have cared if we had got caught and crushed between those wagons. I thought my father would be furious. I hadn't time to bother about the exchange of glances between him and the off-side wagoner. Instead of being furious he was distinctly pleased. I couldn't understand it; or yes, I think I did. I think he was proud.

The fact was that I was afraid of him. Not that I was ill-treated; I wasn't. He occasionally boxed my ears for me or gave me a clout; but my mother did as much — she used to find very useful the little bamboo cane with which the sweets in the bottles were stirred up when they got stuck together. But it was his temper that I was afraid of, his constant irritability. My brother wasn't afraid of him, though he got several severe thrashings, before he finally left home to go to a job in London at the age of sixteen. Perhaps it was all very natural and instinctive — the usual objection of the adult male animal for another male approaching maturity. For when, later, a young relation came to live with us, a little boy of four or five, father was the nicest of us to him, as nice as he had been to me at the same age.

There was a gentler side to his nature. I remember, years before, we had a very much beloved dog called Nell, which used to go away all day with father and the timber wagons from Carclaze and would fetch his slippers for him when he came home in the evenings. One day he came back without her: she had been killed, crushed beneath the wagon. We all cried at this, the whole household, including even father: it was a belief of mine that men didn't cry. Once he asked me to give him some lessons in arithmetic; it would help him with his work in the timber-yard. But he was really no good at taking it in — any more than I was with the screwdriver or plane. I think, too, he must have worried about the future. We made no more money than what we lived on. We paid our way, had good, plain food and clothes, never got into debt and had no savings. What would happen as he got more and more completely deaf, and older, became incapable of working any more? There was not much of a future. His expectations of Uncle, which were reasonably good at one time, had sunk to nothing more than the house we lived in (leasehold property — and in the event he was disappointed even of that). He naturally thought, when I was about fifteen or sixteen, that I ought to be working, helping to earn the family living: he had been earning ever since he was nine. And just about this time he did make an inquiry of his captain at the works if there might not be a place in one of the china-clay offices in the town.

There wasn't one for me. He wasn't 'in' with the captains at the works in the way some of the men were: some of them were relations or had married into their families (my sister hadn't encouraged the attentions of one member of that china-clay family whom she might have married). Others of the 'favourites' danced attendance upon the captains at chapel; we went to church. 'No, Dick', said the captain in his slow, insinuating way, 'you don't want to put the boy into an office in the town; there's not much future in that. Better to keep'n on to school.' That turned out to be much the better advice — if only as altruistic advice it had been tendered. But my father knew it was not; he knew perfectly well that there would have been a place for me all right in a china-clay office if I had been one of their connections, and that they didn't seriously think that there was no future in what they were all engaging in. That was only their Cornish way of putting it.

I think my father understood the position very well, and resented it; and it may have been partly due to that that he raised no more opposition to my going on at school. There was something of a tacit understanding that in return I should look after the shop. And that I faithfully did. All the bookwork fell to me to do (my sister had done it while she was at home, then my brother; mother and father both found adding up an extremely uncertain and tantalizing operation: every time you added the account up the answer came out different. As often as not they cheated themselves. I was not likely to make a mistake of that sort). Then there was serving in the shop, which I did in the evenings when I wasn't doing my homework, and quite often that was interrupted. Thursday afternoons I was left in charge — it was early closing day — while mother drove out to Tregrehan. Friday evenings again I was left on my own while mother went to the pictures with an old crony who dragged her down and up the hill on her arm. Saturdays, as I have said, were rendered abominable by an accumulation of housework and work for the shop: there was chopping sticks enough to light the fire through the week, bringing in coal from the stores, weighing up flour into quarter-and half-pecks, measuring out that infernal lamp-oil, and other jobs. I hated them all. They were all interruptions of *my* work. Then, as the War progressed, there was all the rationing to look after: the making-out of ration-books and checking ration-tickets. All things considered, father hadn't made a bad bargain. And when he went away to the iron-mines in the Midlands I was indispensable at home. In a sense, therefore, I owed it to the War that I went on at school. Neither mother nor father was any more interested than they had been before in what I was doing at school. They never asked, they never bothered; I don't think they looked at my report books; I might have been consistently at the bottom of the form for all the notice they took.

I went on at school. But it had been a narrow shave. I have some-times wondered what would have happened if father had succeeded in getting me a job 'in an office' — height of an elementary schoolboy's ambition — and taken me away from school. I know what I should have done: I thought of it at the time. Consumed with resentment, I should have concentrated on making myself independent and left home. I'd have gone into lodgings and spent all my spare time writing: they'd have got no more out of me. It was very lucky for them that they didn't take me away from school; for later on I was able to take care of them, and in a sense I never left home.

But some years later at Oxford, when my research work was held up by continual illness and I had not the strength to finish the books I planned, I played with the thought sometimes whether it would not have been better if I had *not* gone to the University and my whole development not been turned into academic and intellectual channels. Perish the ungrateful thought! for Oxford has always been the happiest thing in my life. But there was another side than the strictly intel-lectual, which an academic training and career left rather stunted. If Thomas Hardy's fate had been mine, and I had not succeeded in getting through those portals, no doubt — I used to think — I should by this time have half a dozen books — stories, poems, novels — to show for myself. The way of historical research and political thought was much stonier, and for years I suffered from a real feeling of diffidence in writing about either. That very much cramped my natural fertility of mind — that, plus illness and too much teaching in my early years as a don; so the books didn't get written. When I thought of what Q. had written by the time he was my age, I felt like Julius Caesar breaking down crying at the thought that Alexander the Great had conquered the world before he was thirty.

With all this, it was natural that I should regard my father's absence with relief: the coast. was clear. Half-way through the War the china-clay workers, or such of them as were over-age for fighting, were sent up to Oxfordshire to open up the new iron-mines that were being worked near Banbury. My father was first at Bloxham; all that he could tell me about the place that interested me was that the church had a very fine spire and there was an old public school there. Years later, when he was dead, I paid a pilgrimage there, just to see the place where he had been. I found it strangely affecting to see the little streets where he had lived, the iron workings where he had worked, the church which he used to attend on Sundays, until he found it too aggravating not to be able to hear what was said; there was one pillar in the nave which, if he leaned his elbows against, it helped him to hear better. I went round the church and the little village with that same nostalgic loyalty so strong upon me when it is too late: that strange place which had been the scene of an unknown passage in the life of — for all he had done for me — this unknown man.

With all the men away from the village, save for one or two feeble old pensioners, how nervous we were! The village was a prey to scares. All sorts of rumours, all sorts of tales gained upon our nerves when darkness closed in and night came on. There was a half-crazy Salvation Army maniac who lived in the cottages across from Back Lane. One night in his sleep he ran through the village in his shirt screaming 'Murder!'. It was quite unnerving. I really thought someone was being murdered. He was just outside my window downstairs and woke me out of my sleep. My heart beating in my mouth, I ran upstairs to mother, who was similarly, though not to such an extent, frightened. In the other direction — this was later — there was a man who had been invalided out of the Indian Army who used to get drunk and beat his wife unmercifully. It was true she was no better than she should have been; but her screams and crying were heart-rending. Nobody interfered. Lelia wouldn't give them notice — they were her tenants. There was no policeman in the village. Terrified, I used sometimes to try and stop it by rapping on the lighted window; then he would set his dog on me. These excitements were too much for a growing boy, now in the midst of the excitement, and the depressions, of adolescence.

The fact was that the village was becoming a slum: we did not think consciously of it as such. After all, we had always lived in the village; these deplorable people were newcomers — the old Tregonissey characters had almost all gone. A few of the old families held on, who had been there like us all our lives — Blameys and Cockses and Pearces and old Mrs. Kellow, to whom the years made no difference. Together we deplored the changes and the newcomers; but none of us understood what was happening consciously — that the place was becoming a slum; undesirables moving into the cheap-rented cottages. Anyway the process was not complete until after the War — and then the place began to be rebuilt.

There were difficulties in a village almost wholly denuded of men. For example, the awful problem of killing a fowl for our Christmas dinner. My father did this kind of thing with the greatest ease in the world: he just inserted his pocket-knife into the beak of the bird, and behold it was done. From this point of view, even I missed him. For much as I considered the question from all angles, and much as we wanted a fowl for our Christmas dinner, I could not bring myself to do it. I thought of all sorts of ways of performing the operation: my favourite and least disagreeable way was with a sword; if only you had a sword, you could stand the chicken upon a block, whirl your sword round in a circle and clean off with its head without the horrid necessity of looking. But then one hadn't got a sword — and the wretched bird was still unkilled. I couldn't do it; it had to be taken to Tregrehan for my blacksmith uncle, who had no such squeamishness, to kill it. Nor do I think I could do it any better today; though I know one ought. Surely we have got a little too civilized? Then there was the disagreeable business of killing rats, with which the chicken-run and stables at the top of the garden were infested. Under my father's régime kept in a state of respectful repression, with me they became positively insolent. They looked at me out of their holes with that horrible knowing look in their eyes. I hated going into the stables in the dark, they were always about. Occasionally I caught one and wreaked vengeance on him; but I wasn't at all adept at laying gins and setting traps: they always *knew*.

Meanwhile the village was scared by the apparition of a heavy, hulking, unshaven tramp, one Charlie Hancock, who had come back from America and lay about in barns and outhouses and haystacks. He was a fierce-looking customer, bulky and ill-smelling — though I believe his nature was of the gentlest. At night we were terrified of him: 'Charlie Hancock's about' the word went round, and we bolted the doors and fastened the windows apprehensively. He was a less distant terror than the Germans in that war. He seemed to have money and sometimes came into the shop to buy tinned food. I was very respectful, as any Rhineland shopkeeper might have been to a robber-baron in the Middle Ages. The only person who was not afraid of him was Mrs. Pearce, who kept the little dairy-farm at the other end of the village where I went regularly every morning and evening of my life, often followed by the cat, which I had trained to accompany me, to fetch the milk. Mrs. Pearce had been at school with Charlie and said openly that she wasn't afraid of him; the only thing she was afraid of was that he might accidentally set her cowshed on fire, and she would sally out and up the field to order him off. We thought that very brave. In fact the man was harmless: I only relate the episode as an indication of the war-time atmosphere of the village.

There were pleasures, too, of a very simple, unaffected kind. It is astonishing what one was content with—a great ground of strength for one's later life. One wasn't spoiled by an *embarras de richesses*, the restless variety of pleasures open to so many children to-day. Better that life should be simpler, more restricted, more concentrated, opportunities the more highly valued because not too easily come by. Even from the hedonistic point of view they would find their pleasures in consequence more pointed, more intense. I went to the pictures, because we had a free ticket for putting the bills in the shop-window; otherwise I should not have gone, for I had no pocket-money. A cinema of a sort, a very amateurish affair, had just been installed in the old Town Hall. There we went, and invariably brought home a flea. I remember the first moving-pictures I ever saw, which were shots of warships being bombed by Zeppelins from the air, a seascape of a lurid, ominous colour. It was just on the threshold of the War: we were very excited and alarmed. The manager of the cinema was a florid personality, who liked doing turns as a female impersonator: something awful happened to him in the end. Then there was a very temperamental, cross-eyed damsel who played the piano with a mixture of desperate vivacity and languishing sentimentality, and with a distracting discontinuity. The very thought of her brings back the thought of Tchaikovsky's 'Chanson Triste' and the easier, more luscious Preludes of Chopin, which mingled with the terrifying impressions of 'The Clutching Hand' and the familiar figure of Fatty Arbuckle upon the screen, week after week, while the War went on. I am afraid that the cinema did me no good: it merely stimulated my already over-heated imaginativeness, my constant liability to night-terrors, and excited a sexual curiosity for which there was no sufficient satisfaction.

Simpler and more satisfying was the pleasure derived from outings with mother and Neddy in the jingle. I had long got over my nervousness now, and whenever we went out together I drove. We had the roads very much to ourselves, and how well I remember every bend, every turn and twist on the way out to Tregrehan: the splendid, unbroken line of beeches giving us shade in summer all the way down through Holmbush, the roof of the Britannia Inn between the trees, the cool greenness around the Lodge; and as I wandered up the park, dreaming, the blue and gold of sky and leaf. By the end of the holidays the leaves would be turning, and it would be brown against green and gold against brown. Or we went sometimes on a further jaunt down the Pentewan valley to picnic there, the magnificent King's Wood on our left with buzzards mewing above those heights, and with its associations of the Civil War for me, Scobells and Sawles, Menagwins and Penrice; and on our right Nansladron, which centuries ago had belonged to the Arundells, and the high ridge of Heligan Drive, where the Tremaynes had lived since James was king. Arrived at Pentewan there was the smell of the sea, the sun-glitter upon the blue horizon, the green expanse of the Winnick. One Sunday we picnicked all day on the ledrah at Trenarren, mother on the seat looking out to sea (with a depressed friend who wanted cheering up), Neddy cropping peacefully, and I reading all day a book about adventures on the Spanish Main, occasionally looking up and out across that lovely view, the V-shaped valley where the village nestles among the plumed elms, to the bay, Chapel Point, the Channel beyond, the Atlantic, the blue seas of the Caribbean.

Once we had a picnic with some friends at Carn Grey, a new discovery though it was only a mile and a half away: up the tremendously steep hill to Trethurgy which gives such a wonderful view over all the bay, then up a path which skirts a quarry to the carn with its further view across the moors inland to Luxulyan,

> . . . The snake-white road once seen
> Strung with red gems of light under the moon,

to Helman Tors, and on to Brown Willy and Rowtor, blue in the distance. Carn Grey became a favourite place from that time on, to which I took all my troubles and inner turmoil; and it never failed to give relief and solace and renewal.

It was not until the last year of the War, when I was between fourteen and fifteen, that I first went for a long tramp. One of the choirmen, an income-tax inspector of some education and reading, an Anglo-Catholic, took an interest in the intelligent lad with the fine voice and, after sending him a picture-postcard when away on holiday — I, in my innocence, hadn't the remotest idea whose were the initials on it — he proposed to take me for a long walk. I had never been on one, and never supposed that I could walk as much as ten miles. However, one afternoon we went to St. Blazey and then up the valley through the woods of Prideaux to Luxulyan. It might have been the Tyrol, it was so strangely beautiful, and for all I knew that there was such country within half a dozen miles of the place where I was born and had lived all my days. There's immobility and rootedness for you: absolutely characteristic of the people to whom I belonged. I could hardly keep up, I was so unaccustomed to walking. Breathless with nervousness, self-consciousness and exertion I laboured up the valley, among the oaks and ashes, the great granite boulders that strew the slopes, under the splendid aqueduct with the stream dashing noisily down among the withies, this while the shadows gathering fast, until we rounded the nip up into the village and caught sight of the church tower of Luxulyan with its little turret standing black and fortress-like among the trees before us, night fallen.

From that moment Luxulyan was engraved upon my heart. Again and again every year, in spring and summer, in autumn and winter, I have returned to it, often bringing my nearest and dearest friends along with me, still more often, and no less enjoyably, alone. I do not attempt to explain the hold that place has over me, any more than Trollope could explain his passion for hunting. I only know that it is dearer to me than Tregonissey, though I wasn't born there, nor had my family any connections with it, and I had never set eyes on it until that evening. But I know I should be happy to end my days there — my chosen place.

That evening made such an impression upon my mind that I wrote an essay about it for the school magazine, all very Hazlitt and ending up with the passage about the Gentleman in the Parlour from the essay 'On Going a Journey', a favourite of mine. It was my first literary venture. On looking through those old numbers of the magazine I find that this was the prelude to a number of essays and poems in every succeeding number. I wonder if that experience released a hidden spring, and if that is the reason, unrealized till now and long buried, why the place has such a magic for me — because all my subsequent writing goes back to that darkening autumn evening in 1918 and the black outline of Luxulyan church and tower on the spur of its little hill against the night sky.

I was now reading steadily, along the lines that interested me — and some that did not. From the time when I first went to the secondary school I had begun to borrow books regularly from the library: a great advantage over the elementary school, where there was none. There were few enough books at first, but every term added more; and, since I made an efficient and careful librarian, by the time I left school we had a collection of several hundreds. I remember my first struggling with Carlyle, whose *Past and Present* I had taken out for my reading in the summer holidays. I sat there in the shadow of the court outside the shop-door, the flies buzzing in the bay-tree, the light playing in and out the Solomon's seal planted in the rockery of big felspar, china-stones, the sun and leaves making patterns on the white-washed wall of the kitchen. I sat on a hard kitchen chair (nothing else in those days). I read a page and found that I hadn't taken in three-quarters of it, that my attention had slipped and that I had been think-ing about something else. I went back over it again, and so I stumbled on through my first experience of Carlyle. As schoolboy and under-graduate I ended by having read everything of Carlyle — except *Frederick*: nothing would induce me to read that now. I find in my maturity that the young student took far too seriously that disgusting proto-Nazi. Matthew Arnold was quite right to regard him as a 'moral desperado'. However can the Victorian Age have thought he was such a great genius and treated him with such respect? A bad reflection upon that Age, I fear.

One of my earliest admirations, and one which had a great influence

in forming my sensibilities as a writer, was Hazlitt. I owe my intro-
duction to him to Miss Blank. In the corner of the form-room there
was a little bracket bookcase in which were a dozen books, mainly
of hers, including Hazlitt's *Table Talk* and his *Characters of Shakespeare's Plays*. Some of the essays made a great impression on me,
especially that on 'My First Acquaintance with Poets'. I accompanied
Hazlitt with excitement on that winter walk into Shrewsbury, observing what he observed, through his eyes. When, walking home to the
village, I found myself changing from one side of the road to the other,
I suddenly remembered Hazlitt's comment on Coleridge's trick of
doing that, and his taking it as a sign of Coleridge's inconstancy, his
inability to stick to one line. I pulled myself up sharp: I didn't want
to be weak and irresolute like Coleridge. Again, I have only just
realized that in this newly-awakened passion for long tramps, the cult of
the open road, there was an intellectual element that came from Hazlitt: I saw the landscape through his eyes, my sensibilities were sharpened
by contact with his through my reading. That influence is apparent
in all the schoolboy essays I wrote, printed in the school magazine;
and, since it was the earliest, I think it had a lasting, if unobtrusive,
effect on my own writing. At least, there is no writer whom still I
would more willingly follow.

There were no books in our house to speak of at all, except the few
Sunday School prizes which accumulated. But under the flap of the
down-at-heel occasional table (of bamboo) in my bedroom window,
I discovered a torn and not quite complete copy of *Jane Eyre*. I was
very put off by its appearance, but on taking it into bed with me one
night, I was thrilled, gripped, in the end terrified. I was forbidden to
read late by candlelight. I was reduced sometimes to holding the
candle under the bedclothes. When I came to where the mad wife of
Rochester comes down from the attic to set fire to the bed — was it a
bridal bed? — I was cold with terror and excitement. My heart throbbed;
every sound, every creak in the old house, silent enough in the
dead of the night, made me start, ready to cry out. I slept away by
myself downstairs, in the 'lower room' where I had always slept since
we were children. My mother was upstairs, blissfully unaware of the
terrors and excitements going on down below. But such reading,
such tension late at night, can have been no more good for my nerves

than it was for my eyes. I was getting short-sighted. Nobody noticed it.

In that room I had pitched my tent and gathered my cherished possessions about me. They chiefly consisted of orange-boxes, raw and unpainted, into which I had fixed shelves for books (my carpentering went as far). The shelves were a little uncertain and higgledy-piggledy; but those were my bookcases, and I was very proud of the rows of books in bright red cloth and gold lettering. They mostly consisted of Nelson's Classics and Everyman's Library, which was all that I could run to out of my exiguous savings — choir-money and occasional, very occasional, presents. My very first purchase of a book was in the summer the War broke out: it was Scott's *The Abbot*, to which I was drawn by the ecclesiastical picture on the jacket, for I could never read the book. It was a Nelson's Classic, for which I paid the sum of sixpence I had badgered father for. He was distinctly less obstructive on the subject of books than mother. Her attitude was always that of the housewife — that they encumbered the house. 'I'll burn 'em', was her favourite, half-serious threat. Poor dear, she has been much put upon since then — inhabiting a house that now contains some thousands of books. And still they arrive; and still I hear the cry, 'If any more books come in this 'ouse, I'll burn 'em.'

Once in a way father surpassed himself over books. Never shall I forget my surprise when upon his returning on leave from the iron-mines, I dug up all the potatoes in the garden one Saturday morning and he presented me with the money to buy the complete set of Nelson's Encyclopaedia in W. H. Smith's shop-window in the town, 14s. or 18s., I forget which. It was magnificent generosity; it was unbelievable: I was deeply grateful. The potato-digging had given me a sick headache all the afternoon. But on Monday morning I went in and brought home all the volumes in triumph, and wrote 'From father' in every one of the twenty-five.

So my library grew, and my father grew not unproud, in his way, of his son's bookish inclinations.

I had already by now tasted the first delights of authorship. One of those delicious summer days at Porthpean (the Gull Rock and Carrickhowel Point, the view across to Polkerris, one's bare feet tingling with walking on sand and shingle) I found a fountain-pen lying across the path to Mrs. Brenton's. It was as if waiting for me there, for ordinarily I never found anything as other boys did: head in the air or bent over a book, I never looked for anything. Here was this inviting pen lying in my way, as beautiful as a snake, a greeny-black sheen on it, and a gold nib that shone. It was that pen which set me on the path of authorship: a very Valéry reason, but true. Taking my treasure home with me, I tried it out on everything—shop-bills, writing my name on biscuit-tins, on the American oilcloth of the counter. It ended by my dropping it and breaking the nib which had been so smooth and produced a lovely rounded writing (one's writing varied then with the nib one used). But I didn't give up the pen; I scratched out a hideous scrawl with the broken nib: better that than an ordinary pen. It was only then that I thought of devoting my treasured acquisition to something worthy of it: I would write a long story with it.

Father had constructed a small shack of corrugated iron, on top of the rat-infested hedge in the garden — beside the 'green rain-water-barrel' and the elder-tree of my early poem, 'Ireland'. This was referred to as the 'summer-house': our garden always had a summer-house. There was a fixed ledge which served for table, a box for seat, a window that looked out over other gardens — potato and cabbage patches — down the slope to the village. It might have been the old Victor Hugo in his summer-house upon the cliffs of Guernsey looking out over the waste of waters. There all day I sat writing with my scratchy pen in the virginal exercise-book: the excitement of all those pages white and lined and empty that had to be filled up (Valéry again) with whatever I chose to invent. The freedom of it, to be able to say what one liked, go where one chose, to impose one's own form upon events: the boy of fifteen tasted something of the delights of the Creator. But there was the difficulty, too — the fear of not knowing how to go on, what to put in to fill up those expectant pages: the perpetual horror that dogs the steps of infant authors.

And what was the story I chose?

It was the story of Cuthbert Mayne, the first of the Elizabethan seminarist martyrs, caught not far away at Probus and hanged, drawn and quartered at Launceston in 1577. It's odd: as I wrote his name then, I almost wrote Cuthbert Carnsew, for that was the name I gave him in the story. I remember still the peculiar kind of excitement which one got from historical novels — it would be impossible to define — in describing for instance the opening scene, a dark, sullen November day by the quay at Truro, the priest disguised disembarking at that familiar spot, the muddy, malodorous river. (I think I must have got the suggestion for the story from R. H. Benson's *Come Rack! Come Rope!* lent me by my Anglo-Catholic friend.) But I wish I could define that peculiar sensation: the romance of it, its backward-lookingness, its acuity due to something irrevocable in one's apprehension of an imagined, vanished world.

The story was finished, and I embarked on another: I think the second had a love-interest. It wasn't finished; paucity of material (and experience) made me give up the unequal struggle. But the first I rewrote later for a competition in the *Queen*, or some similar woman's journal to which I have subsequently never contributed, where it won a prize, two or three pounds. This was riches. But I was made to buy myself a pair of boots with it. That was the kind of thing which made me sullen with my family, and deprived them of any respect in my juvenile eyes. It offended my sense of justice. Other boys didn't have to buy boots with the prizes they won, I argued. But then they didn't win any prizes: *their* parents would have been only too pleased if they had, and wouldn't have consigned what they won to — boots. (It wasn't really necessary; we weren't so poor as that.) So the argument proceeded. Resentment added to a growing sense of superiority as a compensation for the humiliations I considered I endured, the defects of my family, the loneliness and lovelessness of my life. It was the kind of circumstance, and there were many others, which made me bitterly resent my family background, which made me unyielding, obstinate, proud, determined never to make concessions or yield any respect to these grown-ups I had grown to despise; whereas on the slightest sign of sympathy or understanding or even affection, I should, with such a starved emotional temperament, have melted, become easily sentimental. As it was I built myself a tower of unsmiling resentment, in which I increasingly lived in these years, aloof and almost always alone.

I suppose it had the effect of strengthening and hardening the fibre, as it certainly threw me back upon my own resources of imagination. But it made for an unhappy boyhood — or that is my recollection of it — under a certain strain. The strain was increased in the next few years when I was engaged in a struggle on my own to get to the University. My people hadn't a penny to help me there. Every step of the way had to be won by my own efforts, the whole cost covered by scholarships. It was much less easy in those days than it has subsequently become, and nobody from my school had ever got to Oxford before, or to Cambridge. It undoubtedly produced an anxiety-complex, the combination of working hard with worry, and planted the seeds of the long illness which almost wrecked my young adult life. Over and over I asked unreasonably: What were my people doing to have made no money in all those years? Other people's parents had made money, though their children were such fools as not to be worth sending to the University. Yet they could send them if they wished. And so on. It was perhaps unreasonable, but only because it is unreasonable to expect anything of anybody. It was certainly natural that the adolescent boy upon whom the whole strain fell should have become increasingly embittered and aloof. His consistent attitude at that time was one of loathing his lot in having been born into a working-class family.

My one consolation was my life to myself. In April of that year 1918 I began to keep a Diary. It was started in order to keep a record of the churches which I saw upon the long walks I was being taken by Mr. Booth, the Anglo-Catholic income-tax collector, the series begun by the memorable walk to Luxulyan. My early Diary was, like that of many such adolescents, very architectural, full of holy-water stoups and piscinae, and such remarks as, 'There is a very pleasing apse at the east end.' But as time went on it became something more; it became a real solace to me to pour out in my Diary all my troubles, anxieties, pleasures. It became a secret resource, a companion. Off I would go when upset, through the two glass doors with the muslin curtains, down into the sitting-room — it was always 'down' in the sitting-room with us — to shut myself up with my books and my Diary. As the summer wore on, something of its tremendous events percolated into the school exercise-books and cheap blotting-pads in which I wrote. I was very anti-German; I drew up peace-terms of a Draconian severity. A pity they were not imposed.

In a later, more liberal mood — I should guess during the Locarno period — a little ashamed of the jingoism and naïveté of these early volumes, I destroyed the first seven. What remains is the Diary which I commenced in March 1920, and from then on it is continuous. It gives a full picture of my last two years at school and at home, and of my struggle to get to the University. I shall draw upon it extensively for my next chapter. It might even be worth while to publish selections from it. The English public has become accustomed to *Diaries of a Communist Undergraduate* being thrown at its head from Soviet Russia. Not that they have made much impression. It might with more reason be interested in the Diary of an English schoolboy of the working class making his way to the University: a record as complete, with all its ups and downs, its successes and disappointments, must, I imagine, be rather rare.

There, then, in those two rooms away from the shop and the noises of the kitchen — the rooms in which Granny Collins had kept her school fifty years before — I lived my life to myself. When I came home from school, about five o'clock, I had my tea, did a few odd jobs, and at half-past five settled down to the long evening's reading and writing. I recall now that old, rather unsteady, round table, its beautiful rosewood surface protected by American oilcloth and then another cloth of some indescribable loose material with tassels round the edge. In winter I lit my lamp — I had been given a figured metal lamp with a pink shade by an old lady visitor to the village — and pulled down the Venetian blinds that rattled down with a vigorous snap. I shut out the world, the puddles of the wintry road, the passers-by on the pavement, the disturbing figures of people who were going into town to enjoy themselves. Only the wind rose and fell in the aged elms on the other side of the road, or roared in the chimney: I pulled my rug around my knees — there was no question of a fire — and, opening my books, brought them into the circle of the lamplight.

Beyond, when I looked up, there were all the things I had been used to since I could remember anything: the rosewood chiffonier with the silver teapot that had been given mother at her wedding by Mrs. Doctor; the sporting print that hung above — a wedding present to father; on the mantelpiece, the overmantel with knick-knacks of china, a bright china-orange, a pretty seashell which you put to your ear and heard the surge of the sea in; the uncomfortable armchairs by the fireplace; the old piano with the stuck keys behind me; the horsehair sofa in front of the window; the antimacassars. The evening wore on; mother was getting supper in the kitchen: there was the pleasant sound of cups and saucers tinkling. After supper there would still be the long hours of warmth in the kitchen in which to go on reading and writing in the white light until midnight. I was happy.

Suddenly, one day in November 1918, the Armistice came upon us. For weeks and months the Central Powers had been breaking up: first Bulgaria, then Turkey, then Austria, at last Germany, *fons et origo malorum*. We could hardly believe our eyes and ears; we could not visualize peace, we had become so accustomed to the background of the War going on: it was the normal background of life for a boy my age. With an instinctive impulse we all trooped in droves into the town: everybody left their business and came out into the street. The presiding spirit of the disorder was the vicar, looking more like the Mad Hatter than ever, wandering around beside himself with glee, relief, kindliness. He was also very proud of himself: used to being ordered about by his masterful churchwarden, this memorable day he had on his own responsibility ordered out the bellringers to ring a merry peal. The bells clashed from the tower; the people trooped with an instinctive movement into church, church-people and chapel-people alike, for once the old parish church came into its own and was the place of worship for all the people as it had been in the centuries past. Never have I seen it so crowded: people knelt anywhere in the aisles, on the steps; everybody prayed fervently, thankfulness in their hearts; many were crying. That night, for the last time I can remember, they danced the Flora Dance through the Fore Street; or rather, it was impossible to dance it, there was such a jam. One adolescent boy, aloof and reflective, surveyed the scene gloomily, sullenly, without any pleasure; for him what the Armistice chiefly meant was that his father would be home again from the iron-mines.

CHAPTER VIII

READING, WRITING, POLITICS, POETRY

THE end of the War meant a great waking-up at school. The head-master returned from the Army in which he had been from the very first days. The rumour of his personality had increased to most impressive proportions: it preceded his entry and rendered us awe-struck when at last he made his appearance. The mortar-board awoke from its long sleep in the cupboard and was seen once more about the corridors; a new and flowing black M.A. gown was to be glimpsed emerging or vanishing from the now shut doorway at the end of the dark passage to the headmaster's room. Prayers became much more ceremonious; there was an awed silence when the almost legendary figure stalked with long military stride into the big room; a lectern was installed and the prefects read the lesson according to a rota. As head boy I was moved up to a special place in front near the dais which the headmaster occupied with his kindly deputy, now demoted, on one side and the senior mistress on the other. The fixed stare and the dark eyebrows of the great man were enough to keep a whole school in the strictest order without a word. When he walked into the junior form one day, the little boys and girls were so paralysed that they became quite speechless. But I sensed, or somehow gathered, that in fact he had mellowed as the result of his years away at the War; and it was not long before I began to suspect that the stern exterior, the dry, military voice, concealed a kind and considerate heart. Uprightness, honour, duty — the insistence upon those rather public-school virtues (he was a public-school man) I expected; what I had not expected, for I too shared the general alarm, was his personal kindness and under-standing, his tact, the gentleness with which he handled me. I was very anxious to please him, and from the very first I was devotedly his: with the old deep-rooted loyalty of temperament and a pathetic gratitude for any kindness or understanding, I gave him my absolute trust and confidence.

There were other changes in the staff; men made their appearance once more. Now came the long and melancholy pale Irishman (he might have been one of the early kings of Connaught) who succeeded Miss Blank, with her subject, in my affections. He worked very hard, sat up half the night correcting our essays, was an R.C. (which I found very intriguing), a poor disciplinarian; he had a very deep dimple in his chin, which fascinated me, it was impossible to shave in that declivity. He was gentle and kind, and I was fond of him. He it was who first introduced me to Hardy, for whom I fell at the first moment. Here was a writer who wrote for me—he joined the company of *my* authors, my schoolboy admirations to which I have remained constant ever since— Daudet, Q., Hardy. Even while at school I added Swift; it was not until later that I added those other writers who speak specially to me— Newman, Joyce, Rilke, Proust, Flaubert. Reading *Jude the Obscure* increased my growing exasperation with the circumstances of my home-life and with the difficulties, indeed the improbability, of my getting to Oxford. I find from my early Diary that I was 'fascinated' by *Jude*, but that it was *The Trumpet-Major* which really delighted me. The last sentence about the steps of the Trumpet-Major leaving the village, fading away until they were to be heard no more upon what field of Spain, made an undying impression upon my mind. There is a reference to it in a line of my poem, 'Duporth Camp: September 1940'.

There follows an analysis of the plot, and then the following school-boy comments which perhaps I may quote from that early volume of Diary (August 20th, 1920):

> The book is built up out of what actually did happen in Dorset at the time of the Napoleonic War, more than any other of the Wessex novels. This makes the book all the more interesting to me, for in going about the countryside and in talking to old folks I always have my mind bent on knowing little incidents of the past from those who witnessed them. I think Uncle and Auntie were the best people for 'telling up' stories of the past. But they are now dead — before I appreciated the importance of gathering first-hand information from them. What I did learn, however, was by no means small, though I gathered it from casual listening more out of interest in the past than in preparing for my future. I still remem-

ber Auntie's description of the great occasion when the first train passed through Mount Charles. The scholars at the dame's school were given a holiday to view the wondrous locomotive with its train of trucks as it passed beneath the bridge. But for 'telling up' Uncle far exceeded her. He has related to me so many anecdotes of village life here in Tregonissey more than fifty years ago that I can reconstruct it in my mind.

Then there follows a picture of life in the village very much on the lines of an early chapter of this book, with some stories and rhymes which I had forgotten and do not appear there. But it is made clear in several entries that my very first literary ambition was to write a book about life as it had been in the old village, with the old characters and stories; and my aim at this time — I had apparently ceased to entertain my earlier designs upon the see of Canterbury — is stated in so many words, to be the English Daudet. Again and again my passionate admiration for the *Lettres de Mon Moulin* is expressed, and the idea of the book becomes associated with my obsession for Luxulyan Valley, to which I now walked regularly as a sort of Mecca. One such walk followed a reading of Stevenson's *Travels with a Donkey* — I was gradually reading all I could get hold of of Stevenson, another favourite author; and I saw the wooded slopes of Luxulyan as my Cevennes, where one day I would sleep among the oak-copses *à la belle étoile*. I saw my Daudet book more and more in terms of the Valley rather than our village. It is strange to me that I have only returned to do justice to the village in this book, after twenty years, after what wanderings in the realm of politics and political thought, of history and historical thought, of poetry, French and German as well as English. It pleases me now to find, for I had forgotten if it had not been for the Diary, that my early bent towards collecting stories and information about old Cornwall was confirmed and made conscious by reading Hardy.

We got a new science master, son of a blighting old martinet of an ex-elementary school headmaster, an unattractive family man, who went regularly to chapel, and lived for a while in Uncle and Auntie's old house: he did not interest me. He was succeeded by a young temporary recruit, who, in spite of his being a scientist, did interest me more and more and ended by becoming a life-long friend. This was J. G.

Crowther, then not much more than twenty, who had had the great success of winning a mathematical exhibition at Trinity, Cambridge, had been pushed very young into hectic war-work at the mathematics of gunnery, and had had a breakdown from overwork. He came to us by way of convalescing, and I was much mystified by so distinguished a person having so little idea of how to conduct a class. The fact was that he couldn't take it seriously. One heard an uproar whenever one was in his vicinity, went into the room to find everybody having rigs of fun, and Jimmy sitting in the middle of the disorder in fits of laughter, enjoying it as much as anybody. I, who modelled myself on the headmaster, and was at this time a severe and baleful personage of whom the young stood more in awe than they did of these new masters, could not but disapprove. (It had struck me as early as this that there were two ways of influencing other people. One was to be like them, to share their interests, to be good, if possible rather better, at the things they were good at, particularly sport, athletics, the girls — in short, to be popular. In the nature of things this could not be my way. But there was a second, and far more powerful, way of dominating them: to be as unlike them as possible, not to share their interests on an equal footing, to hold oneself aloof. This had to be my way, and I found it vastly more effective than ever the first could have been.) Jimmy explained that it was his misfortune to take the periods after the form had had a visitation from the headmaster or the senior mistress, and that the boys and girls simply had to let off steam afterwards.

Though my contact with him was not very close while he was at St. Austell, he lent me books and continued very kindly to take an interest in me, write me long letters and send me more books when he left. His interests, being intellectual rather than purely literary, were rather above my head. He lent me Santayana, whom I couldn't understand: there is a note in my Diary hoping that perhaps some day I should. That juvenile aspiration has since come to pass; I now find in myself a very close sympathy with Santayana's position, his aesthetic naturalism, his Latin affiliations, his distaste for Protestant utilitarianism, Anglo-Saxon moralism, Teutonic barbarism; I find I can subscribe with almost complete agreement to the critical point of view expressed in such books as *Egotism and German Philosophy*, *Character and Opinion in the United States*, *Winds of Doctrine*, *Soliloquies in England*, though at that time the schoolboy found his *Little Essays* unreadable, unintelligible. The fact was that on the intellectual side my education was not begun; nor was it to be until I went to Oxford. Crowther gave me a Shelley too, whose philosophical doctrines I could not understand, though I liked the poetry; he thought Shelley much superior to Keats; I stood up for Keats, whom I preferred. He lent me regularly the numbers of *Plebs* as they came out with letters by his friend Ralph Fox on Shelley as revolutionary poet: I could not understand the points at issue in the discussion. In reading this highbrow, left-wing periodical, I felt rather like Keynes about German economics — that I could only rightly understand what I understood before. However, all this had some influence in corroborating the natural inclinations of an ambitious, sensitive working-class schoolboy at that period of industrial unrest and political hope in a socialist direction.

He was not responsible for 'turning me into a socialist', as the fatuous phrase ran among the more foolish of the middle-class elements, with their very narrow and restricted prejudices, their almost total lack of any education or culture or taste or sympathy of mind, in this small provincial town. (Flaubert's *bourgeois*.) I gathered afterwards that he was regarded as having subverted my ideas. That did less than justice to my own independence of mind: I wasn't, even then, likely to follow anybody's lead unless I agreed with it. In so far as I was 'converted to socialism', if the phrase means anything, it was by reading Ruskin, who had been set as a text for the examination for the County University Scholarship, and by Ramsay MacDonald's little book on *The Socialist Movement*, which had found its way into the school library, and whose irrefutable platitudes were well calculated to impress a sympathetic, adolescent mind.

The truth was that there was a wave of radicalism which swept through the working class in those years, while the mean-minded, small-propertied classes, fearful for their particular security, went more reactionary and deserted Liberalism for Conservatism. That movement underlay the whole post-war period of the next two decades and was responsible for the permanent Conservative majority which led this country to disaster. One may well ask now, Who was right? the intelligent schoolboy, with his intuitive grasp of the future, or the mean and miserable middle-class people of his home town, who, in their anxiety not to lose a shilling, ended by throwing away the lives of sons and husbands and jeopardizing the security and well-being of us all?

As a matter of fact I was not very political, understood very little about politics. It was just that my emotional sympathies were with my own people. There was the miners' strike in 1921, for instance. The headmaster, who was a Conservative of the most conventional views, who took his line from the *Daily Telegraph*, talked to me at length one morning in his study about the deplorable behaviour of the miners. It suddenly came over me how little I should like working in their conditions, and that men who had such hard lives well deserved the best that could be given them. It was a very simple ethical view, expressed eloquently, somewhat hotly; I felt my cheeks burning. The headmaster was rather taken aback; he had never seen it in that light before, and, gentleman that he was, didn't push his own view any more. I think for the moment he was quite affected; it was my turn to be taken aback. The conversation ended.

Other people were less considerate. I find in my Diary, for example, that the good-hearted wife of the pompous auctioneer 'damned the miners to the heavens and vociferated that their leaders ought to be shot'. There follows the naif comment: 'She cannot get rid of the idea that she is dealing with people below her rank, or of a different class, or inferiors.' This kind of thing only hardened my opinions against them. I find a reference to a long argument with the daughter at the farm, a girl a good deal older than I, with whom I used to go to church and hold long colloquies under the lilac-tree, she standing among the camellias inside her garden, I under the lilac branches in the road outside. I had apparently lent her some numbers of *Plebs*, which she proceeded to run down to me; then, 'she couldn't be reasonably expected to enjoy detailed articles on out-of-the-way revolutionaries, neither could she be expected to appreciate the statistics regarding the accumulation of capital'. Poor girl, how right she was!

Next year, January 1922, I took my father to our first Labour meeting: it was held, appropriately enough, at Carclaze in my old elementary school. It was addressed by Joe Harris, a trade-union organizer, whom I was to succeed, at a remove, eight years later as Labour candidate for Penryn and Falmouth, our constituency. But it is curious to see that even then I had no illusions about my own people. I watched the face of each man that came into the room, and upon every one was a look of blank incomprehension. There was apparently one man who looked as if he understood what was being said — and he did not agree. No wonder my Diary comments: 'I come away from a meeting such as that held to-night in deep despair.' The prescient despair of the juvenile diarist, who was to succeed the trade-union organizer as Labour candidate, was only too justified, in the event.

But that did not make the selfish middle class any more right; it only showed their selfishness up the more. In my then idealistic view, they ought to have been ready to extend a helping hand. That was all that my supposed socialism came to at that time. I made a few youthful gestures in the right direction, such as sitting down when people sang 'God Save the King' and taking no notice of Empire Day at school. The former infuriated the old Tory women of the town, and the latter brought down upon my head a protest from the old ex-elementary schoolmaster who had become a governor of the school and whom I hardly knew. This was passed on to me by our headmaster's successor, a kindly, liberal-minded man, with the sage advice 'not to run my head up against a brick wall'. That was his attitude towards cantankerous reactionaries, the line of least resistance. In his way he was right.

But when did that sort of faint-hearted advice ever do any good to an impulsive, generous-minded youth, who would have despised himself for not having the courage of his opinions against a lot of small minds for whose prejudices he had complete contempt? The years have only corroborated the contempt, and extended it to their whole personalities and everything they have and are. For years now I have pursued them and their foibles with the loving hatred with which Flaubert for twenty years kept his *Dictionnaire des Idées Reçues*, or with which Swift compiled his *Polite Conversation*. I, too, have kept my *Dictionnaire des Idées Reçues*, more than a score of little pocket-books in which I have carefully recorded their clichés, their characteristics of make-up and behaviour: the conversation of human idiots, as the book is sometimes called; sometimes, more simply, the Book of Life.

So characteristic of their meanness of mind was something which happened when the County Scholarship was being discussed. Q. was making a speech in my favour when some member of the Education Committee, some landlord, farmer, butcher, speculative builder or mere rentier, passed up a note saying: 'Do you know that this boy is a socialist?' Q. just tore the note up and went on with his speech. This story I never heard from him; but I have no reason to doubt it. It is so characteristic of the meanness and smallness of their minds, of the Bouvards and Pécuchets of Cornwall. It is the same kind of mentality which I have had to contend with throughout the decade during which I was a Labour candidate there, and which has gone far to thwart and embitter my whole relation to my native county.

However, my reaction has not been a passive one; I always hit back at them actively, with interest and pleasure. I have paid my compliments to that sort in the poem 'Sunday Cinemas' in my *Poems of a Decade*, and shall do so again. This book, all my writing, is so much evidence of how deeply Cornish I am, so inextricably rooted — I had never even been out of Cornwall until at the age of seventeen I went to Oxford to try a scholarship. Nobody has done more to celebrate the Cornish past and make it intelligible to and valued by English readers than I have done, certainly in my generation. Yet there is little enough appreciation of that in Cornwall, and when I consider the type that is dominant in the county — conventional, narrow, nonconformist, hypocritical, uncivilized — I am perpetually irritated by it. Deeply as I love every field and lane and hedgerow, here where a gateway gives you a view of the sea, there a line of plumed Cornish elms watching by a stream, or a neck of headland, the lovely lines of the moor, I have again and again been tempted throughout my political experience to cut away from the place and never see it again. But that loathsome, sterile mentality, so uncreative, which has been for long on top in Cornwall is losing ground and going downhill at last.

But, I repeat, the main interest of my mind was very far from being political. In politics I was a complete *ingénu*; it was just a question of emotional sympathy, the generous impulses of a youngster for those who had had a raw deal in life, anger with those who, well enough off themselves, had no feeling for the 'most numerous and the most poor'. For myself, everything took precedence of politics in my interests; it came in a very lame hindmost. What with my school-work, work at home, church, my love of literature, reading and writing, tramps across the countryside with friends, my time was fully occupied. And to these interests I now added another, which absorbed the most intimate impulses of my emotional life and became my secret passion, a sort of hidden touchstone for all the rest of my life—the writing of poetry. It took the place which in another age, and if my fundamental impulses had not been aesthetic rather than of an ethical character, might have been taken by religion, in especial the act of prayer. What happened was that, now I had 'found' poetry, I needed religion less, in the end not at all.

The mere reading of poetry would not have been enough; it was the fact that I had discovered the writing of poetry which made the difference. That became my secret religion, the activity which I hugged to myself, the tower into which I could always retreat for consolation for my troubles, my angers, my disappointment, for it was the activity in which I was most wholly myself, untouchable from outside. I knew no more intense excitement than this, except perhaps for sex; it was wholly absorbing, and the thrill was only matched by the difficulty. I was never satisfied with the verses I wrote; they always fell so far short of the intensity of the experience I had been through, and of which, in the cold chill of after-reading, I invariably felt they were unworthy. It was endlessly exasperating, this struggle to write poetry. There was no one at all I could turn to, no one to consult, for nobody I knew cared about poetry in that way sufficiently to be any use; no one to tell one where one was going wrong, how to turn a difficult phrase or fetch a needed rhyme. But even that was not the real difficulty, for I was used to being for ever on my own — though I often complained to myself about it — in these things of the mind that so interested me. No, the real difficulty, of which I was constantly conscious, was that my intense desire to write outran what I had either of experience or ability to express myself, technical capacity. I suppose the case was a usual one with young authors.

I was not one of those who from earliest childhood had 'lisped in numbers, for the numbers came'. Throughout childhood and youth I had naturally never had any poetry read to me by my parents; I had never read Hans Andersen, or *Alice in Wonderland*, or *Just So Stories*, or *Dream Days*, or any of the children's books with which educated parents amuse their children. My friend, Lord David Cecil, in the fastnesses of Hatfield was having Shakespeare read to him at the age of five. Not so at Tregonissey, where Shakespeare had not yet been heard of. The result was that I came to writing poetry all at once, with adolescence, and that what I wrote was extremely literary, imitative, following the models of what I was then reading, Italianate and Shakespearean sonnets with formal rhyme-schemes. Until I was sixteen I had never written a line — and then the experience came quite suddenly. It was all so vivid and moving that I remember it quite well — though the first volume of my Diary that remains begins with the poem that resulted.

Once when I was coming home from choir-practice — as usual alone, for my brother and earlier companions had grown up and gone — I was overcome by, I was possessed by, the beauty of the night. It was the very beginning of March 1920; it was frosty and the sky was alive with stars. I must often have noticed starlight and moonlight before; indeed I remember still occasions from my childhood when I noticed them, the stars flung out over the hill-side that bounded our view to the north, the moon bathing the fields below the village with a soft misty glow, or lighting up the bay with pathways of silver. But never had I noticed before with such intensity; the sensation of being possessed was a physical one: I *was* 'possessed'. In spite of there being a bright moon the stars shone clear like jewels; I saw them entangled among the wintry branches of the hedgerow, as I came up the last bend of the road by the farm before entering the village. I noticed that in spite of the clear, glittering brilliance, there was colour in the sky: it was frost-blue.

I hurried home, my mind on fire, went straight to bed to be by myself and think of nothing but writing my poem. I wrote until midnight and finished my first poem, a very Keatsian sonnet, which I called 'Star-Jewels':

> The full moon, floating high in the frost-blue sky,
>   Bathes the world in a flood of silver light
>   Whose haunting splendour making day of night
> Forbids the numb rest of Sleep . . .

It was very rich and literary, not a good poem; but it was my first. I was both proud of it and exasperated: it was so much less good than the experience which had gone into it. Indeed that was unrecapturable, inexpressible. And yet, years later, I can say that it was the fact of writing the poem which fixed that night for ever in my mind.

That year there appeared an anthology, *Public School Verse*, edited by three original and enterprising Oxford men, Martin Gilkes, Richard Hughes and P. H. B. Lyon. It had an introduction by Masefield, whom I subsequently came to know at Oxford. I don't know how I came to hear of this: the headmaster may have told me of it. But I sent in my poem and it was accepted. It appeared in the next volume; I saw myself, if not in print for the first time, at any rate published: the now so familiar name staring strangely out at me from the printed page. I was childishly proud, too, of seeing my own school appearing, if under an inaccurate form — St. Austell's County School — along with Rugby and Wellington and Marlborough and Eton. (It strikes me now that I must have got in under a misapprehension, all the others seemed to be public schools.) What struck me then was the incredible cleverness, the sophistication of the other people, which I could never hope to rival: it made me wonder the more at my own poem appearing there at all. And indeed these volumes of *Public School Verse* were distinguished by the very remarkable early poems of Peter Quennell, elegant, graceful, self-conscious, of a most discriminating and precocious craftsmanship. They were far the best things in these books: it is sad to think that he should have written no more poetry, or hardly any, since. He was much the most talented of the boys who contributed. There were others whom I came across afterwards, some of whom have made their mark: R. C. Matthews, J. L. Gray, D. R. Gillie, and — the best known of them all, a household name in every sense of the word — Joseph Gordon Macleod. In the next volume we were joined by Graham Greene and Christopher Isherwood.

To that volume I contributed another sonnet, a better one, which has something of my own idiosyncrasy in it: the first poem which was recognizably mine. It was originally called 'Black Mood' — I was often in one at that time, and the whole suggestion was to convey a mood of temper in terms of nature. The editors didn't like that, and I altered it to a plain description of a 'Winter's Night', under which title it appeared. It still brings back those hours of winter darkness in the village, myself at the table in the circle of lamplight, reading, writing, listening to the wind roaring in the old elms outside:

To-night upon the world has fall'n a mood
   Of hideous blackness: mists of driving rain
Have quenched the stars; the moon in solitude
   Fitfully, wanly glimmers o'er the plain,
Where roadside puddles catch a fleeting gleam
   And bare the reflex to the sightless skies;
Foul, distorted figures throng and teem
   Amid the darkness; shapes of horror rise
And beckon in the trees with writhing limb;
   Around the house, the winds in fury race,
Waking shrill voices at their every whim
   And tiring not as night moves on apace;
And at the coast there beat unceasingly
The thunderous breakers of the wintry sea.

There is something odd about the twelfth line; there are various versions of the last lines in my Diary: I think the editors must have altered it a bit. Anyway it marks an advance on the first sonnet; though, of that, I was very pleased when J. C. Squire in a review of the volume in the *London Mercury* mentioned my poem much more favourably than it deserved.

These poems, though not very much in themselves, sprang out of a real and pressing experience; and that has been the case with all my later poems that have been any good. Apparently poets differ in this respect. T. S. Eliot told me quite recently that in his case he could never write a poem unless he tricked himself into the belief that it was only a technical problem to be solved. With me, I have to be really moved for the poem to be any good. Perhaps it is a more exhausting way. In those early volumes of Diary poetry comes to have more and more place. There are a great many verses all told, most of them not much good. But unsatisfactory as they are, they served the purpose of exercises, and I notice an increasing command and greater facility as time goes on.

My poetry was associated with the places which I went to for consolation and renewal. (I have always found such places — or such a place, for usually there has been only one — wherever I have lived. At Oxford, it is the walks of Magdalen, Addison's Walk especially.) At home there were two, Carn Grey first and foremost, and secondly, Lost House. Ever since the walk to Luxulyan, I had made Carn Grey my evening walk when I could take one: up through the village and the raw, ugly granite squalor of Lane End, breasting the great broad slope of Trethurgy Hill, the view over all the bay expanding on the right from the Gribbin to Trenarren; until when you got on the level road on the top of the plateau, the romantic view away across the moor to Luxulyan, Helman Tors and Brown Willy opened out, on the right the country of the Civil Wars following the course of the River Fowey from the woods of Lanhydrock and Boconnoc to Lostwithiel and so down to Fowey. When I looked across to the heights the other side of the Fowey, my mind influenced from elementary-school days by *The Splendid Spur*, I thought of the melancholy King sleeping all night in his coach surrounded by his guards in the park at Boconnoc, the watch-fires burning under the hedges, Bevil Grenville there and Hopton and Lord Mohun: I saw the figure of the King on his charger, as he appears in the picture, bestriding all that peninsula, towering above the horizon.

Those evenings at Carn Grey were a feast of solitary sensuousness. I walked up through the village, books under one arm, a large military mackintosh, relic of my brother's service in the army, over the other: a curious figure I must have presented, but the village people were accustomed to me from childhood and it never occurred to me to care what anybody thought anyway. My favourite place was on the bank under the shelter of the Carn right on the edge of the quarry — a splendid vantage-point from which I could look down into the bowl of the amphitheatre, with its deep glass-green pools in the corner at the foot of the cliff; and out over beyond to the beloved Valley, the round camp above Prideaux, the dark woods of Tregrehan, the darker woods of Crinnis, the steeple of St. Blazey Gate Church pricking up among the trees on its hill. (It is the country of my poem 'March Landscape in Cornwall'.) There was the keen, shrill music of the moor-wind in the grass; there was always a lark singing somewhere in those skies; there was the scent of bracken, the tang of camomile among the moorland herbs; dogs barked in the distance as the evening wore on; the cattle lowed across the moor; the sun went down behind the clay-pits where my father worked; the shadows grew immensely long; the colours of the bay, which had been so vivid, deep blues and greens, softened; a haze came up over the Gribbin and one star came faintly out. Time to go home; it was getting cold. I had been reading and writing, looking up at the landscape at intervals all through the evening. Here, nobody could get at me: in this pure air I threw off the vexations, the disappointments, the moods of my life down below. In all the years in which I went regularly, deliberately, to Carn Grey, as to a high place in which to 'blow away the cobwebs', that beloved spot never once failed me. In whatever mood of temper or impatience I left home, I came back from Carn Grey at peace with myself, happy.

Naturally, therefore, a good many of my early verses were about that place; and when, a year or two ago, I was near, as near as one could be, to dying, my mind was haunted with the wish, that goes back to my schooldays, that I might be buried there.

There was another spot, which took second place in my affections: Lost House. This was much nearer and more convenient; for whereas Carn Grey meant a walk of a mile and a half up a very steep hill, to get to Lost House you had only to climb over the hedge on the other side of our road and go down to the bottom of the field. For all that, it had an atmosphere of its own. There was something queer about that place. It was just a paddock, hedged in by high stone Cornish hedges, in the middle of the fields below the village. On one side there was a cowshed. It was surrounded thickly by trees, elms, sycamores, ashes, thorns; it was always green and shady there, however hot it was; the sun only came through filtered by the leaves, or latticed by them into pretty, moving patterns. But its atmosphere was not cheerful all the same; it was watchful, as if waiting, like so many places in Cornwall. You might get frightened down there if you stayed too late. My post was on the outskirts of it, on the hedge, under a big sycamore tree. There I spread my mackintosh and sat back against the trunk, books all round me. Often I had the cows for company: I used to feed them with the branches of choice leaves they couldn't reach up to. With the insatiable curiosity of cows (in that as in other respects so like the Cornish) they nuzzled at the mackintosh; and once, when I was away for a second, they pulled it right off the hedge, scattering books, papers and pencil in every direction. Mrs. Lewis, at the farm, used to see me on my way down, mackintosh trailing, and say that nothing would induce her to go down the fields and sit for hours on that snake- and rat-infested hedge. This didn't add to my confidence, but all the same the spot had a charm, and a mystery, for me.

The mystery was its name. When we played there as children it was called Lost Wood: all the boys of the village knew it by that name. But behind that name there was the shadow of another, by which I think my father and the older people at our end of the village knew it: Lost House. What could possibly be the explanation, I wondered. Which was its proper name, Lost Wood or Lost House? What was the story which the latter name suggested? Had there once been a house there, some habitation which had fallen into decay, become waste, its very site lost among the trees? There are few things more moving than the site of an old vanished house, with its potent memories, its suggestion of a once crowded life, the voices of children that are heard no more. Lost House was very silent now: there was only the murmur of summer leaves there. But perhaps that was why I always had the feeling that the place was waiting and watching — not that it was unfriendly, but that there were so many eyes looking out at me among the myriad tongues of the leaves. What did it mean?

There was the curious circumstance that connected my name with that shadow-name. (One knows well the fascination that one's own name can exercise upon one: a sort of hypnosis. Robert de Montesquieu's obsession comes to mind, and his saying, when ill: 'Je ne m'intéresse pas même dans mon propre nom.') The first time that the name Rowse appears in the parish registers of St. Austell — when they begin in the reign of Elizabeth — it appears as Le Rowse, or Lescowse, so I read in Hammond's history of the parish. Could there be any connection between Lost House and Lescowse? The first word 'Lost' would seem pretty clear: by analogy with Lostwithiel it would be the old Cornish word 'Lis', meaning court or palace. With this in mind, I summoned up courage to write to Henry Jenner, the venerable doyen of Cornish scholars, with the appearance of a patriarch, whom I, of course, had never met. (He was already the friend of the young Charles Henderson; and years later I was summoned to his death-bed — he looked like a Hebrew prophet with his magnificent profile and long white beard — to receive, in a manner, his blessing and the word to carry on the work, since Charles, on whom it should have rested, was already dead. His sister went with me: a sort of ceremonial laying of the mantle on my shoulders. But I had my own ideas as to the course I should pursue.)[1] However, Jenner replied very kindly to the unknown schoolboy, agreed that he, too, thought 'Lost' must be a corruption of 'Lis', and felt sure that 'House' must be a form of 'cowse' or 'coose', the Cornish word for 'wood'.

It was a curious story. For it looks to me now as if behind the English word 'wood', by which we knew the place, there lurked in the memories of the oldest village family, which we were, the shadow of the old Celtic name: a mere shell meaning nothing to us since the death of the language, but of which the English word was the translation. But whose was the 'lis' that had been there? The word 'lis' always referred to the court, the 'place' of some personage, as at Liskeard or Lostwithiel. Is it possible, I wonder now, that that was the site of the house of the original family that owned the village, in the dim past beyond which no man has any remembrance, of that Cunedwith whose name Charles Henderson thought was perpetuated in the name of the village? How it came to be part of the manor of Treverbyn in the hands of the Courtenays there is no knowing; presumably when the original family died out. All this is purely imaginative reconstruction, for no records remain of so small a place from so remote a time. But it was a good site for a 'place': the stream ran freshly, vigorously by it, through those fields, by those trees where in the hot summer nights the nightjar croaked and in winter the owls hooted. I could never explain its hold upon me; perhaps some very remote thread from the past held me to it. I longed to be rich and buy it: there would I build my house, I determined. But when the time came I found my house elsewhere, on the sea-coast; and no one of our name remains now in the village. For all that, I think I have done it justice in my mind and that my name will not go unconnected with it into the future.

Here is one of the Lost House poems, written in May 1921:

---

[1] It is pleasant to record, since writing the above, that the Royal Institution of Cornwall has awarded me the Jenner Medal, founded in his memory, for my historical work, particularly *Tudor Cornwall*. So that the ceremony that day by the old patriarch's deathbed had its effect. In a sense it may be said that Henry Jenner won.

Lost House: another place that I have found
   Wherein to dream and be at rest, a nook
Of leafy quiet, where great elms abound,
   Lifting their heads aloft as if to look
Into the depths of heaven; above me sways
   In the soft noon breeze, a canopy of leaves,
And ever and anon the sun's bright rays
   Glint through the green, printing upon the eaves
And moss-grown roof of the old cattle-shed
   Their flickering, laughing kisses. O'er the grass
The dappled plots of shadow-leaves are spread,
   Where sinuous waves and long-drawn ripples pass,
Repass and merge, as o'er a moorland lake
At night-fall, when the moorland winds awake.

There are several such poems from this time: not exciting, but no worse than the worst Wordsworth. And there are many more verses, all faithfully entered into the Diary. I didn't get any encouragement at home. I find a note that on reading one of these poems to mother, a Rupert Brookeish piece about the things I loved (all very pastoral), her only comment was: 'Gid along — taakin' up all that time to write a few little ole verses.' One can hardly suppose oneself to have been spoiled by an admiring family. When, years later, after my illness in 1938 I came upon this and read the poem to her again, she thought it 'do sound very nice'. She must have become reconciled, after so much poetry in the interval! According to a note, she went on to explain that when I was always 'writing away' she thought I 'ought to be workin'', i.e. tending shop, chopping sticks, helping with the house-work, etc., and as a concession, or an excuse, she adds: 'I didn' knaw I should 'ave such a clever son.' The poor old dear, at over seventy, appears at last broken in to this oddity (anything but an angel) in the house.

Encouragement or no encouragement, it made no difference to my going on trying to write poetry. My attitude to that was deliberate, determined, *voulu*. It was not like that of my young relation, who came to live with us when his father died. He wrote a poem when quite young at school, much younger than I, and a very good poem, and was content to leave it at that, a flash in the pan. I was determined to go on, disappointed as I was almost always with what I wrote. In the absence of anybody to help or encourage, I made my own attachment to the Irish school of poets. It was rather pathetic. I thought of Dublin as a kind of Mecca, and would go up in the garden sometimes in the evenings and look over the hedge where the rose-bay willow-herb grew, up the green slope of the Doctor's field to the edge of the skyline, where the sky in the north-west was turning a strange shade, half-green, half-blue, and say to myself: 'There is Ireland.' The word, repeated several times, had a hypnotic effect. By this time I was reading some modern poetry in the anthologies *Poems of To-day* and Methuen's *Modern Verse*, and in the *London Mercury*. And what I liked most were the poems of Yeats (these were the early Yeats), of Padraic Colum and James Stephens, and, among English poets, Robert Bridges and Walter de la Mare. My taste was forming itself, for these were the poets who spoke to something in me.

But there was a more serious antinomy for me ahead than that between poetry and my mother's idea of what I should be doing with my time. As the time drew near for me to be taking my examinations and trying for scholarships at the University, I find my Diary expressing the fear that the pressure of school work would make it impossible for me to devote any time to writing poetry. I was terribly afraid that I would get out of practice. And in fact, in my last year at school, 1921-22, I wrote very much less verse: there was no time to; I was very hard-worked. That antinomy was repeated later at Oxford, both as undergraduate and when I became a Research Fellow of my College. As an undergraduate I was deflected into taking the History School, instead of English Literature, as I intended. It meant so much harder work, so much leeway to catch up in reading, that I dared not devote much of my time to poetry. And again, later, when as a Research Fellow I was immersed in the drudgery of gathering original materials for history, and such time as I could spare in vacation I wasted upon the idiot people in the field of politics, it meant that poetry — which was the dearest interest of my mind, the touchstone of my mind's life — had to take second place to drudgery in time, though it always had first place in my emotions.

But that is another story. So much for the most intimate concern of my mind. There was much else going along on the surface, in addition to my school work; for example, a great deal of miscellaneous reading. The headmaster, with his *Daily Telegraph* almost *Morning Post* mind, introduced me to Kipling. He was rather surprised at my never having read any of him. A batch of his books were ordered for the school library, and I read *Kim*, the *Jungle Books*, *Puck of Pook's Hill*, *Stalky and Co.*, and others with great enjoyment. But he did not appeal in the inner way that some authors did to me. Hardy, for instance, was from the first a great experience and his sombre view of life had a deep influence on me. With my temperament, adolescence was a disturbing and over-emotionalized affair; I was very prone to moodiness and ups and downs of elation and depression. I had no reason to take a cheerful view of my future; everything would have to be achieved by my own effort, with no help from home: with a strenuous programme of examinations and scholarships before me, I was already under a sense of strain. The combination of poetry and pessimism in Hardy was irresistible: it was exactly what I felt about life. From that time I have always loved him with a personal love that I have felt for no other author.

There were other writers whom I was specially drawn to; one's affective choices both reveal and help to form one's personality. For example, I admired, I felt akin to, the Brontës as against Jane Austen, whom I did not appreciate. I was certainly not a Janeite — unlike some of my later friends contemporaneously at their schools — David Cecil at Eton, Richard Pares at Winchester, both devoted Janeites. That difference between us tells a lot; it was very natural; the Brontës were essentially poets in their attitude to experience. Or rather, perhaps, it was the difference between Beethoven and Mozart. Q. and R.L.S. I was always reading with pleasure: they both had special places in my heart. I was immensely struck by Nathaniel Hawthorne (also quite right); that particular quality of nostalgia, not merely for the past, was one which I shared; there was something else, too, hidden in his temperament which spoke to mine: I understood intuitively that sense of evil springing out of an emotional nature under the strain of Puritan repression.

From my Diary I find I was reading Renan's *Poetry of the Celtic Races*, Verlaine, stories of Anatole France; Rupert Brooke, Santayana,

Dickens, Edward FitzGerald. One day, when I was reading Turgeniev, I dreamed at night about Jesuits. On New Year's Eve 1920 I was reading alone in the kitchen Colonel Repington's *War Diary*, my hair standing on end at the levity and frivolity of his circle in London while hundreds of thousands of men were being killed on the Western Front. The bells from the church-tower, ringing out the old year, came up over the hill-side. I went out into the cold night for a moment; there were the subdued voices of one or two of the villagers in the shadows; the matron of the Scattered Home for Children opposite looked out of her lighted bedroom window and wished me a Happy New Year (she was kind to me then: politics had not yet come in to poison this relation, as so many others). I went in, back to my book, and to bed in the early hours of the morning. Later I read Gilbert Murray's *Stoic Philosophy*, which opened my eyes wide to the intellectual questionings I was already beginning to feel about religion. I was ready for such an impulse, and the little book had a corresponding effect: it acted as a precipitate.

Among my greatest pleasures were the tramps which I was now regularly taking across the countryside alone, sometimes with friends. They were also an unconscious preparation for the historian, observing the lie of the land and invariably making for the churches or any other object of historic interest. I had now struck up a sort of friendship in the Sixth Form with a lad called Mander, who had joined our lot later in the school and stuck out as an oddity. He wore pince-nez; he was the child of an old man, an educated man, who had married his nurse — an ill-assorted pair; the old father was dying of cancer. Mander had an odd jerky way of speaking; he spoke an educated English with no trace of Cornish accent; he was superior and as such unpopular, aggressively on the defensive, eyes burning and dancing rapidly with anger. He was a curiosity, extremely High Church, played the organ at St. Mary's, Par, for ever pressing his amenable vicar into further extremities, such as burning incense in a converted tin, and altogether alienating more and more of the already exiguous congregation. With my Anglo-Catholic sympathies, I envied these amenities; Mander and I were inevitably drawn together. In this curious relation he took the lead: he was rather older than I, he had the advantage of a more educated home, he had a tame vicar on the lead, a church in which he did as he liked, and he was very impulsive and headstrong, more so even than I, and with no sense of caution at all. I was at bottom a little uncertain of him; but I was prepared to go along with him a good deal of the way, and, with little real affection on either side, we joggled along till he left.

To him I owed several interesting tramps at this time: he was more of an organizer than I was. He took me on a long walk to Boconnoc, most splendid of Cornish parks, with its great beeches and oaks, its memories of medieval Courtenays, Mohuns, Pitts, Fortescues. For me, my head was full of the Civil War and my Diary of historical notes about the place, for it was the King's headquarters in the campaign of 1644, whence the surrender of Essex's army was brought about; there is a note for a story about a boy who warned the King to sleep in his coach because of an attempt to be made on his life. We ate our lunch beside the running water not far from the house, and trudged along the splendid straight drive across Bradock Down where the battle was fought, Hopton and Bevil Grenville against Ruthven, in 1643. Everywhere we explored the churches, and seem to have enjoyed playing the organ and trying on the parson's vestments.

Another day, accompanied by Mander's vicar, we walked from Bodmin out across the moor to Blisland, sweet grey granite village around its beech-strewn green, the church with its painted screens and images a sanctuary of Anglo-Catholicism. The parson asked us all to tea in that comfortable low dining-room with its exquisite view over the valley with its trout-stream and the woods beyond. There was honey for tea; but not even this reconciled me to the occasion: I was acutely self-conscious of not being with my own people, angry at my nervousness, the signs of a social inferiority-complex which persisted with me for years. We walked back to Bodmin to find the last bus and train gone and had to face, already tired, the prospect of another fourteen miles home. I elected to go with them for company by the Lostwithiel route, which added another four miles. From St. Blazey onwards, where I dropped them, I went on alone, too tired out to be nervous of the dark woods of Tregrehan, past the Lodge, where I could see a warm light in granny's bedroom, to arrive home at midnight, the key thrown down from mother's window upstairs.

There were prefects' picnics, too, which involved long tramps, organized by the new senior mistress, Miss Griffiths, a Welsh woman with a good French accent. One day we all walked together from Fowey across that lovely coast to Polperro, through Lansallos. I was appointed guide to the party, took a wrong turning once above Polruan, recovered myself and spent most of the day in conversation with Miss Griffiths. The little Ebenezer chapel at Lansallos, dated 1852, outside which we ate our pasties and sandwiches, excited my novelistic curiosity: I imagined the generations of country people, farmers and their stalwart sons and daughters, sitting Sunday after Sunday in those high-backed pews. It was not until our return that evening and crossing the river by the Polruan Ferry that I learned that the large house by the waterside was 'The Haven' itself, where Q. lived. Always after that, whenever I spent an afternoon at Fowey, I walked by that house with reverence and veneration. There used to be a large sponge placed out upon the window of the bathroom upstairs (a good deal of the house you could see into from the street). I think I paid to that sponge the vicarious worship which Sir Charles Oman told me he found the citizens of Hanover paying to the cream horses of the old royal family at Herrenhausen, in the absence of the dynasty. Q. himself I had never so much as seen.

At other times, making a habit of my passion, I walked alone to Luxulyan and the Valley, sometimes on to Lanlivery and Lostwithiel, immersed in my dream of the seventeenth century. There was a young fellow, an architect, a little older than I, whose family had come to the village and for whom I had a romantic *schwärmerei*: I took him to these favourite haunts; I remember now his telling me the name of the hembagrimony which grows along the road out of the valley to Lanlivery and upon which the Red Admirals feed. My older friend, T. C. Bennett, took me on a tramp home from Truro, going down first along the river to Malpas, crossing over the ferry where Tristram crossed to find Iseult awaiting him on the other bank, and so into the deep woods of Lamorran. Here my companion paddled in a cool rivulet: I was too shy to do that, and trudged the more weary on to Tregony and tea in the inn and writing verses in the innkeeper's book. I wonder what has become of them now? Ah, those delicious summer days of my youth, when the senses were never so keen, and one walked in a trance of summer scents and white dust on the roads, clear streams and the illimitable prospects of the future — alluring, veiled, unknown.

Or I would, on a rich November day (November 6th, 1920 — just twenty-one years ago to-day), walk out to Tregrehan, as in childhood but now a youth of seventeen and, with all my successes and prizes at school, held in some respect by granny and grandfather: the only one of her innumerable grandchildren of whom the old lady stood in any awe. The clearings in the woods were blue and purple; the tops of the trees lit up with gold. Granny and grandfather were having tea in their large kitchen; and after tea I got them to tell me scraps of the old songs which they, like Auntie and Uncle, used to sing in days gone by. Granny:

> Old 'uman Whiddle-Whaddle jumped out o' bed
> And out of the window she popped her head,
> Saying 'Run John, Run John, the grey goose is gone,
> And the fox is run out of the town — O.'

Grandfather:

> Farmers with their breeches on
>   Their boots filled up with straw;
> Miners with their pick and gad
>   An' powder for to blaw.
>
> The more the miners sing,
>   The more they fill their quarts;
> The more the sailors sink,
>   The more the achin' hearts.

Such were the verses the old pair remembered for me; I think it pleased them that I was interested and wanted to write them down. Some were very fragmentary; but it was wonderful what they could call to mind from that previous age when folk had to provide their own entertainment.

I too provided my own entertainments. I find my Diary recording my first French conversation, a long talk with a Breton onion-seller all the way into town: he told me about his service in the army, and I told him of my brother's, and added, of the Germans, 'Ce sont des bêtes.'

I showed him my donkey in the field as we passed. He understood what I said, and I understood him; I was greatly elated with this success. Mixed up with this, there is a fierce outburst against having been made to take somebody's luggage to the station in the donkey-jingle one Whit Monday: did father think I was a porter, etc.? The money with which I was rewarded for my sullen submission — I never spoke a word to the people in question all the way in — I flung on the floor as soon as I got home: I wouldn't have kept it for anything. My day was ruined; that sort of humiliation left a deep mark in my attitude to my father. My mother explained subsequently that he used to think I was lazy! It was true that I had developed a technique of keeping out of his way. I used to think, and say, that 'if he couldn't find something for me to do, he'd *make* something'. He had no conception in fact of what I was doing with my time, with all this reading and writing. Sometimes I would bring my beloved Diary, my refuge, up into the kitchen, and write down under their noses the conversation that went on round the kitchen-fire with their visitors and cronies. I find several such conversations faithfully reported: they did not object when I told them afterwards — like sitting for their photographs. But it was useful literary practice, and led directly to my subsequent habit of endless pocket-books, the series 'The Book of Life'.

For our second Speech-day after the War the headmaster decided that we should do a Shakespeare play, and chose *Twelfth Night*, in which I was to be Malvolio. After a few ineffective beginnings with one of the women on the staff he took the thing in hand himself, gave us a good shaking up, and electrified us with his demands and expectations. It had a prodigious effect on me; it was a revelation. I had often enough had a child's part in some childish pageant or spectacle at church Sunday School. But this was Shakespeare, the first time I had seen Shakespeare treated as anything but a text to pass examinations in, and I had an adult part to play. I was very self-conscious at the demands made on me, and then, entering into the spirit of it, found myself growing into the part. It was a new and thrilling experience: I find my Diary here voluble with pleasure — the fun of trying on my costume when it arrived, mainly black with gold braid and white ruffles at the wrist, which I thought very fetching. There was the entertainment of the rehearsals growing to a pitch of excitement as the performance drew near. In the last lap I had a cold and stayed at home for a few days, which brought many anxious inquiries from the headmaster and staff. (I had been helping out during a 'flu epidemic by teaching at school for three weeks, which I thoroughly enjoyed, but it ended by wearing me out, and my Diary has for the first time the entry 'Unwell—a new experience for me' — an experience which was to become all too familiar as the years went on.) The headmaster sent along a deputation of prefects to see me and find out what really was the matter; all sorts of rumours were about and he was afraid for the performance. I thoroughly enjoyed all the fuss. Mander, however, did not come: 'It might be something infectious, you know', one of the prefects reported, and added: 'If that's Mander's friendship . . .' I began to talk hurriedly about something else; but in fact I was hurt.

I emerged from this retirement — partly due to a cold, partly over-work and precautionary stage-fright — to a triumph in the performance. It was indubitably *my* play. The fact was that the character of Mal-volio answered to something in me: the pride, the loyalty, frustration, defeat. As early as that I saw my own life in that light. Perhaps it was a very adolescent way of seeing it. I took the part seriously, as a tragic one; I felt its pathos. Sir Toby's question: 'Dost thou think, because thou art virtuous, there shall be no more cakes and ale?' went to the root of the matter. Other people had their fun; not so me: for me there was the ceaseless strain of effort, ambition, work for distant objectives. In a dim, unconscious way — or perhaps not so dimly — the boy who played the part of Sir Toby felt the point of the question, too, addressed as it was against my view of life as well as Malvolio's. It gave a real twist of feeling to the situation. But my sense of the pathos of Malvolio's character carried the day: the auctioneer's wife declared that never had she seen Malvolio played so sympathetically. I, of course, had never seen him played at all and could not have con-ceived of him in any other light. It was a performance which, I have found, people remember in the district.

That kind of success, whether in examinations or winning prizes for essays or publishing poems, I needed to carry me on; though I might not have desisted even without such encouragement, the way would have been too lonely and depressing. The excitement over the play carried me along for a bit; I find pasted in my Diary the programme for the performance, which mother had proudly kept, and the love-letter, smeared with grease-paint, with which Malvolio was baited. Olivia was played by Noreen Sweet, a girl a year or two younger than I, whose acquaintance I thus made. Next year, I find a copy of gay verses inscribed to her under the title of 'The Tragic Muse': the Muse we called her, a nickname of mine. Afterwards she became perhaps the closest of all my friends going back to schooldays, and certainly the most remarkable, and distinguished, of the girls produced from the school.

But as yet my friends were among the older girls, especially two who were now leaving to go to college, one at Exeter, the other at Truro. With these I exchanged immensely long and effusive letters. There was another girl, who had now left the school for another, for whom I entertained a callow feeling. It came to no more than a cold, wet kiss exchanged under my Uncle's lilac-tree (another lilac-tree from the one at the farm). Whenever I think of this episode, I think of Alissa in Gide's *La Porte Etroite*, that story of frustrated love, coming out into the dark garden saying: 'Est-ce toi, Jérome? Est-ce toi?'

I have said nothing about examinations, for their real importance was only in so far as success justified my going on at school and gave me encouragement and confidence. I passed my School Certificate with first-class honours, and distinctions in English at one time and History at another. But my friendship with Mander had a curious consequence. The Sixth Form, a small body of eight or so, was to take the London Matriculation. Mander used to come to school telling me how he was getting up at six o'clock in the morning to swot Latin grammar and mathematics, which we were weak in. I began to get quite worried and think I had better do something about it, too. Much as I loathed getting up in the mornings — an inability from which I have always suffered, along with many of the great and good — I began to get up to work, too, before breakfast. I started at seven; and then, as Mander's reports became more and more impressive, I got up at half-past six, then at six, and finally at half-past five. It was very bleak, sitting huddled in the sitting-room, a greatcoat round my knees, trying to staunch the gaps in my Latin and mathematics. All that I remember of the examination was that I did a very good essay, with which I was pleased, on Dickens.

But there was an odd sequel. One Sunday morning, after church, the headmaster came round to the vestry with the news that I had got through in the first Division, while all the others had been ploughed. The mystery to me was what had happened to Mander? It did not strike me until much later, such was my innocence, that he was by no means so wholly addicted to work as he had given me to suppose: he had quite an eye for the girls. However, his rivalry had been useful; without it I should never have got up to work before breakfast.

Meanwhile, village life was not without its excitements. There were two murders within half a mile of us. The first was of a little lad about seven who had been born in Back Lane, just behind our house. He had been lured away one evening up on the downs by an ugly lout of fifteen or so, of a difficult and abnormal temperament given to mischief, who, tired of his life, wanted somebody to accompany him out of it. So he murdered the lad, whom we knew well as a baby, and threw the body and himself into a lonely disused clay pit full of water. A great suspense hung over the village for days — search-parties, dragging of pools, and so on, until they were found. Then, some time later, a man at Lane End poisoned his wife. She was a woman of gallant spirit, who had borne a difficult life nobly: had been a teacher, with an adoptive daughter; hers was a story for a novel. Later in life she married a man much younger than herself, an insurance agent, who poisoned her slowly. It was a pitiful affair. The man was a member of the church choir, also a St. John's ambulance man; and I remember one evening when we were coming home together alone up the dark lane his saying that he knew the spot in my body which he had only to put his hand on for two minutes and he could kill me. I felt a certain uncomfortable thrill.

Next door, the tragic family life by the side of which we lived all my childhood and youth in the village was proceeding to its melancholy conclusion.

CHAPTER IX

GETTING TO OXFORD

THE headmaster had it in mind that I should go up to Oxford, or at any rate to some University. In that he determined my fate, for I did not know what was to become of me: it did not seem that I should be able to go to University College, Exeter, into which at most a few of the more intelligent scholars from our school had percolated. My people hadn't the money even for that; it was very aggravating to stand by and watch much less successful schoolfellows go off to Exeter, or even to London, while I didn't know that I would ever be able to go at all. It didn't improve my temper at home. I was very morose about my station in life and my prospects at this time — until in fact the way was clear. And then illness, after so much anxiety and effort, filled the foreground; so I had even less time for enjoyment after than before. However, that belongs to the Oxford part of my story.

Something about my work, perhaps the combination of firsts in examinations with writing poetry and winning prizes for essays, decided the headmaster at this time that I should try for Oxford. He was an Oxford man himself, and his brother, killed in the War, had been a distinguished scientist, a Fellow of Exeter. After some preliminary inquiries of that college, it was decided that I should go up the very next month (March 1921) and sit for their English scholarship. I wasn't expected to get it; I was much too young. It was simply by way of getting 'to know the ropes' — that was the phrase. But indeed I owe everything to that first attempt; for little as Oxford meant to me up till then, I fell in love with the place from that moment, and after that nothing counted with me compared with the desire to get there. My headmaster fulfilled the same role in my life as Emlyn Williams's schoolmistress in his play *The Corn is Green*. (Emlyn Williams and I were to arrive at the same college, Christ Church, within a year of each other, and both had rooms in Meadow Buildings.)

There was the further difficulty, in addition to my not knowing the ways of scholarship examinations, that the headmaster himself wasn't

at all clear about the steps necessary to get a boy who had absolutely
no funds of his own to the University. No one from our school had
ever got a University scholarship, or ever gone to Oxford or Cambridge. And in those days it was much more difficult than it has subsequently become. I should need to win three scholarships to cover
the whole cost of my going to Oxford—a minimum of £200 a year.
This was my first try.

The whole thing was a bit of a rush. For a month I was faithful to
my resolution not to write up my Diary, while I worked hard. On
the very eve of going there is an outburst about the shop:

> 'Father has just come home from work, with a sore head as
> usual; is grumbling at present because I neglected to ask the baker
> the price of flour — as if I cared for the damned price of flour!
> It's bad enough to have to remember to ask the price of lard. I
> don't care a scrap for these little details, which keeping a half-
> penny shop entails. I hate the shop.'

That made a good set-off for leaving home and prevented me from
being too sentimental, though it was the first time that I had ever
crossed the Tamar into England. I was to stay with my headmaster's
sister-in-law's charwoman in a little red-brick working-class street
called Hayfield Road at the extreme limit of North Oxford, beside
the canal. It was the country of Flecker's poem:

When you have wearied of the valiant spires of this County Town,
Of its wide white streets and glistening museums, and black monastic
  walls,
Of its red motors and lumbering trams, and self-sufficient people,
I will take you walking with me to a place you have not seen —
Half town and half country — the land of the Canal.

Later I wrote a poem on those lines, though what has become of it,
I don't know.

There I was completely comfortable, as I should not have been
stopping with the too superior. Good Mrs. Colman supported the
household on her own shoulders, going out every day and all day to
work and bringing back parcels of washing to occupy her at home;
she had a ne'er-do-well husband, whose chief occupation was drink,

though for the rest he was not a bad man—merely not grown up; and she spoiled him like the boy at over fifty he essentially was. It was a situation I was used to: not unlike that next door at home. I recall how she looked: her head all curling-pins, beady black eyes like a frightened rabbit looking out upon the world. Mrs. Colman had no children, and took to me; together we went down once or twice to St. Barnabas to high, very high, evensong, or perhaps compline. To me, with my head in a dream all those days, it was Hardy's 'ceremonial church of St. Silas'. The service I thought 'pleasant', the architecture of 'a disagreeable Italian style'.

Oxford, on its first impact, was too much for me. The first morning in Exeter Hall I could not write for looking round at the Jacobean screen with painted armorial bearings, the walls hung with portraits of the eminent—wigs, lawn-sleeves, ribbons, garters. Some, I noticed with pride and envy, were westcountrymen. Never had I been in such surroundings; never had I had such difficulty in concentrating in an examination before. Unfortunately it was the essay paper that morning, and a most uncongenial subject: 'Has the development of material civilization been accompanied by a corresponding increase in human happiness?' What a subject for a lad of seventeen! How was I to know? I answered an emphatic NO. Perhaps my No would be less emphatic now; I might even answer 'Yes'. I had the greatest difficulty in putting down what I wanted to say. I was quite clear that it was the worst essay I had ever written.

After that the other papers went better. On the Friday afternoon, those of us who were left took a paper in a lecture-room looking out upon the lovely Fellows' Garden, very green and quiet, the Bodleian on one side, the Radcliffe Camera appearing behind the trees at the end. That serene and exquisite scene, the heart of Oxford, made a great impression on me, and on returning I wrote a triolet about it. It is now my view from the other side, from All Souls. In the evenings I went about the streets of the city, sight-seeing in a daze, with a boy from Truro, older than I, son of a parson, who greatly impressed me: he seemed 'to have read everything from Montaigne and Pascal to Bernard Shaw'.

One evening, we arrived at Christ Church as the bells were ringing for Cathedral service; blue shadows were winding themselves in and out the doorways of the great quadrangle; a few white surplices flitted by in the twilight; the lights began to come out here and there. This magnificence, we decided, was too much to hope for. But at the very moment of that precautionary thought I had the curious presentiment suggesting — what if one day it should be my luck to come here? In that moment I felt a sensation of quasi-certainty, which I dared not entertain seriously, that I should. It was very Cornish.

At the end of the examination I was given a brief *viva* by an elderly don who asked if I played games and guffawed when I said 'No'. On my last day there was a visit from the Queen, who was receiving an honorary degree. The Broad was packed with people, but I got a very good view of her coming out of the Sheldonian accompanied by Lord Curzon, very splendid as Chancellor. In that crowd all unknown to me was Charles Henderson, an undergraduate in his first year, who was to become my great friend in later years: in his diary he describes the scene outside the Sheldonian that day. The afternoon I spent burrowing in the bookshops, and bought myself Arnold's *Essays in Criticism*, Wilde's *De Profundis*, and two volumes of the unreadable Emerson. They are unread to this day.

I did not get the scholarship, but the headmaster got a report on my work from the Senior Tutor. Apparently I was the youngest candidate in; my essay was too dogmatic, my opinions considered too forceful for my age. In fact my dogmatism was due to all-round immaturity. Great indignation is registered by me in my Diary, along with resolutions to tone down my views. There was this consolation, had I known it, that my work had clearly made an impression, if an unfavourable one. There is the further reflection that that reaction on the part of the Senior Tutor represented an out-of-date attitude at Oxford, as I was to learn in subsequent years, both as undergraduate and don. Younger Fellows were interested in expressions of opinion by scholarship candidates, and didn't hold it against them if they themselves didn't agree. The attitude has quite changed in my time. And the joke of it is that I gathered R. R. Marett was the Senior Tutor in question, the most dogmatic man in Oxford. In time I have come to appreciate *his* dogmatism: it has a charm all its own.[1]

[1] cf. my review of his autobiography, *A Jerseyman at Oxford*, *New Statesman*, September 27th, 1941.

But this failure never prejudiced me in any way against Exeter, unlike Birkenhead's grudge against Eton for not electing him to a scholarship: not even Alington's assuring him that it was Eton's failure would pacify him. My attempt at Exeter fixed that college in my mind as my objective, to which I held through all the efforts of the next year. And though it was ultimately my fate to go elsewhere, by the accident of a scholarship, connections of friendship have always bound me to Exeter both as undergraduate and as Fellow of another college; in addition to the natural westcountry loyalty which has always made me look upon myself as an honorary Exeter man.

Back from this glimpse of Paradise, I plunged once more into my usual routine — school, house, shop, church. I discovered the delights of playing mixed hockey. At school the boys didn't play hockey; so I got up scratch teams of boys and girls on Saturday afternoons when there was nothing else to do and played with rapturous enthusiasm and unrewarded ambition, until finally it was discouraged, I think by the miserable women on the staff. My Diary mentions early church and sausages for breakfast: there is a jejune Kilvert-like passage describing the burnished silver of the bay that Easter morning, a few dark clouds about, the breeze from the moors across the dew-wet fields, the church-bells ringing, birds piping in the bushes on my way to church: Easter twenty years ago!

I was deeply moved by an article in the *Round Table* on 'The Passing of Woodrow Wilson': I read its conclusion over and over with tears, and copied it out in my Diary. Ironical to read now, after all we know of the Harding régime, that on Wilson's defeat 'speculators are already buying property in Washington in the belief that the City of Magnificent Distances will once more become the social centre of America under the courtly and benevolent direction of President Harding and his wife'. Harding's benevolence proved to be exerted in quite another direction. Really, the American governing class and their instrument, the Republican Party, have no more to be proud of than the English governing classes and the Conservative Party in the period between the two wars. But now that in later years I have come to know almost all the *Round Table* group, so closely associated with All Souls, I wonder who wrote that article that so moved the schoolboy: was it John Dove? or perhaps Philip Kerr?[1]

Family life went on unchanged. I had got used to my loneliness in the bosom of it as if I were an only child—the consequence of being so much younger than my brother and sister. Hilda had left home when about seventeen or eighteen to become half-lady's-maid, half-governess, to a Mrs. Thomas Peter at Perran-ar-worthal. It was not more than seventeen miles away, but to us it might have been Peking. It was the first breach in the family, and the day she went away we turned our chairs to the wall and cried all day. For days the house had a funeral atmosphere. And indeed it was a turning-point—the end of her life at home. There was nobody to spoil me now. She had another charge—a pretty, elf-like child with lovely hair, called Nancy Peter, about my age, who danced with the prettiest grace. The doings and ways of 'Miss Nancy' became a property of ours: we were proud of having a share in her. Once when they took a house at Carbis Bay for the summer, Hilda invited mother and me down for the day, and I was allowed the privilege of playing for an hour with this little girl with the wonderful, long hair and fairy appearance. I wonder what has become of her now?

After this Hilda took a job with a Baroness Bouck. I remember the Sunday morning when the Baroness, then staying in Cornwall, called in her motor-car: the jammed and never-used front door was specially opened for her; I was kept out of the way. My sister did not stay long with these foreigners. After a spell near Kettering with a Mrs. Thurburn, looking after another exquisite upper-class daughter with an exquisite upper-class name, Rosemary, Hilda came back to Cornwall with the beginning of the War and went to live with one of the Dorrien-Smith daughters at the hospitable, friendly Tresco Abbey in the Scilly Islands. There she was treated with the greatest kindness and consideration, and remained the whole period of the War.

That had its excitements, for the Scilly Islands were a rendezvous for German submarines. Innumerable ships were torpedoed within sight of the islands; strange cargoes were constantly coming ashore:

[1] I learn that it was by Whitney Shepardson, an American Rhodes Scholar of great ability.

one ship had a large consignment of sewing-machines, and in consequence islanders were able to set up grand new sewing-machines in the home. Then from one high cliff you could look down into deep water and see a cargo of golden maize lying there; at another time barrels of lard rolled in upon the beaches. Such and still more fantastic were the stories we heard of war-time in the Scilly Islands. Mother and I were invited over; but I think nothing would have induced us to face that passage — our minds, if not the seas, infested with German submarines. More terrifying to my sister — for in fact the Germans never attacked the little steamer, the *Lady of the Isles* — was the inevitable sea-sickness of those horrid upheaved crossings where all the tides and currents meet. The Dorrien-Smith ladies were never ill: they had been used to the sea since childhood, and made nothing of going across to St. Mary's and catching the little boat, whatever the weather. Just as well when your home is an island: you might otherwise wait for weeks.

My sister travelled to London each year with them, but we saw very little of her. I remember in those years of war-time scarcity, 1917 and 1918, the welcome presents of food that came across from those friendly islands: the delicious tomatoes — never have I tasted such tomatoes as they grow on Scilly — the lobsters already cooked for us, occasionally a rich crab, a fat rabbit. At that time, in spite of the shop, which meant that we did not go short of sugar and tinned stuff, we were hard put to it for variety in diet. The flour was so bad in 1917; it was dark and unappetizing, frequently musty. Mother tried to disguise it by making cocoa and coffee buns, till we were sick of them. I have sometimes wondered whether my digestive troubles weren't partly due to that war-time diet.

Then a Royal Naval Air Squadron was based upon Tresco to help tackle the submarine menace. One day there was an explosion on the beach: some fool had hit the detonator of a depth-charge on the head. Two men were killed and several injured. The women of the house rushed to the scene with pillow-cases, towels, bandages. It was a bad moment. Then there were the concerts and dances for the men marooned in this remote, but not wholly unenjoyable, spot. Here my sister met her future husband. She was married at his home at Reading; his father had a business there as a cabinet-maker, in which the sons were brought up. They rejoiced in the name of Cattermole. Later when the War ended she brought her baby home and stayed for a month or two before joining him at Reading. Naturally I had long lost first place in her affections. But I did not expect the outburst of maternal fury when I came home from visiting my friend, the income-tax inspector, with 'flu on me, and gave it to the baby.

I remember the fearful weakness of body and mind on recovering from that visitation: it was the 'flu epidemic of the last year of the War which carried off thousands of people — in one case near us both parents, leaving a family of small children. I went to bed a fat and strong-looking boy, and got up a lean and gaunt adolescent. My mother wept. I remember acutely the sensation that overcame me one afternoon at the kitchen table at tea: the weak, wan light appearing for a few instants around the corner of the thick ivy upon Uncle's shop, the feeling of listlessness, the emptiness, the sense of being on the edge of things, mixed up with some other existence which I had been reading about. In other words, the well-known feeling of convalescence; but in my case fused with what I have come to call aesthetic experience, the sense of life passing under another, less temporal, aspect. In that strange moment I was not unhappy.

My sister left with her baby to join her husband and cross the Atlantic to try their fortunes in America. They have been there ever since — without a fortune, on the outermost rim of our family horizon.

My brother's career was not dissimilar. Three years after Hilda left home he left too, for a job in London with an old-fashioned firm of wholesale merchants, John Howell's, in St. Paul's Churchyard. He was only sixteen; the lads of the firm were paid a mere pittance and lodged together in an annexe in Wardrobe Place: I suppose theirs were the conditions of old-fashioned apprenticeship. I imagined mistakenly the place where they lodged going back to the Wardrobe of the medieval kings. I had visions of my brother making his fortune in business in the City, like Dick Whittington, or Sir William Treloar among the tale of Cornishmen who have 'made good' in London. Not so my brother. At eighteen he went into the army and, being classed B2 owing to his sight, was put on the land, which was much more to his taste. He went tractor-ploughing in Dorset, near Lyme Regis, and there — in Hardy's country — picked up a girl, in the normal way. The course of that affair ran true to Hardy.

Upon the Armistice George went with the Army of Occupation to Germany, was stationed at Düren, where he was quite happy and comfortable. Like others of our uneducated, he liked the Germans and got on well with them. The defeated enemy, particularly the women, made up to the British Tommies. The usual things happened, the landlady where he was billeted taking the opportunity of her husband's absence to come into the young Englishman's bedroom. (The horror of the German *Frau*! I quite agree with Henry VIII in that respect. I've always thought Anne of Cleves sufficient justification for the execution of Thomas Cromwell.) My brother quite enjoyed himself.

On demobilization he came home for a bit. I longed for an understanding with him: he had now the prestige of experience, of being grown up, of London, Germany, the War. There was no understanding. I waited about pathetically to be taken some notice of. I even volunteered to take him, a sign of great confidence, to the beloved Luxulyan Valley. We went. I do not think he saw anything special about the place. We had a quarrel about coming back. There was the choice of walking back the way we had come, the shortest and most direct; or we could walk two or three miles out of our way in the (faint) hope of catching a train at Par. If we did the latter, and there was no train, it would about double the distance we should have to walk. My brother insisted, against my better judgment, on doing the latter: it was just like the quarrels of our childhood over again — he five years older, I with fifteen years more sense. I gave way. We walked miles out of our way, and of course there was no train. We had another four miles to walk in pitch darkness, uphill, rain coming on. After that, I never addressed him another word; I walked like fury — after all, gone were the years of physical disparity. He arrived quite worn out, which wouldn't have happened if he had followed my advice, and swore that he would never go for a long tramp with me again. He was never invited to.

The next time he came home complete with girl, whom I did my best to like, but failed. After their marriage, they came again before leaving for Australia. It was, it seemed to me, a very questionable venture to marry a tricksy girl, and on top of that to embark on the gamble of taking up a block of land and clearing it for corn-growing in the speculative wheat-belt of Western Australia. The sort of enterprise, or combination of enterprises, that I with a more impulsive temperament, but greater caution, would never have dreamed of undertaking. They were very sure of each other. They went to early Communion together for the last time in our church before leaving next day. Father and I went to the station to see them off. Coming back over the railway-bridge, I said to him: 'Do you think it will be all right?': I had had that same inexplicable intuition which I had had with Miss Blank's marriage. It was a failure.

After more experience of life I have come to the conclusion, when I think of that frightful walk to Luxulyan, that failed venture, that it is a mistake to defer to other people's judgment, even in matters concerning themselves and their own well-being: other people never know so well as one does oneself. But when I think of the early impressions made upon my mind by these marriages, reinforced by others no less unfortunate later, it goes some way to explain, if not wholly, the savagery of the poems about marriage which everybody noticed in my *Poems of a Decade*. There will not be any more such to give offence in the next volume: for I am no longer even interested in the subject.

About this time there came to live with us a little boy, Len, whose relation to the family I did not know. His mother had been married off by the indomitable Grandmother Vanson to a South African miner she wasn't in love with: another tragic marriage, another story. He came home after the War to die, like so many others, still a young man, of miner's phthisis. It was a miserable affair, of which I knew very little and kept clear: I was too young to take in its full tragedy and they lived in a village off my track. Of the two children left, the little boy came to live with us. At first I resented his intrusion into a sphere where I had built myself an almost impenetrable preserve. But after the first difficulties of adjustment, I found he did not intrude: he was a sweet-natured child, who had an instinctive tact, and I soon grew fond of him. He can have been no more than five or so, and, when asked who he was, he used to reply: 'I'm a little Africander.' (He was born in South Africa.) Father was very good with him and very fond of him — especially so long as he remained a child. He had a deplorable tendency to fall down in the mud, walk in the stream, etc., which was an early bone of contention. He was fair, with remarkable, wide-open, easily frightened, blue eyes; he had a dreaming, absent-minded, artistic temperament, with a talent for drawing early developed. He is the 'child of the daydream blue eyes' of my early poem 'Saturday' in *Poems of a Decade*.

From the first I noticed that his temperament was a great deal like mine, where my brother and I had nothing in common, though Len was much quieter, more placid and good-tempered. But he was imaginative and had all the same tendency to night-terrors. I saw to it that he was never frightened off to bed, as I had been as a child and suffered agonies of fear in consequence. I explained to him that everybody felt frightened, and that in reality you knew that there was no reason for it. This mixture of confidence-trick, suggestion and good sense was entirely successful, and Len was delivered from the fears which haunted me at night and, right up to manhood, made me sometimes look under the bed or behind the curtains — particularly when my mind was overheated with working late. I was very proud of this success with him, and I think he grew to have confidence in me. I find touching little notes in my Diary about how upset he used to be when his mother came down from Plymouth for the day, where she was earning her living as housekeeper to a couple of old ladies; or again: 'Leonard has just been in to kiss me good-night; my cheek is wet now, where his lips have been.' Or there was his excitement when the street-lamp outside our shop was lighted again after all the War years:

Sunday, December 18th, 1921

As I write, I can hear father scolding about something in the kitchen; somebody else — Susan Pellow, next door, I expect — is chopping up wood; Basil Loam and another boy are holding a conversation outside my window; and the church-bells are ringing.

The gas-lamp outside our door has been lit again for the first time since 1914. . . . There was great jubilation when the lamplighter arrived at tea-time. Lennie skipped about and did his best to persuade father to come out into the court and have a look. Mother was quite excited. The Rickards' children from over the way shouted 'Hurrah' and danced for joy. . . . To me the lighting of the lamp meant much more than an additional conveniency, and even more than renewed acquaintance with an old friend. I thought again of the years that followed 1914; and all that the War means, the relighting of our lamp this evening has meant to me.

The baby-girl next door was as often as not in our house these years; if it had not been for my mother and the good-hearted girl at the farm I doubt if she would have survived, such was the state of affairs. In spite of Jack's poaching and snooping things by night, they never had enough to eat. He would even take things from us — anything handy, like a scrubbing-brush left out in the bay-tree overnight — though we were feeding his children.

He was a thoroughly bad lot. Still, there is this to be said for him, that his life was a tragedy to himself: he had been made to marry the wrong woman. He had got her in trouble and her family made him marry her. His mother, a Linkinhorne woman, told Jane that he was the black sheep of the family, and yet, in spite of that, he was the nearest of all her children to her. He was never in love with his wife. Honest, hard-working, clean, paying her way every penny she could, she had no temperament for him, no imagination, no sensuality, nothing to hold him. He needed something exotic, a passionate woman with a flaming temper, who might have kept him in order. Good-looking and sensual himself, with those cold, steely-blue eyes, he had a great attraction for women. There was one of his 'fancy-women' who came up from Holmbush after him one day; she was another man's wife, hot-tempered, gipsy-dark:

All the fires of hell were in her eyes,

and she was not afraid to tell Annie Courtenay, respectable soul who did not hold with such goings on, that she 'loved the very ground he trod on'.

There was another woman in the town whom he was in love with and with whom he lived as much as he could. She had a little boy by him, exactly like his younger boy by Jane, so people said. When conscription came in, he was determined not to go into the army. He knew a thing or two. He wore pennies round his legs to bring out varicose veins; before his medical examination he swallowed soap to give himself palpitations. Not surprisingly he was rejected, but was sent to work at a munitions factory in Limehouse. His woman went to London to work at the factory, too. He never let his wife know his address. Occasionally, very occasionally, with no regularity even, he would send her a pound or ten shillings. For the rest she had to get on as best she could. She went out to work every day; she did our washing and scrubbing for us, she worked at the farm. My mother, increasingly crippled by rheumatism, looked after and fed the baby, a very pretty little girl, fair curly hair and blue eyes.

They were often reduced to straits for food; they lived very largely on potatoes, fried in some fat. My mother was always adding something, or giving the baby dinner; other people were kind, particularly the good farm-folk. One day there was the sort of minor tragedy which loomed as a major one in the circumstances of that house: the cat carried off and mauled the little scrap of meat that went with the potatoes. This broke Jane's nerve, unshattered by other and graver disasters: she had become so inured to the disaster of her life. I don't believe she ever looked outside it: she just held on, keeping herself honest and spotless all through. Perhaps that was the only way to support it. My mother made up the dinner that day, as on so many other days. Jane was a good worker, and at the end of it all she wasn't in debt.

With the end of the War Jack came home to die on her. Things got worse and worse. Whereas in earlier years he had taken an interest in his garden, if not in his house, he now stayed away for weeks on end. He had been a very good gardener, and he had a wonderful way with animals, as with women: both worshipped him. I remember in his earlier years his garden, unlike ours, was beautiful with roses. My father, an honest worker, didn't go in for fancy things: he fed his family. Jack would take a briar cutting from the hedges, plant it, graft on to it shoots of lovely, velvety roses which he had begged, or more likely stolen, and on Saturday nights take off the most handsome blooms to his 'fancy-women' in the town. No roses for Jane. Sometimes there were blows when he came home drunk on Sunday afternoon, after a Saturday night out, and realized the misery of their existence. But he was not often drunk: sex was the great interest of his life. Once, in his later years, he showed me a wooden phallus, carved and painted, which he had made. There was something Greek about him, even his fine profile, which would have done for an Emperor on a coin, the clear pallor of his skin.

He was very good, too, with birds and ferrets and dogs, which all adored him. In earlier years, the court would be alive with the singing of his finches, which he had caught or bred himself. He was a great adept at the art of bush-beating (i.e. for birds at night); my brother, when young, accompanied him surreptitiously on one or two of these expeditions, and then was forbidden by my father, who disapproved of such things. I wouldn't have gone bush-beating for anything in the world: I should have been furious and tortured by the cruelty of it. But that was Jack all over: he was cruel, and he had a magic hand. He was a completely pagan character, a survival from an older world.

I have seen him take a maggot out of the ear of a ferret in poor condition with the greatest aplomb and not the slightest fear of the ferret biting him. Once he brought home a snake and, holding it by the neck, exhibited its convolutions and twistings and turnings to our horror in the court. I wouldn't go near it; but Kate Courtenay, who shared Jack's liking for animals and wasn't afraid of him, didn't mind having snake or ferret round her neck. Though we all regarded Jack as a 'blackguard' — the usual name for him — he wasn't an outcast: we all spoke to him, and, often enough, in no unfriendly fashion — perhaps a genuine difference between working-class and middle-class behaviour.

But his conduct towards his family was past all endurance. One time he didn't come near them for weeks: they had nothing to live on. Jane left home with her children and went back to her own people, who were not much help to her. Late one night he came back ill and miserable to find a cold hearth, an empty house, not a crust of bread. My father, who did not approve of him but never went on about him as all the women did, took pity on him and asked him in to have a cup of tea. I see him now standing there in the kitchen, his clothes hanging round him like a tramp's; there were tears in his eyes, and all he said was: 'You mustn't think that the fault is all on one side.' I remember

feeling pleased at father's act of kindness, and, in an odd way, at the
scamp's being there: perhaps a feeling of superiority at a disinterested
good deed, perhaps something else — a tinge of excitement at looking
through a window into someone else's life. In the town one day Jane
passed the other woman, who held brazenly on her way — Jane knowing
that she was keeping her husband and at the same time afraid to say
anything; she had no evidence and went in fear of him. When it
couldn't go on any longer, mother lent her the money to get a main-
tenance order against him. The policeman went to the house where he
was; the woman shouted upstairs: 'Jack, you had better come down.'

He was brought home, very ill. He didn't live many months after
this. He was fond of his little boy, Cyril, who in turn adored his
father. They would sit solemnly one each side of the fire all day, while
Jane was out working, the father hawking and spitting consumptively
into the fire. The child was an intelligent lad, who would get worried
at night-time, and shout down to his mother such questions as: 'Who
would bury the last man when he died?' One day, when the father
was almost too weak to walk he went up Down Park to Look Out, to his
last rendezvous with the woman he must have loved. He took his
little boy along with him, and she brought hers: they were extraordinarily alike. Somebody saw them sitting on the seat there in the
fresh air of that familiar spot, looking over all the bay. Then the little
boy, Cyril, sickened. We were convinced he had caught his father's
complaint; we tried to tempt him to eat with the choicest things we
could think of, I with dates and oranges, as a sort of a bribe, in despair.
He died of meningitis: he must have been about nine. I remember his
mother asking me if I thought there was any hereafter in which she
would ever see him again. I was a scholar: I was supposed to know.
It was very touching. I hope and believe that I answered 'Yes'. Her
real consolation was that he was best off where he was: she told herself
and us that over and over again. Then, not long after, Jack himself
died, Jane looking after him faithfully and doing everything for him.
On his deathbed he gave her one word of thanks, a crumb of comfort
for all the misery they had endured: she had been a good wife to him.
He was thirty-five.

Nor was this the worst, or the most squalid, tragedy in the village;
it was that with which we were most concerned, since we lived beside

it year after year all through my childhood, until the year we left Tregonissey and I went to Oxford. Really, when I think of the illusions of Left intellectuals about the rationality of human nature, it is very clear to me that they know nothing about human beings. I know in my bones what the facts are; and it is interesting, at any rate to me, to see that even in my schooldays, when I had hopes and some ideals, I still had no illusions about human nature. I took father to Labour meetings, because I thought it was good for him; at the same time I was writing in my Diary:

> I find my thoughts and conversation turning ever more and more towards Socialism. The present system of affairs (1921) is terrible; but, being young, I have hopes of helping to reform it. At the same time I know what has happened in the past. The young men of the time have started out to revolutionize things, full of hope for the future and of confidence in mankind. They generally end in disillusion. Think of Carlyle's later years.

Carlyle, at that time, was a great hero of mine; a few pages later is the first mention of Swift, who has remained a more constant admiration.

In fact, in all these years, there was not a soul in the village who understood the first thing about politics or the society he lived in, or who had even the slightest interest—with the exception of a radical tailor, crippled and crazy, of an apocalyptic mentality, who talked of politics in a vocabulary drawn almost exclusively from the Book of Revelation.

Such was the background to the last two years of my life at home. But it was no more than the background; the foreground was occupied by my work at school and constant worries about scholarships and getting to Oxford. A propos of Froude's 'Words about Oxford', which I read— it describes his return to Oxford years after he had left, coming up the High and turning into the quadrangle of All Souls, which meant nothing to me then but was to come to mean so much—my Diary says that to go to Oxford was now the sole end and aim of my life. And it was to Exeter College that all my thoughts and hopes turned. Then I was worried by the sudden contraction of the County Education Committee's offer of scholarships to the University, as the result of the economy campaign of the Rothermere newspapers at that time and the activities of the Big Business Geddes brothers. Instead of four scholarships, one of £140 p.a., another of £100, and two at £60, the first two were axed, and we were left with two miserable scholarships of £60 p.a. for the whole county of Cornwall. It was very worrying; I had to be sure of winning one of them, and even then £60 a year was a very little way to the £200 I should need to go to Oxford.

Two scholarships of £60 p.a. were a disgracefully small allowance for a county like Cornwall, whose schoolchildren were above the average of most English counties – the midlands around Birmingham, for instance, habitat of the Baldwins and Chamberlains. If there were two scholars produced a year from Cornish schools worthy of a University education there were surely a dozen – I do not say more than a dozen. But the number of scholarships remained at two for fifteen years after the War; until, a few years ago, after a persistent campaign on my part, the Education Committee doubled the number, with which I was very pleased – one small thing that future scholars coming from Cornwall to the University will have owed, in part at any rate, to me. But it was no use to me in 1921: my struggle was all before me; and it is because of the remembrance of that struggle and all its worries, that ever since, I have always gone out of my way to help Cornish candidates along the same path to the University.

That summer I had my first attack of appendicitis. It happened on sports' day at school, when I had been fool enough, after a heavy, indigestible dinner at home, to allow myself by an appeal to house-spirit to take part in a race. The excruciating pain of an acute attack of appendicitis – so many people know just what it is like – came on suddenly and grew worse. I didn't let anybody know what had happened: I could hardly understand what had overcome me; but, feeling green with pain, I crept away by myself to the friendly proximity of our donkey-field: there was some consolation in Neddy's familiar company, though he was not much use in the present circumstances. The pain in my bowels – that hot searing pain which became so recognizable later – did not stop; so I walked home up the road, slowly, cautiously, holding my stomach. It was a good thing I went cautiously – I might easily have brought on a perforation. I was terrified to hear that it was appendicitis I had, and was above all frightened of the prospect of an operation. Anything rather than that: I had all the working-class fear of being operated upon. Our doctor was away on holiday; when he came back, my temperature had subsided and he let me off the operation. That happened again a second time in the next year; and a combination of obstinacy, wheedling, and a terrified determination to avoid being operated on — a form of moral bullying of my doctor, who was a nice man and probably unable to cope with such a character — got me off again. The third time I did get a perforation, and a really bad appendix, and had to be operated on in the dangerous conditions of peritonitis. But by then I had got to Oxford.

I recovered with a spate of convalescent reading of one or two plays of Bernard Shaw, one or two of the remoter reaches of Stevenson (*The New Arabian Nights* and *The Merry Men*), some essays of Matthew Arnold — I was very much struck with that on Maurice de Guérin, and with a phrase from Bossuet: 'On trouve au fond de tout le vide et le néant.' That was very much my mood at the time; oddly enough, in 1941 I do not subscribe to it. 'One soon tires of Francis Thompson', my Diary, correctly, opines; but I was immensely taken by a long poem by an unknown Miss Dorothy Sayers, 'Obsequies for Music', which I copied out almost in full, such was my enthusiasm, from the *London Mercury*. Dear old Dr. Lea made an idiotic allusion to Russia and the Russian Famine in a sermon, which much annoyed me. (Unknown to me, my later friend Ralph Fox was making his first acquaintance with Russia by going out with the Quaker Relief Mission to help in the Volga district.) One day I was showing the pictures in the big *Home Preacher*, which had so excited my imagination as a child, to baby Loam seated on my knee. She was a sweet little creature with amusing ways, and we were all doing our best to be kind and helpful in the black time next door. Another day I was very angry and upset at Basil Loam's keeping goldfish in a small jar in the window and going away and never feeding them. One of them was dead and the other little creature gulped wildly at the crumbs I fetched him when I found out. This minor tragedy was the kind of thing that rent my heart then, more than the deeper disasters of which I was a spectator.

I had too many worries of my own. I find notes in my Diary stating that the alternative was either a scholarship or suicide — a curious dichotomy it seems now. At other times I asked whether I wasn't going mad.

I was certainly very gloomy. My last friends and contemporaries at school had gone off to college, and I was left to face the future alone. I used to mope about the corridors and rooms of the empty school at night, in the summer holidays, more and more. To all this was added a more serious cause of worry, which might have proved fatal to my hope of getting to Oxford: the headmaster was leaving.

He had never been happy with the dreary set of uneducated, almost illiterate governors with which the school was provided; under the lead of the formidable Sidney Hancock they made things as uncomfortable as they could, and were very unsympathetic to him. Now the County Education Committee added a last blow. Under the inspiration of the Economy Ramp sponsored by the worst people in English life, the County Council refused to pay school-teachers the full scale which had been settled by the Burnham Award. It was very disgraceful — the act of a lot of short-sighted, close-fisted, miserable farmers and butchers and business men, who had done well out of the War. I do not suppose it was the responsibility of the Education Committee or the wish of its redoubtable Secretary, who had to bear the brunt of the unpopularity. It meant that a number of the very best secondary-school teachers left the county, and their places were taken by inferior ones who took the opportunity to insert themselves while they had the chance. We lost our English master, to whom I was specially attached. It was a very awkward moment for me: there was no one now to oversee my English work. Since the failure of our London Matriculation experiment, there was no regular teaching provided for the Sixth Form — as is often the case in these small, inferior secondary schools. If I had not been now used to working on my own, doing my own reading and, so far as I could, directing my own course, it might have been disastrous. We were all fond of the long, pale Irishman; and small as our resources of pocket-money were, the Sixth Form clubbed together and presented him with some nice books. He was much touched; and I made a nervous little speech on the verge of breaking down.

But the departure of the headmaster was a far worse blow. I felt it, in a sense, as a desertion. I did not know what was to become of me, or what course I was to pursue to get to Oxford. If he had not kept his eye on me from Yorkshire, where he went to take on a new and soon very successful school, at Hemsworth, I should have been lost. But he kept in touch faithfully, writing me letters of encouragement from his new charge, where he must have been very busy laying the foundations, suggesting the steps I should take and handing me over as a special legacy to the new headmaster who came in his place. In the end, long after, when he had built up a fine secondary school in that sound-hearted colliery district, I went down to present the prizes at his Speech Day, and was able to get Lord Halifax from All Souls to go down the following year – the last Speech Day before my head-master's retirement.

Mr. Jenkinson's departure was the occasion of a row with the senior mistress which, added to the overwork and strain which I was under, quite unnerved me. For some time my relations with her had not been good. I think she thought that I was uppish – which I certainly was not in intention: I admired her and wished to stand well with her; I liked her subject, which was French, and did well in it. She was quite proud of my winning the prize in the journal *English* with an essay on a French book, the *Lettres de Mon Moulin*, which we were reading in class with her – at a crab's pace, suited to all the duffers who could not keep up. I read the book for pure pleasure at home. She kept my essay, and years later gave me the printed cutting of it which I had improvidently lost.

She was an excellent teacher; being Welsh, she had a pure French accent. She was a fine-looking woman, tall, with an admirable car-riage of shoulders and hips, large, dark eyes and a curve of wavy hair; but she had a small, biting voice which she used to great effect. I was really afraid of her; she had an uncertain temper and a most sarcastic tongue. Still I was spirited and not giving way. She had an eye for a tall, good-looking fellow with golden curly hair who was in my form— hopeless at her subject, he had a way with him where women were concerned. I sensed that, and realized I had not. There are difficulties that occasionally arise in a co-educational school between women members of the staff and adolescent boys. One or two of the mistresses thought that I was superior with them; there was a certain feeling of instinctive rivalry which was a surprise to me at the age of seventeen.

One day when discussing the difficulties of getting to the University, Miss Griffiths was very discouraging. And when I said that Crowther, after all, had got a scholarship at Trinity, Cambridge, she said: 'Oh, but you see, he was very brilliant.' A little later she came to me in the draughty basement passage which I inhabited as a room to myself and suggested that I should write a letter to the local paper, on behalf of the prefects, as a farewell tribute to the headmaster. I wrote a nice letter, but what with one job and another in this hectic week, and having to rush to catch the paper before going to press, I completely forgot to submit it to the other prefects.[1] They would only have said 'Yes' anyhow. When she learned this she came in to me in a towering rage. I had been driven past endurance that week, and in an equal high temper answered that 'What she had said was ridiculous and unjust'. I was rather pleased with the adjectives, which exactly expressed my sense of the injustice of the attack, but at the same time terrified of the consequences. She flung out and went straight off to the headmaster. He, wise man, must have calmed her down, for he never mentioned the incident to me, much less called me over the coals. I was not re-pentant, and during the whole of the rest of the term she never addressed another word to me nor looked in my direction, though her eyes and mouth spoke guns whenever I looked her way. But afraid of her as I was, I was not going to give in: I felt an outraged sense of justice; I didn't speak to her, and when she left at the beginning of next term and a presentation was made to her, I neither contributed to it nor was present at the proceedings: somebody else had to do it in my absence from school.

It was a small incident, but like those small incidents in our earlier years it had an effect out of all proportion to its importance. It un-doubtedly gave me a complex: I harboured the resentment and a sense of injury, and for years after I used to dream about that woman. There was probably some delicate adolescent equilibrium which was deeply disturbed by this row with a woman who was much older than I: the boy who was not quite a man was afraid of her and yet was man enough not to give way. That may be an incorrect psychological explanation. But I have often wondered what the explanation was why this should have had such a deeply disturbing effect. She came

---

[1] I was charmed to find only the other day that my old headmaster had remembered my little letter of so many years ago and the phrase in which I had described him as the *ressort de l'action* of the school.

back next year, and again and again, to St. Austell and Mevagissey for her holidays from Hemsworth. She came to see me at the shop — I was out. Apparently she was quite unaware of the psychological injury she had done me. For I was possessed of a furious hatred of her. Once when I was at home from Oxford for the vacation, she was on the beach at Porthpean, where I was, and sent a message that she would like to see me; I ignored it and shortly after left the beach. Another time she arranged a picnic for the prefects of the old Sixth who were in the neighbourhood; I half said that I would go and then absented myself. But I went on dreaming about her.

Later at All Souls, I spent my holidays abroad a good deal and was ill off and on all the time; so I did not come home much in the summer and lost sight of her. When, some years later, I went to present the prizes at Hemsworth, still more under the weather with duodenal ulcer, I wondered whether I shouldn't be upset by meeting her again. Not at all. She was on her very best behaviour. I saw at once, with the experience that years had brought, that she was not at all the great lady I had thought her, that she was not really well dressed, nor possessed taste. But she more than made up for that by being very human: she now obviously wanted to stand well with me. Ill as I was, she had had a good, if rather indigestible, supper cooked for me at her house. And afterwards told me a curious story — of the headmistress at the school where she had first taught, for whom she had a great admiration. Then things began to go wrong: the headmistress was a fine woman, but was secretly drinking. She lost her post, and later they learned what was the cause: she was dying of cancer and had taken to drink to alleviate the pain. Within a year Miss Griffiths herself, still only fifty, was dead of cancer. The headmaster went to her funeral one March day in a little bare churchyard on a windswept Welsh hill-side.

The day of the headmaster's farewell was a very sad day for me. There was first the ceremony of unveiling the Memorial Window on the staircase to the old boys who had been killed in the War. I had the job of accompanying the singing, which made me nervous, and playing 'God Save the King', which I didn't much relish but wouldn't have refused the headmaster. After the 'Last Post' and 'Réveillé', my

Diary records: 'A little man came up to me and started talking in a rambling way about his son who was killed. I think the poor fellow was for the moment carried away with sorrow. He said, "Sidney Herbert — Sidney Herbert — you know they called him Sidney Herbert, but really he was called Sidney Hubert: he was my boy. He was killed in the War — yes: I thought you would like to know." And he went on like that till I dared not stay any longer with him.' The Diary continues with a passage about the lost generation of 1914-1918, the first expression of what later became a cult in my early years at All Souls, with the photographs of the young Fellows who were killed upon the walls of the common-room, their books in the library — a cult of their memory from which sprang my book *Politics and the Younger Generation*.

Then followed the prize-giving, which was performed by that noble, if somewhat gnarled, Cornishman, John Charles Williams of Carhayes, then Lord-Lieutenant of the county.[1] I noted: 'The governors — most of them egoistic fools — tried to pass over the occasion as lightly as possible and to talk of anything else under the sun rather than our headmaster's going. Sidney Hancock rambled on for a quarter of an hour, talking about his own education, his life, his opinions; and — colossal cheek — in conclusion he said that as for the love and pride of his native town, his own life was a record of that.' In a way the old man was right; but at that time no large experience of school Speech Days had yet revealed to me the fact that they are the prize hunting-ground of the local bores.

That affair over, the school made a presentation to the headmaster. I remember we were naively surprised at his choosing an old mahogany table and a breakfast service of old Staffordshire ware. He was a man of taste. We were very innocent. The senior master made a speech for the staff, and I had to speak on behalf of the school. Unbearably nervous as I always was, I was this time near bursting into tears. Fortunately I had learnt my little speech by heart, and the headmaster was visibly touched — gratified, I thought, that I hadn't broken down.

[1] I should add, what I learnt subsequently from my old headmaster, that his attitude to my going to the University was very unhelpful: he, too, thought it better that I should go into the china-clay industry. In view of that, perhaps the adjective 'noble' which I apply to him above is a trifle over-generous. Still I allow it to stand, for in his defence I should say that he can have had no idea who one was.

The next day there follows an interesting passage which reveals two things: the nostalgia which was a deeply characteristic note in my temperament and the increasing command of literary expression which the Diary reveals and which no doubt keeping it was a main factor in achieving:

> This afternoon I went to school. To-day was an extra holiday and the place was quite deserted; only the back door was left unlocked. I looked into the big room, and there were all the chairs as the visitors had left them after yesterday's doings. Some were in little groups of three or two, some remained very straight and prim and severely in line with their fellows. In one place was a regular heap of chairs all crowded together, some overturned where parents and pupils had scrambled up to shake hands with the headmaster and wish him good-bye.

I was now working for the County Scholarship — not so hard as I thought I ought to be. My Diary records: 'There is nothing that embitters one so much as continual suspense and a sharp struggle all the time.' I was reading Ruskin, one or two of whose books were set-texts for the examination. His essay on War made a great impression: I could 'think of nothing else for the time'. *Sesame and Lilies* I considered 'very fanciful and would make an excellent sermon for a Girls' Friendly Association Festival'. Reading Ruskin — under the aegis of a reactionary County Council! — inevitably increased my socialist tendencies. I was fortified in my views by passages in my reading such as this from Bury's *History of Freedom of Thought*: 'Of those to whom socialism is repugnant, how many are there who have never examined the arguments for and against it, but turn away in disgust simply because the notion disturbs their mental universe and implies a drastic criticism on the order of things to which they are accustomed?' That clinched the matter for me.

From Oxford the news was depressing. I got letters from Exeter and Magdalen to say that no English scholarships would be awarded that year; the communication from Jesus was so confused that I could not make head or tail of it. There was an English scholarship to be offered at Balliol. But what chance was there of my winning a Balliol scholarship, I asked. I put the thought out of my mind. I was quite right to do so. Peter Quennell was in for that scholarship and would inevitably have won it. It was a good thing I didn't go in for it. Balliol was not wrong in electing him.

At school I took dinner-duty on Mondays, and came home tired and depressed with all the jobs and tasks which are imposed upon head boys in all schools, and of which their sense of self-importance at that age makes them victims. It is called, by those to whom it is very convenient, 'learning how to run things'. I was beginning to suffer seriously from indigestion and sleepless nights — the beginning, I fancy, of a duodenal ulcer. I was doing a mass of miscellaneous reading in French and English, and was particularly drawn at this time to Verlaine and Edward Thomas. I hoped it wasn't waste of time. In the end it wasn't. Very Cornish, I took a money-spider which crawled over my arm while working for the County Scholarship as a good omen. It was.

In black December weather I went down to Truro to sit for the examination. I lodged for four or five days in a small house in a street going down from the railway station, and trudged uphill every day to the uncomfortable grandeur of the Council Chamber at the County Hall, where the seats were very far off from the desks and you sat on the hard edge in a half-leaning, half-stooping position for three mortal hours, while the iron entered into your soul — where ordinarily, and more suitably, dreary County Councillors made their ineffable speeches. In these circumstances I was very dissatisfied with my essay; it was on a difficult subject: 'The effect of the late War upon English Literature', and I could have made a much better job of it. But on the last day of the examination I had a question which was right in my hand. It was a Cornish question, and there were two alternatives: the importance of Sir Bevil Grenville, or Archbishop Benson, in the history of the county; or Q.'s literary work. I longed to do them all. But, after some regrets, I settled down to what I knew was my best work, on my beloved Q. By this time I knew his books almost from A to Z; the difficulty was to know where to stop. I stopped with a sentence which brought together my two chief loves: 'What Thomas Hardy is to Wessex, Q. is to Cornwall.' I knew when I finished that day that I had at last done the best that I was capable of.

One evening I went to a performance of the 'Hymn of Praise' in the

Cathedral. We waited in a queue in the dark, the darker mass of the building looming above us as we were pressed up against the entrance in the south-west tower. '*I* was in a crush like this at the Zoo', said somebody; 'Oh, Mummie, s'pose if it all fell down', said a little girl. The habit of literary reporting was developing in me. Inside the building I was surprised at being recognized and smiled to by a girl from Carclaze. I never travelled anywhere: it might have been 'Dr. Livingstone, I presume?' in Darkest Africa, it was so unexpected. Another afternoon I went to tea at St. John's vicarage with my friend Carpenter, whom I had met at Oxford and who was now happily installed at Exeter. I was envious of his good fortune in having a family that could provide for him. He had very nicely tried to do me a good turn by telling Dr. Farnell, the Rector of Exeter, about my poem in *Public School Verse*: much impression that would have made upon that curious, insensitive martinet, who was now launched upon his fantastic career as Vice-Chancellor at Oxford. My last afternoon I spent in the bookshop in Boscawen Street, tormenting myself with the thought of how like the street was to the Broad, and trying to persuade myself that Jordan's was really Blackwell's and Boscawen Street really the Broad.

After so much strain I was ill for weeks. Nobody at home knew what it was; I didn't know what it was: we called it indigestion. I know now that it must have been an ulcer forming. There are entries like the following in my Diary:

Wednesday, January 4th, 1922

Another night of agony for me. From three o'clock till nearly eight this morning I had fearful pains in my stomach: I was afraid that another attack of appendicitis was coming on. And now, after hours spent in pain and without sleep, I feel quite exhausted. I should be in bed; but have to get up in this house as nearly everybody else suffers in the same degree. Mother can scarcely walk, her rheumatism is so bad; father suffers with indigestion. Yet we have to go on and on; it doesn't matter how ill any of us may be. There seems no pleasure in our lives as compared with other people's; and when the present state of things will come to an end and we shall be comfortably off, the devil only knows!

That blessed state was to come in time, but only as the result of my own exertions. Meanwhile, I leave that passage from the Diary to stand for its pathological interest — there may be doctors among my readers who will be interested in the growth of symptoms of duodenal ulcer, that scourge of the intelligent, the highly-strung, the literary; the passage will serve to stand for scores of others in the years of illness that were to come.

My reading continued: now it was Jane Austen and Rupert Brooke; reading Edward Marsh's Memoir of him made me angry at his death, as he had been angry at Walter Headlam's being snatched away suddenly, senselessly. I was not now composing much poetry — I was working too hard; but the notes of conversations in the kitchen continue, and I took down a few sayings from father, such as the belief that the coldest water in Cornwall was that in the well in St. Ewe cemetery. When I had recovered a little, I went for a long walk there with my friend the young architect to see if it was. It was deliciously cold. We had tea in the big kitchen of the inn — a nice old lady with spectacles to look after us and cut the good farm bread and butter; and we walked home in the tingling winter darkness, climbing up signposts to find our way. For that January afternoon I was happy.

The new headmaster made a kindly, friendly impression from the first, though much less august than the old. He had no style. I noticed that his first address to us prefects was about picking up waste-paper about the premises, a casual affair compared with the formal meetings we had been used to in the Sixth-Form room, the addresses and admonitions on an altogether higher plane. (Once, after I had been caught tickling one of the girls — by the senior mistress, of course — we had a whole half-hour's lecture on being *Sans peur et sans reproche*, while I wished that the whole earth would open to receive me.) However, the new man's intentions were evidently good; he called me into his study and told me of the excellent report he had had of me from his predecessor and that he hoped we should work together. From that moment he had my complete confidence and I came to regard him with a more intimate feeling of fondness than I had the old headmaster, for whom I had the greatest respect and affection; but he always looked a little too austere and stern for fondness, which for the rest he did not invite.

My Diary shows that I realized my affairs were at a crisis: 'one of the few crises that come in one's life. Everything now may go wrong, or everything may go right. Fate has struck me two or three severe blows lately. I have been ill; I have had news from Exeter College which means the end of all my hopes of getting there; the editors of *Public School Verse* have refused my contribution. May everything come right!' The new headmaster decided that I must try for a scholarship in the next group at Oxford. There was none in English, except that at Balliol, so I must try for one in history.

I had been concentrating upon English literature and reading no history at all. For the next two or three months I read as hard as I could at history, with no one to advise me, no one to give me any idea of the standards required in a much more competitive subject. There would be scores of candidates competing in that history group, most of them from the better public schools, practically all of them from schools which could give their candidates some training in scholarship work. Had I known what I know now I shouldn't have gone in for a history scholarship at all. With Exeter out of the running, we didn't know what college to put down first: I put down St. John's out of the blue, because (I think) the new headmaster's college was St. John's at Cambridge! Needless to say the gamble was a failure. I hardly remember anything about it except that the essay was set on John Morley's dreary subject, 'Compromise', so suitable for a late-Victorian Liberal, and of which I could make nothing. I had been working too hard to keep up my Diary, in which there is no entry from January 19th to April 4th; and nothing of that time remains in my memory.

For all my efforts I was still without a scholarship, and the academic year in which it was necessary to get one was nearly gone. It would soon be too late. I came home to face a new blow. I had based my hopes of getting to some University or college, perhaps Bristol or Sheffield or Exeter, upon the extensive scheme of State scholarships awarded upon the results of the Higher School Certificate, which had been in operation the previous years under H. A. L. Fisher's presidency of the Board of Education. Now without a word of warning they were suspended, owing to the economy ramp fomented by the loathsome Northcliffe and Rothermere and their henchman Lovat Fraser. I was nearly sunk by this, since of the large number awarded over the whole country there was some chance of my winning one. My friend, Noreen Sweet, certainly suffered by this measure; she was going to the University, but for her this meant taking the first chance and going to Reading instead of to Oxford. (Is it any wonder that we both became supporters of the Labour Party? And we were not wrong. Twenty years of the rule of business men have wellnigh ruined the country, brought us directly to our present pass.)

One crumb of consolation was that I had now won the County Scholarship: I heard the news in my shirt, running from my bedroom into the sitting-room to receive the telegram early one morning. I was rather bowled over, but too tired and unwell to be particularly elated. 'What is £60 a year to take me to the University?' says my Diary. 'But I intend to go', it goes on; 'I shan't invoke the gods to bring everything right, as I did at the end of the last entry. Damn the gods! What I want to do, I am going to do! And what I want to do first of all, before I can think of any ultimate aim in life, is to go to Oxford. Then to Oxford I am going!' Next day there was a hockey match such as I liked, between staff and prefects, in honour of the event – the first time the school had won a University scholarship. A letter from my old headmaster followed, bidding me stick to it. But 'What is the good of it?' I asked next day, depressed.

For the Easter holidays Mr. Jenkinson came down, and there was a concentration of friends in the town, who came to see me: J. G. Crowther and his sister, T. C. Bennett and others. Mr. Jenkinson was very worried about my prospects of getting into Oxford and insisted that I should try for the English scholarship at Christ Church the very next month. I was alarmed at the prospect, for I had now dropped reading English for several months past in order to read history; I had only a fortnight's clear preparation. He ended up by proposing that I should obtain an interview with Q. and get his advice about it all. I jumped at the idea of going to see the great man at his home. My enthusiasm for him was at white heat; I had just been re-reading *The Delectable Duchy* and *Troy Town*, and went about saying over and over to myself the concluding words of the Prologue to the former: 'Oh my country, if I keep for you your secrets, keep for me your heart.'

Mr. Jenkinson arranged the interview before he left, and one fine day at the end of April, with the kind Crowthers to hold my hand, I went over to Fowey. There is a long and elaborate account in my Diary, from the primroses that were thick upon the embankment between Par and Fowey to the daffodils upon Q.'s writing-table. It was the first time that I had ever so much as seen this man who had meant so much to me from the time when, a very small elementary-school boy, I had read *The Splendid Spur*. The Crowthers sat reading the *Daily Herald* (Lansbury's *Daily Herald*) upon the Esplanade in front of Q.'s garden, while I, with beating heart, made my first call at 'The Haven'. Many as are the calls I have made at that familiar, hospitable house since, it always has something of the excitement and timorousness of that first call still.

I felt horribly confused as to which door to ring at. The large front door seemed too grand for me; so I made for the little private entrance at the side. The moment I rang I knew it was wrong. Q. was just inside in his study, that looks out to the harbour-mouth and the open sea. I put my foot gingerly on the mat and it slid along with me on the polished floor into the doorway and Q.'s presence. That made me feel rather more at home; it was a very informal mode of arrival, and Q. was very kind, though he let me know that that was the wrong door. He gave me a chair and then marched up and down the room himself (that pretty room, the gay chintzes, the brass candlesticks, the views of the river and across to Polruan, the sea). He walked in the way I have come to know so well with the years — hands behind his back, head leaning forward, eyes on the ground, 'and then took each step in a curious way as if half-halting and half-deliberate'. Q.'s appearance reminded me of something very strongly, I could not recall what. And then it struck me that it was Charles I: it was the Stuart-looking breeches, true without rosettes at the knees, the long stockings, the shoes. On identifying Charles I I wanted to laugh; 'but Q.'s habit of darting a glance at you suddenly, just when you didn't expect it, dissuaded me from grinning'.

I had brought with me a little book of interest to Q. and of which I was extraordinarily proud. A school-friend of mine in rummaging the bookstalls of old John Dungey — a great character, a retired sailor — in the market-house at St. Austell, had found a school-text of Aristophanes' *The Clouds* with the neat initials A. T. Q. C., the handwriting hardly differing now from his schooldays at Clifton. My friend had given it to me; and Q. was pleased to see it and, not unnaturally, at my obvious pride in possessing it. He talked to me of the Cambridge English School ('which I invented, you know—so to speak'), and at last we got down to the Christ Church scholarship. Q. said there would be strong competition for it, which depressed me a little. He said he had once coached a boy for it who wrote like an angel ('And talked like poor Poll?' I put in, by way of letting him know that his reference wasn't lost on me); but he didn't get it. This was depressing news indeed. Many years later Q. gave an account of this interview to the westcountry press a propos of my *Sir Richard Grenville*, which I dedicated to him. He was terribly afraid that he had nearly put me off trying; for, man of extreme sensitiveness and delicacy as he is, he saw that this passage about the clever boy whom Q. had coached but didn't get the Christ Church scholarship had an effect upon the schoolboy before him. I can reassure him about that. It did have its effect; but the effect was to make me say to myself, with a sort of defiance, half-devilment: 'Well, we'll see whether I won't get it.'

There was some more talk of a very helpful character, about scholarships and ways and means, while I longed to talk to Q. about literature and about his books and about the Prologue to *The Delectable Duchy*, which I found so moving. And then, at the end, before I left, Q. advised me quite definitely that I was to go in for the Christ Church scholarship.

Before going up I spent one glorious early summer afternoon at Lost House, tramping round the fields reading poems aloud from the *Golden Treasury*; and I read Ibsen's *Pillars of Society*, which stood me in good stead at Oxford; for, years after, Roy Harrod told me that it was what I wrote about Ibsen which so impressed the examiners — when I had completely forgotten all about it. On the morning I left home, with my heart in my mouth, I found half-way down the road to the station that I had forgotten my shaving gear. I ran back, and was almost pushed away from the door by mother, who said it was the unluckiest thing possible to come back. However, I hoped the three-penny bit I had carried round in my pocket for weeks would counteract the ill-luck. It did.

With such success that I remember nothing about the examination, nothing whatever—except the grandeur of Christ Church Hall, where it was held; the portraits all round, the far greater air of opulence and splendour than my so long desired Exeter possessed. One thing I do remember very clearly — the interview which I had with J. C. Masterman, then Junior Censor, at the end of the examination. He was extraordinarily kind and sympathetic. I liked him at once, not only for his handsome good-looks, but because he began to ask me about Cornwall, and that put me at my ease. From that he went on to poetry and talked of *Public School Verse*, in which some of my poems had appeared; asked me if I liked music and French literature. Of course, I did. (I forgot to say that one of the few things I do remember from that hazy week was this: as I walked round the streets of Oxford in a dream once more, I kept saying to myself over and over again the last line of Verlaine's sonnet:

Grêle — parmi l'odeur fade du réséda.)

I was so elated with the kindness and friendliness of this interview that I could not go back to the dingy street on the outskirts, Hayfield Road, the crampedness of my bedroom at Mrs. Colman's, the children screaming outside. I wandered round Tom Quad, watching the undergraduates going in to dine in hall, wondering whether it would be my lot to join them. Then I went through Peckwater out through Canterbury Gate into Merton Street, turning back often to look at Christ Church, upon which now all my hopes were centred, and glimpsing across the green lawns and trees in all the glory of their May flowering, red and white chestnut candles, hawthorn pink and white and red, the figures of men playing cricket in the Meadows in the level, evening light, serene and quiet.

I could not help feeling as I went home to Cornwall that I had won the scholarship.

On my way home from the station I met a friend who told me that mother was anxiously awaiting my return. It was, my Diary says, 'the shock of my life'. Hitherto, I had always supposed that I was unwanted; mother always seemed to be glad to get rid of me, and with a literal honesty of temperament I took that *au pied de la lettre*. Nor can I suppose even now that her attitude was that of the Mother towards Michael Ransome, her favourite son, in Auden and Isherwood's *The Ascent of F6*: it was too instinctive and unconsidered for that. To me it was very surprising that anybody had missed me at all; the years taught me to set such little store upon my worth to them. But Lennie too had missed me, and said the place was quite lonely without me: this was very endearing.

They had to get used to that in the years to come; for I had won the scholarship. Somebody first saw the news in the paper; I am not sure that it was not dear old Dr. Lea, who caught me with the news just by the station one morning, and was as delighted as if he had got it himself. All his real standards were academic, of the University—he ought to have been a don; I rather think that in that moment the old boy went back in his mind to the day, some time in the seventies, when he had first gone up from the country rectory in Herefordshire to his adored Oxford. His dark tan flushed with pleasure, as I had seen him only once before flush with anger at an injustice. He called up the curate, a long, thin Oxford man; they were both very impressed that it should be Christ Church, of all colleges, that I was going to. At school there were great jubilations: tennis all the afternoon and evening; ice-cream and tea at four o'clock, and, I think, a whole holiday. That evening I had a touching, intimate conversation with the headmaster, who told me of his own troubles, and my heart went out to him: I regarded him with real tenderness, and looked upon him in the light of a father to me, a father who could understand and help me. So much my Diary makes clear, as I wrote by the light of a candle in the sitting-room, before going to bed. It was a profound pity that with the years there came an irreparable breach.

In later life it has been a source of gratification, after my failure to get in at Exeter, to know that it was J. D. Beazley to whom I chiefly owe my election at Christ Church—one of the most distinguished of Oxford scholars, a man of genius. He discerned something in my work. So, too, J. C. Masterman, who gave me so friendly a *viva*: a man of a fine and discriminating nature.

I now had two scholarships making £140 a year towards the £200 I needed to take me to Oxford. I had to get a third. My old head-master was very delighted about Christ Church, and it was he who suggested that I should try for one of the City Companies' scholarships. He wrote to the Drapers' Company, and at the end of the month father and I were summoned up to London for an interview. I went up for a day or two beforehand, in a great state of trepidation, for it was my first visit. The place came up to expectations: I was for ever on tenterhooks lest I got lost and never knew where I was. Fortunately there was an old St. Austell schoolboy, L. H. Tippett, soundest and most sterling of men, who became one of my lasting friends, then up at the Imperial College of Science. He found lodgings for me in Bayswater, with a Welsh couple from Merioneth whose chief pleasure was reading their local Welsh newspaper; I was fearful of the cost, compared with good Mrs. Colman at Oxford, in spite of the fact that the rich City Company was paying our expenses! My friend took me in tow over the week-end. For the first time I went to a London theatre — to Barrie's *Quality Street*, with which I was entranced. St. Paul's, of which my preference for medieval Gothic had hitherto made me disapprove on paper, effected an immediate conquest the moment I set foot inside it; and I have always known it ever since for what it is — one of the world's most wonderful churches.

But the great problem in London was finding one's way round. I couldn't believe but that I should miss father on his arrival at Paddington Station. My eyes could hardly credit it when I saw him there on the platform in that vast cathedral-like space. Dear Paddington, regarded by me at eighteen with a baleful eye as such a strange, hostile world, when now it has become one's home station, as familiar as St. Austell itself. Our troubles began when we had to find our way round by ourselves. The streets had such a provoking way of looking quite different, according as you went up or went down: not much use retracing your steps, you only lost your way worse. The buses always very inconsiderately overshot the mark and went on for miles; I wouldn't have got off while one was moving for anything. (We had no buses at home then.) Besides, through some misunderstanding, one always got on the wrong bus. We didn't dare go by Underground; there were such stories at home about people getting caught down there and travelling round and round all day. The only safe thing, I decided, was to walk everywhere. So we treated the place as it might be St. Austell district and trudged about the day long. It was very tiring.

Next day we went up to the City early to identify Drapers' Hall in Throgmorton Avenue beforehand, in case it moved away when the time came. I had banked on spending another hour in St. Paul's, but

it was closed, and we mooned about, both horribly nervous, went into
a restaurant for some lemonade, and then sat in the little garden around
St. Paul's Cross, where the Elizabethans listened to sermons, watching
the pigeons wheeling round the Cathedral in the yellow fog. At noon
we presented ourselves at Drapers' Hall, my heart beating fast as I rang
the bell at the Clerk's Office, that feeling of the irrevocable upon
me. I was taken aback by the eighteenth-century opulence of the interior — the heavy pile carpets, the oil paintings on the panelled walls,
a river scene near London Bridge, some Georgian Lord Mayor's procession. An elaborate candelabra hung from the ceiling of the room
where we all waited in silence. (Alas, to think what has happened
since, the *furor Teutonicus* having passed over the City.)

There were several couples of anxious fathers and sons waiting; and
it was not for nearly an hour that our turn came. We were shown
into a fine, large, sombre room where eight gentlemen, half of them
old, half young, were drawn up in a semi-circle round a shining mahogany table. Father and I were given seats confronting this barrage of
eyes and ears. They started to put their questions to him; apparently
their conception of the proceedings was that the fathers were there to
answer for the sons. I said that father was deaf and that they had
better put the questions to me. They sat up a bit at this. Then the
Clerk of the Company put me a lot of questions, very nice and kindly:
I was very taken with him, Mr. (now Sir E. H.) Pooley. He knew all
the ropes about the University and had to explain to a very surprised
old gentleman that there was such a thing as an English Literature
school at Oxford, which I was intending to take. He asked if I had
any ambition to write, and of course I said 'Yes'. The Clerk asked
what scholarships I had already got. I told them, and they seemed
very impressed that I had won an Open Scholarship at Christ Church.
Then each gentleman put pen to paper and did for himself the little
addition sum of

I was very amused by this. Then one of them said: 'You'll want a good deal more than that to go up to Christ Church with.' How much did I think was necessary? I said I thought I could do it on £200. The Clerk said he had received a letter about me from the headmaster of my school — it turned out to be from the faithful Jenkinson — and asked quizzically if I ran the place. I said 'No, the headmaster did.'

Meanwhile father, who couldn't hear all that was being said, was vastly entertained by all the by-play which he observed. At the end, the chairman turned to him and said: 'Do you want your son to go up to the University?' I had to interpret. So I said to him, a bit afraid he might get the answer wrong: 'Do you want me to go to the University? You do, don't you?'; and he said, rather hesitating, 'Well — yes; I should like for'n to.' I think we must have given the gentlemen of the Drapers' Company their money's worth of entertainment that morning. Years after, mother told me that when he came home he said to her: 'Les spoke to 'em like a lawyer — I couldn' get a word in edgeways. [!] They asked'n several questions that I couldn' answer. No trouble to 'ee: 'ee answered 'em all like a lawyer.' Again this interesting old-fashioned respect among country people for the skill, if not the person, of the lawyer. To me he never said a word, then or after. It is very odd that he shouldn't have done. Perhaps he was too shy, or afraid of turning my head. But if my head has been turned at all, it was not by excess of encouragement in my youth, but for the want of it.

After the interview we were told to wait on, so I knew there was hope. We went down and walked in the pretty little courtyard, which had a statue in the middle and arcades all round. It was a surprise to me, after the plainness of the exterior of Drapers' Hall. Then we were called in and told that I was awarded one of their scholarships of £60 a year. The friendly Clerk shook hands and congratulated me, hoping that I would get on; then he added, 'And I think that you will.' Later experience of these things tells me that I owed my scholarship to him.

We went out into the light of the afternoon, I light-headed with suspense and success and from having had no dinner. Now that it was over, poor old pa was quite overcome with it all and had to go in and have a drink at the first pub we came to (which was something very unusual with him), while I waited outside on the pavement — I had never been inside a pub yet. That afternoon I dragged father along to the Sons of the Clergy Festival at St. Paul's: there was a splendid procession — the Bishop of London, the Lord Mayor and, at the end of it all, a resplendent figure in scarlet with a long train, the Archbishop of Canterbury. As he passed us by, father and I exchanged a smile: I think in that moment he remembered what had been my earliest ambition from my childhood; in that moment I realized that I had already said good-bye to it. Poor father, there was not such a gulf between us then as there was later! After tea, I hunted out Carter Lane and Wardrobe Place, where George had lived those years in London, very poor; having no money for anything else, he used to amuse himself tramping the streets sight-seeing until nearly every alley and by-way in the City was familiar to him. I found out where he had lived: the whole place was alive for me with his memory. I determined to write him a long letter when I got home describing how it looked and how it was getting on — some memento for him the other side of the world in the wilds of the bush in Western Australia, where every morning he would have to get up and round up the horses 'as wild as cats', and work all day from dawn to sundown.

That evening I took father along with me to see *The Beggar's Opera* at the Lyric, Hammersmith — a wonderful production by Nigel Playfair, which I much wanted to see. But we had to come out before the end of the second act, he was so bored with it and so frightened we should not get back to Bayswater that night. The one man he knew in London had come with us and put us on a bus: 'After waiting at various places for half an hour, we got No. 28, which took us within half an hour's walk from Powis Gardens. So much for the guidance of people who "know" London', I added mistrustfully. 'I would prefer to steer my own course; and I am sure I'd get about more quickly.' Father went home next day: I don't think he had more than three days off from his wretched clay-work. The men at the works, I gathered indirectly — not from him — were proud of Dick's son's success. It was nice of them, and in later years they were very faithful to me when I put up as their Labour candidate for Parliament.

I came home as usual in a black mood at the circumstances in which we lived, after a glimpse of something better elsewhere. While we were away mother had had a severe attack of arthritis, which made it

almost impossible for her to walk about the house. I tended her in bed
and did the housework, and as much cooking as I knew how – the
simplest things, fried and boiled eggs, stewed rhubarb. The most
tedious part of all was washing up; I never knew what to do with
myself while wiping the plates and cups. I tried doing two things at
once, like reciting Verlaine's 'Aprés Trois Ans' aloud:

> Ayant poussé la porte étroite qui chancelle
> Je me suis promené dans un petit jardin –

and then I broke a saucer. Mother tried to get up and carry on with
the work, but the pain was excruciating. It got on my nerves; my
Diary has pages of anguished protest: 'Every step she makes causes
her such pain that I could cry out. For two nights now I have stood
at the top of the stairs with the candle in my hand to light her way up;
and each night I could have cried. I have just come into my room, and
when at length she reached the top to-night I could have screamed out.'
Fortunately the attack subsided and she got better; for I was anything
but well myself. I had been under too great a strain. At the beginning
of July I had my second acute appendicitis. My Diary says: 'I am just
(7 July) getting over another attack of appendicitis. I am afraid, afraid
of an operation. The thought makes me shiver: I have no nerves to
face such a prospect at all. I would almost [that 'almost' is a concession
to my superstition: very Cornish] face more attacks, though they are
too awful to have any more of. What a coward I am!' Apprehension runs all through this passage; and indeed for the next few weeks
I was in constant fear of a recurrence of the attack.

The Oxford Higher School Certificate examination, which was to
have been the coping-stone of my structure of scholarships, according
to the original plan, by qualifying me for a State Scholarship, came
on before I had properly recovered from the attack. The headmaster
suggested that I need not take it seriously, and indeed I had had no
time to prepare for it properly. Putting off an examination did not
enter into my scheme of things, however; and it was my own fault
that I sat for it in a kind of weak haze. However, I got through it all
right, even though it didn't matter any more.

I had got my £200 a year clear now, and even a little extra. For
the great panjandrums of the County Council, perhaps a little shame-

faced at the meanness of their £60 a year scholarship, and I think incited by Q., put together an additional small sum out of their own pockets. The Lord Lieutenant gave a lead, and various people like Q., C. V. Thomas, G. T. Petherick, F. R. Pascoe followed, and from this fund I received an additional £15 a year while an undergraduate. It was very nice of them. But it would have been better had they made their scholarship the full value of £80. I am opposed to things being done *qua* private charity which should be done as a matter of public duty. And I am afraid I never considered that small addition to my scholarship for an instant in the light of charity, but merely as my due.

When in the Election of 1931 I was adopted as Labour candidate for my home constituency, against one of the Pethericks, small-minded people on the other side were mean enough to put about the cry that my education had been paid for by the family. That is the kind of thing that happens with the stupid electorate. This chapter, with the whole record of struggle to get enough scholarships to pay my own way at the University, is the answer to that. But, of course, it is impossible, by definition, to answer fools I must say that that disgraceful cry was never given the slightest countenance by the family itself, which was much too generous and public-spirited for such a thing. But I at once made out a cheque for £20 to the headmaster — the utmost that I could have received from that source — for scholarship boys like myself to come to the University and try their luck. I am glad to say that in several cases it was useful. As for the county, I do not suppose that they think their money was wasted now.

August I spent very idly, noting in my Diary that I had been 'too lazy to do any work lately'. And no wonder, after a year of such exertions and two or three bouts of illness. I played tennis a little at school in the evenings, went for some of my favourite walks — to Trenarren in the moonlight, to Luxulyan, Lanlivery and Lostwithiel. I went to read at Lost House; I read under a favourite tree at the top of the school field, while a friendly greybird[1] came quite near and tried his first notes at me. I read Walter Savage Landor, Stevenson's Poems, Wells's *Kipps* and *Bealby*, Samuel Butler's *The Way of all Flesh*, *Sinister Street*, Anatole le Braz's *Au Pays des Pardons*. In spite of its Breton attraction, I could not admit that it was on a level with Daudet. I wrote a sonnet

[1] i.e. the Cornish for a thrush.

on recovering from illness. I noted that I was getting more and more interested in Cornwall and Cornish things — our history, customs, churches, dialect; and I thought that in variety and extent my knowledge of Cornish things was greater than anybody else's of my age. There I was wrong. I had never even heard of Charles Henderson who already knew far, far more.

One day I read a pompous speech by a fatuous Tory diehard, a judge called W. T. Lawrance, who had been M.P. for Truro. He apparently thought the Act of Union of 1801 the be-all and end-all of British politics, and said that the country had gone to the dogs since the Liberals came in in 1906. So I wrote my first political letter, to the *Western Morning News*, taking him up on a few points. Very young, very innocent, I 'was sick of seeing such rubbish appearing day after day in the newspapers, and nobody venturing to write against it'. I did not realize that tackling human foolery would be a whole-time job, all day and every day; that God alone could deal with it — and he had apparently retired.

My mother meanwhile was collecting together my things for Oxford — sheets, towels, table-linen, cups and saucers, plates, cutlery. It was quite a strain; but I think it interested her. One or two kind friends added some useful articles for setting up in rooms of my own — a cruet, an egg-stand, table-napkins. Not a thing from my fatuous family, uncles and aunts and cousins in every direction, ignorant and uninteresting — with the exception of my kind-hearted Aunt Bess.

When term started again at school, the headmaster told me that he wanted a play for Speech Day. I said in bravado that if he had told me before the summer holidays I'd have written him one. That gave him a very good idea — he suddenly thought of getting Q.'s permission for me to dramatize *Troy Town*. My mind was on fire with the idea at once; and I went off to town to get a copy, and there and then set to work in the cool silence of the church to plan out the acts and scenes. 'This was the hardest part of all; several times I came near to desperation.' After that it was easier going: so much of the admirable dialogue was already in play-form and could be incorporated straight off. I worked at it for a week, easily and enjoyably. Then I had some bad moments worrying about how to draw together the various strands at the end: I had to write in some dialogue of my own, and I couldn't make it go anything like so well as Q.'s. But in the end it was done, and I took it round to the headmaster a week or so before going up to Oxford.

They put it into rehearsal under one of the women on the staff, who proved an excellent producer. Most important of all, it happened that there was a boy in the school who was a born comic-character, and who, in spite of being called McCoskrie, spoke first-class Cornish dialect. So there was our Caleb Trotter. He was the making of the play. But the girls were very good, too, and beautifully dressed in bustles and silk of the sixties. When I came home from Oxford for the Christmas vacation, I was astonished at the revelation the play was. The production was admirable. Caleb just walked away with it. I was enormously excited as I sat there and saw the puzzling work of construction in the silent church that September day come to life before my eyes. But my name was not on the bills. Dear Q. was as good as his word and came over for the first performance, dressed to the nines. When, at the end, some of the boys at the back called for the author, for they knew who had made the dramatic version, Q. took me by the hand and led me on with him.

One of these last days at home, F. R. Pascoe, the County Secretary for Education, and a St. Austell man by origin — a man of great administrative drive and ability — came up to the school and asked to see me. A meeting was arranged, and we sat out in the garden on a green bench discussing everything under the sun — just as I liked and as I learned he enjoyed. He had a formidable reputation; he was a hard fighter and at this time none too popular, because of the county's refusal to pay their teachers properly. But I enjoyed his informality and hard-hitting, and his positive liking for getting one back, where smaller people curled up and resented an argument as a personal affront. I think he held the same opinion of them as I. That was the first of many such rambling, racketing talks, and the beginning of a friendship, based on the mutual regard of two buccaneers, which has lasted without a breach to this day.

Shortly after this he took me down with him to Helston to visit my namesake R. G. Rows, a very remarkable old man, who at over eighty, and blind, was still the directing and inspiring force in county education. He had been Chairman of the Education Committee since the great Act of 1902; he and F. R. Pascoe, as Secretary, had together driven through a programme and a policy which in twenty years had provided a fine girdle of secondary schools all round the county. Rows was a born orator and a natural philosopher, a most formidable-looking old sage, with those blind eyes, dead-white pallor and white Victorian side-whiskers. While F. R. Pascoe and he discussed educational business, I walked in the formal garden, watching the pigeons circling about the house, the church-tower behind the trees, marking the noises of a little country town that was strange to me.

Then my turn came. I was led again into the presence, where the old man sat beside his books, all the latest philosophical works — Bergson, Croce, Wildon Carr, along with Bury and Gilbert Murray. We talked about our name; we talked about Q.; we were surprised together at Q. putting Keats and Byron before Shelley. The old man was not interested in Cornish history, but he was very proud of an early protégé of his, a Helston lad whom they had sent to South Kensington, and who, after a brilliant career as geologist, was now Principal of the Imperial College of Science — Sir Thomas Holland.[1] Rows drew the moral — he was nothing if not a moralist — of Holland's career for me. This was the first of a number of such meetings I had with him, each vacation that I came down from Oxford, until he became too ill to receive visitors. Though his activity was confined to the small field of Cornish education, he was probably a great man, and certainly made in a big mould.

My leave-taking from school was spoiled by a wholly superfluous fuss which was the making of the headmaster, and marked the difference between him and my real headmaster, the old one. My getting to Oxford had been noticed in the London papers: 'China-Clay Worker's Son Goes to Christ Church', and so on — it had some small news-value as a story, more then than it would have now, when that kind of thing is much more common. The week before I went up, the local journalist returned to the charge and wrote up a whole column on the subject; some of it he wrote in the first person, as if it were I speaking. He may have had a few words with me, but he certainly

---

[1] Now Vice-Chancellor of the University of Edinburgh.

inflated them with his own fuddled superlatives. It was no fault of mine; the man had just written up a local story — and that was all there was to it. Somebody may have drawn the headmaster's attention to the fact that there was nothing said about the school in it: there were a few people about in the district who were jealous of success — there always are — and ready to do me the disservice of making me responsible. Of course, I had nothing whatever to do with it, and was as annoyed as the headmaster when I saw how annoyed he was. He had asked me to tea; the row raged for an hour. I spent sleepless hours that night. I can only hope that it had a cathartic effect and made me glad to go, when, with my backward-looking temperament, the moment of departure would have been filled with melancholy regrets and memories: my first days there, the thrill of a new place, Miss Blank and her going away, her kind Irish successor, my friends among the girls — Marion, Dorothy, Amy, Noreen — my dead friend, John Clark.

Now I realize that the fuss· was due to a streak in the headmaster's temperament, upon which my regard for him and the very real affection I had for him at one time — my Diary bears witness to it — in the end foundered. Not so my friendships with the old headmaster, Q., F. R. Pascoe, J. G. Crowther, L. H. Tippett, Noreen — all of which have held constant and true through all the changes that the years have brought.

Before I left home we had already left the village. For the last year or two the shop had been nothing but an encumbrance and a nuisance to us all. It made no money, and I was urgent that we should leave it. Father and mother must have discussed it and come to the conclusion that without me they could not carry it on anyhow, and were ready to go. We applied for one of the smallest of the council houses which were building in the fields below the village, just beyond my grandmother's old holding. One summer week-end we shifted our things down to the new house. The donkey and cart came in very handy, and father and I were very busy. For some time Neddy had not been much in use: the roads were being made up and tarred, and getting dangerously slippery for a little quick-trotting donkey; the motor-traffic was beginning to blow us off the roads. Once at the dinner-table we were asking what we kept the donkey for. I replied brightly that 'father kept the donkey to bring home straw for the donkey'. My brother was much amused by this sally; father suspected some impertinence or other, but couldn't exactly lay hold of it. And in fact the donkey went on bringing home straw for himself for years and years.

But that week-end he worked manfully carting away our things from the village: the big brass bed which was to be mine, the round rosewood table on which I had written so many essays and letters and poems and pages of Diary, the old piano on which my sister had played me to sleep, the firelight leaping upon the ceiling of my bedroom, the sitting-room chairs which were so knobbly and uncomfortable, my books and home-made bookcases, the lamps by which I had read and written till morning, the pink-shaded one in the sitting-room, the white by the midnight kitchen fire. Gone now for ever and for ever were the old days in the village with their memories — of Granny Collins keeping school in the house where I was born, my father a little boy in the ABC class, of Uncle and Auntie singing 'I will sing you one, O' on Christmas morning; my own memories of Hilda, of walking off into town as a child, of starlit nights in winter coming home from choir-practice, of smoke-blue autumn evenings when I played rounders in the village street with the boys.

The village itself was changing; across the road the elm-trees, in which I had often heard the winter winds roar while I wrote at night, were coming down to make way for new, unfamiliar houses; the thatched cottages in the garden, where I had looked through the apple-blossom and seen the blue sky of the Civil Wars, had gone. I was not sorry to be leaving. After all, we were only going a couple of stone's throws away, to the other side of Lost House. But it was a profound break in our lives, nevertheless: leaving the village coincided with my leaving home for Oxford. My eyes were turned to the lights of the town, as you see them mirrored in the moving water when the train draws in from the west at night; as Jude saw the haze of those lights reflected in the sky from his lonely field in the uplands of Wessex. More fortunate than Jude, I was going to Oxford. Those lights have held my eyes ever since.

INDEX